# CALDERÓN

CALDERÓN

# Calderón de la Barca
## FOUR PLAYS

*Translated and with an Introduction by*
### EDWIN HONIG

*With an appendix on Spanish Golden Age Customs*
*and Drama by*
### NORMAN MACCOLL

A MERMAID DRAMABOOK
HILL AND WANG  –  NEW YORK

FIRST EDITION AUGUST 1961
SECOND PRINTING DECEMBER 1966
THIRD PRINTING FEBRUARY 1969

Manufactured in the United States of America
by The Colonial Press Inc.

*In memory of a Spanish grandmother*
Esther Mulliver Honig
(1869–1943)

## The translator

Edwin Honig, Professor of English at Brown University, is the author of two volumes of poems, *The Moral Circus* and *The Gazabos*, the critical work *Dark Conceit: The Making of Allegory*, and a well-known book on Lorca's poetry and drama, *García Lorca*. He has published stories and essays in the quarterlies and has translated Lorca and Cervantes, and with Oscar Williams he edited *The Mentor Book of Major American Poets*.

## The playwright

The eminence of Pedro Calderón de la Barca (1600–1681) in Spanish drama is equaled only by that of Lope de Vega. Calderón wrote more than two hundred dramatic works; of these 108 were full-length plays and some 70 were *autos*, the type of religious and mythological one-act play he brought to perfection. Lope, who wrote at least seven times as many plays, is proverbially known as "the monster of nature"; Calderón's equivalent title is "the monster of ingenuity."

Born into a well-established Castilian family in Madrid, where his father was secretary to the Council of the Treasury, Calderón was educated by the Jesuits, studied law at Salamanca and Alcalá, and was complimented by Lope de Vega in 1623 for some verses celebrating the patron saint of Madrid, San Isidro. Made a Knight of Santiago in 1637, he served as a soldier from 1638 to 1642 and became a priest in 1651. He was favored by three Spanish monarchs; his plays, many of them commissioned by the Court, were acknowledged the best dramatic work of his time. His contemporaries besides Lope included Cervantes, Velásquez, Murillo, Gracián, Quevedo, Tirso de Molina, and Góngora —the most celebrated artists and writers of the Golden Age. A French diplomat who met him in 1669 gathered from the conversation that Calderón knew next to nothing generally, and perhaps least of all about the rules of drama, which he mocked. It is said that Calderón died while writing a new play.

# ACKNOWLEDGMENTS

These translations, begun in the wet winter of 1958 in a Mallorcan garden of ever-blooming rosebushes and a yellow-fringed mimosa, were completed in the summer of 1960 in a pine grove on the Maine island of Vinalhaven. During that period the work profited most by Eric Bentley's alert and literally far-reaching enthusiasm for making Calderón, among a score of other foreign classics, viable in English; and, to my own considerable advantage, I was always in touch with his hopeful and clear-cut opinions on the subject. Without Arthur Wang's thoughtful concern for the drama and his courage in publishing the dramatic masters of the great periods and countries, this manuscript would not have seen the light of day so soon or so attractively. I am indebted, finally, to the John Hay Library of Brown University, and in particular to Miss Sara De Luca, for making available, often at very short notice, all the odd and hard-to-come-by items I ever asked for.

E. H.

# CONTENTS

Acknowledgments vii

Introduction xi

Selected Bibliography xxvii

SECRET VENGEANCE FOR SECRET INSULT 1

DEVOTON TO THE CROSS 73

THE MAYOR OF ZALAMEA 141

THE PHANTOM LADY 217

Appendix 307

# INTRODUCTION

In the crude engraving prefacing Calderón's collected works, the distracted look of an elderly melancholiac stares out at the reader. The portrait seems an unintentional caricature of an earlier one done by Juan de Alfaro, showing a somewhat younger disdainful head emerging from the dark cape and tunic of a Knight of Santiago. Disdain softened by resignation dominates still another portrait revealing a clerical gentleman, in severe habit and flowing cape, holding a copy of his plays opened to the title page of *Bien vengas, mal, si vienes solo* (*Welcome, Evil, if You Come Alone*). And still the haunted, indrawn stare prevails. For a man who lived eighty-one years (1600–1681), and more than fifty in close touch with Court society, the record is sketchy, the relevant facts of his existence singularly bare. As if to emphasize that all this is due to the playwright's characteristic reserve, unmarred by legend or exploit, the commentators have coined a phrase, "the biography of silence."

I

Pedro Calderón de la Barca was born in Madrid on January 17, 1600, the third child and second son of María Henao y Riaño and Don Diego, the Secretary of the Council of the Treasury, a fairly substantial minor post at Court. The family followed the King to Valladolid and back to Madrid before Calderón's matriculation at the Imperial College of the Jesuits in 1608. The college curriculum at the time would have included readings in the Latin of Cicero, Virgil, Seneca, Catullus, and Propertius, and enough Greek to read St. John Chrysostom. His mother, who wanted her son to become a priest, died suddenly in 1610. Four years later, he enrolled at the University of Alcalá to study logic and rhetoric, and that same year his father was remarried. But in 1615 his father died, leaving a will which admits the paternity of an illegitimate son, Francisco, thereafter accepted by the Calderón household as a relative and servant; as for Pedro, "I charge and beseech [him], under no circumstances to quit his studies, but rather to continue and finish them." From 1616 to 1620 the young Calderón divided his time between Madrid and the two university cities of Alcalá and Salamanca, where he had embarked on a course in canon law; but there is no record of his having completed the course, as is sometimes maintained. His earliest known verses date from this period, and in 1620 he entered a poetry competition held in Madrid in honor of the beatification of San Isidro. Lope de Vega, one of the judges on this occasion, bestowed some general words of praise on Calderón's efforts. During this time there was a litigation between the Calderón brothers and their stepmother, which was settled satisfactorily upon her remarriage in 1618. In addition, there is a record of a suit against them for having killed a relative of the Duke of Frias, of a huge fine being levied, and subsequently of an exonerating settlement effected out of court.

Calderón's literary career began in earnest in the early 1620s with the winning of several poetry prizes. His first play, *Amor, honor y poder* (*Love, Honor and Power*), was performed at Court in June 1623; another, *La selva confusa* (*The Tangled Forest*), in July; and a play about the Maccabees in September of the same year. There is no record of his whereabouts in the next two years, though he is believed to have been soldiering in Italy and Flanders, this mainly because of the vivid geographical details which turn up in his play *El sitio de Breda* (*The Siege of Breda*), the same subject as Velásquez' celebrated painting, *The Lances*. Of the fifteen plays he wrote by 1630, at least two were destined to become world-famous: *La dama duende* (*The Phantom Lady*) and *El príncipe constante* (*The Constant Prince*). It was in the latter of these that Calderón undertook to satirize the florid Gongoristic style of the Court preacher, Hortensio Félix y Arteaga. The playwright was motivated by the preacher's attack upon him following the second and last of the cape-and-sword escapades in which Calderón is purported to have engaged. Seeking revenge on the actor Pedro de Villegas, who had wounded his brother in a duel, Calderón pursued him into a nunnery where he is said to have molested the nuns. One of the nuns was Lope de Vega's daughter Marcela, and her father complained about the incident to the Duke of Sessa. Calderón was put under house arrest for a few days. But the incident only spurred the young playwright's growing popularity and brought him into higher favor at Court. By 1637 he had written forty-one more plays, among them almost all the great secular dramas by which he is best known.

When Lope de Vega died in 1635, Calderón succeeded him as director of all theatrical functions at Court. Two years later he was made a Knight of Santiago after a magnificent *zarzuela* which he had superintended at the opening of the new palace of the Buen Retiro. "This was a musical play," as Gerald Brenan reports in *The Literature of the Spanish People*, "on the theme of Ulysses and Circe, which was later printed as *El mayor encanto amor*. No play had ever been given under such splendid circumstances. A floating stage was built on the large *estanque* or oblong pond and lit with three thousand lanterns. Cosme Lotti, an Italian stage machinist, designed the décor, which included a shipwreck, a triumphal watercar pulled by dolphins, and the destruction of Circe's palace to the accompaniment of artillery and fireworks. The king and his suite watched from gondolas." By 1637, two volumes of his plays had been brought out under the nominal editorship of José Calderón, his brother.

If his star was fixed in the 1630s, the following decade saw it overcast by national and personal misfortunes. In 1640 Portugal successfully revolted against the Spanish crown, and in the

same year Calderón went off with the army to put down a
rebellion in Catalonia occasioned by outrages against the peasantry
committed by Spanish soldiers stationed there. The disillusioning
experience is strikingly borne out in his play *El alcalde de
Zalamea*. The closing of the public and Court theatres, his own
ill health after the military campaign, and his withdrawal from
military service caused him to become a member of the Duke of
Alba's household, where he stayed for four years (1646–1650).
Within a relatively short period both his brothers were killed and
his mistress died, leaving him a son. His resignation from his post
at Court (1650) was immediately followed by his entrance into
the priesthood. By 1653 he had written thirty-three more plays—
a few, as before, in collaboration—and twenty-one *autos*, the
allegorical dramas to which he was to devote the remainder of
his life. He was given a chaplaincy in Toledo until prevailed
on by the king to return to his former post at Court in 1663.
Here he remained until his death. The third (1664), fourth
(1672), and fifth (1677) volumes of his collected plays were
edited by friends, but in the latter year Calderón himself also
collected and published his *autos* and wrote a preface to them.
In 1680 he answered a request to provide a list of his plays,
which he determined as 110 secular dramas and 70 *autos*. In 1669
a French diplomat reported that he had spoken with Calderón
and had gathered from the conversation that the playwright had
almost no general knowledge and, despite his hoary locks, knew
least of all about the rules of drama. On the other hand there
is a contemporary report that on the day of his death, May 25,
1681, Calderón was writing a new *auto*, so that "he died, as they
say of the swan, singing."

II

OUR four plays belong to Calderón's most productive period,
roughly from 1625 to 1640. In these works the honor theme
predominates, as it did earlier in the popular drama of Lope
de Vega, Tirso de Molina, and Mira de Amescua. The theme is
central to *Secret Vengeance for Secret Insult* (1635); it runs
parallel to the religious thaumaturgy in *Devotion to the Cross*
(1633); and it is closely interwoven with the principle of the
liberty of individual conscience in *The Mayor of Zalamea* (1640–
1644). Though muted by concerns for plot intrigue in cape-and-
sword comedy, the honor theme enters crucially, with serious
implications concerning incest, in *The Phantom Lady* (1629).
It is the exploitation of this theme by the Golden Age dramatists
generally and by Calderón in particular which gives Spanish
drama its indelibly national character as well as its peculiarly
forbidding look to foreign readers. In enactment always close to
the bizarreness of melodrama, it is still widely mistaken for a
kind of primordial version of French classicism, which it in fact
influenced.

Honor, a virtue built on pride, obedience, fealty, adoration, and self-sacrifice deriving from feudal customs, was turned into a combative ideal and a preservative of caste society. In Spain of the Counter Reformation, subsisting under an autocratic, Catholic, imperialistic rule, the medieval notion of honor was reinforced and rigidified with typical Iberian fervor. The Spanish instinct to preserve gains righteously wrested in military-religious missions gave the notion of honor both a repressive and an idealistic character. The three Spanish synonyms for gentleman, *señor,* *hidalgo, caballero,* suggest as much. *Señor* also means God, lord, sir, sire, and owner; *hidalgo,* the member of a privileged class, a nobleman; *caballero,* a squire, horseman, rider. And these are the figures of authority who actively sustain the rule of honor. The word *hidalgo*—a contraction of *hijo de algo,* "son of something" —suggests the patrilinear law of inheritance. But it also carries particular implications of polygamy in Moorish society, where the sequestration of women in a harem insured the breeding of numerous sons. Each son inherited a portion of his father's vast lands; and because each held exclusive dominion over his portion through pure-blooded affiliation with the patriarchal lord-owner, he could be expected to defend it to the death against any foreign or extrafamilial encroachment.

As seen at work in Spanish drama, the honor code represents certain prepossessions and obligations. First, there is pride in one's class, family, good name, blood, or heritage. Secondly there is the safeguarding against sexual assault of female members of the family—wife, sister, and daughter. There is the articulation and defense of the principle of the freedom of individual conscience. Then there is the obligation to redress an offense or insult, usually involving a woman, by secretly murdering the wrongdoer and dispatching the implicated woman to a convent for the rest of her life or killing her on the spot. Finally there is the need to be vindicated for such actions by the highest prevailing authority, usually the paternalistic king.

In his *New Art of Writing Plays* Lope de Vega prescribed writing about honor because the subject had wide appeal. Such plays were popular because they concerned acts of violence, the contortions of jealous rage, infringements on sexual taboos, and plenty of high-flown language aimed at a chilling ethic which, though often battered, could never be overthrown. This convention, offering itself to Calderón at the start of his career, was enormously fruitful. For he seemed to be a man temperamentally inclined to the psychological and esthetic treatment of the honor theme. His training with the Jesuits no doubt prepared him to exploit the implications of the subject, and his fondness for a complex, allegorical view of action permitted him to shape his plays with unusual subtlety. These characteristics of his art have been memorialized in the sobriquet "the monster of ingenuity," though affixed to him partly in order to balance Cervantes' magniloquent title for Lope, "the monster of nature." Yet theological training and dramaturgical astuteness were surely less crucial to his rapid development as one of Europe's greatest dramatists than a particular capacity, amounting to an appetite, to dramatize the paradox of honor as a universal figure for human fatality.

The four plays in this volume illustrate Calderón's diversified treatment of this theme and his originality as a thinking dramatist. Their arrangement is thematic rather than chronological so as to show a typical development applicable to other plays given to the treatment of the same problems. Thus *Secret Vengeance* comes first because it defines the laws of honor in the most unmitigated terms. Among other plays of this sort are *Amor, honor y poder* (*Love, Honor and Power*); *Un castigo en tres venganzas* (*Three Judgments at a Blow*); *El médico de su honra* (*The Surgeon of His Honor*); *El pintor de su deshonra* (*The Painter of His Dishonor*); *El mayor monstruo del mundo* (*The World's Greatest Monster*).

*Devotion to the Cross* presents a modification of the honor code through the countervailing movement of the principle of mercy. The mercy principle, part of a theocratic code, triumphs in the end without, however, destroying the structure of the honor system it opposes. Other plays of this sort are *El príncipe constante* (*The Constant Prince*); *El purgatorio de San Patricio* (*The Purgatory of Saint Patrick*); *El mágico prodigioso* (*The Wonder-Working Magician*); *La exaltación de la cruz* (*The Exaltation of the Cross*); *Las cadenas del demonio* (*The Devil's Chains*).

In *The Mayor of Zalamea*, a further modification of the honor code occurs when the mayor, a rich peasant, undertakes to judge and execute a nobleman who has raped his daughter; but instead of being punished, he is rewarded by the king. The peasant's emergent cause—the freedom of conscience and justice for all—is permitted to triumph not by violating the honor code but by extending it. Though Lope de Vega, among others, showed partiality to the peasantry in many plays—*Fuenteovejuna* and *Peribáñez* being the most famous—Calderón rarely treated the subject so favorably again. On this subject he wrote *Luis Pérez el gallego* (*Luis Pérez the Galician*) and *El alcaide de sí mismo* (*Warden to Himself*), but in the latter his view of the newly rich peasant is deprecatory.

In the last of the four, *The Phantom Lady*, not usually considered an honor play, the code is mocked under cover of comedy, where a pastoral dispensation allows for the triumph of love. Other romantic plays of this type are *El galán fantasma* (*The Ghostly Lover*); *El escondido y la tapada* (*The Secret Swain and the Veiled Lady*); *Guárdate del agua mansa* (*Beware of Smooth Waters*); and *Casa con dos puertas, mala es de guardar* (*A House with Two Entrances Is Hard to Protect*).

The critical cliché which has long impugned Calderón's drama for being fashioned on morally dogmatic lines, for dealing with types and flat characters, and for sacrificing organic interests to surface complications of plot is only now being gradually disproved. Albert E. Sloman's authoritative work, *The Dramatic Craftsmanship of Calderón*, A. A. Parker's analysis of the *autos* in *The Allegorical Drama of Calderón*, and Valbuena Briones' introduction to the Aguilar edition of the *comedias* represent the most eloquent vindications of his grave and complex art. W. G. Chapman's introductory study to the mythological plays, the investigations of Valbuena Prat and Frutos Cortés in the same area, William Entwistle's inquiry into Calderón's Thomist psychology, E. M. Wilson's studies of Calderonian imagery, and Bruce Wardropper's work on the unconscious motives of Calderón's honor victims indicate persistent elements in the whole range of Calderón's drama which need to be further explored.

Like Ben Jonson's, Calderon's dramatic art has been poorly understood, and for similar reasons. Taking Jonson's humour theory as a rigid application to drama of a medieval psychological principle, critics missed the profoundly fruitful purpose it served in the development of an art based on character typology. And they were thus prevented from seeing how the logical requirement of his esthetic came to flower in his allegorical and mythological masques. Similarly with Calderón. The critics who have given limited approval to the art of realistic portraiture in *The Mayor of Zalamea* or *The Phantom Lady* are like the critics who commend the Jonson of *Volpone* or *The Alchemist*. They do not see that the realism overlays a deeper typological design which they object to when the realistic patina disappears in the dramatists' other works. Jonson's mythological plays and masques are natural developments of an earlier typological realism much as Calderón's mythological plays and *autos* are condensations and fulfillments of a dominant symbology at work in his earlier honor plays and well-known cape-and-sword plays.

III

In *Secret Vengeance* the classical honor situation occurs in its barest form. Don Lope de Almeida, the Portuguese king's military commander, has married by proxy a Castilian lady, Doña Leonor. The king releases him from military duty so that Don Lope, according to his own request, may consummate his marriage. Leonor was formerly betrothed to a Spanish nobleman, Don Luis, whom she believes was killed in the wars. As Lope is on his way to join Leonor he is met by Don Juan, an exiled friend, now secretly returned from Goa where his rash murder of the governor's son over a question of honor has forced him to live in disgrace. Lope takes him into his protection as he joins Leonor, who has meanwhile also made a discovery: Don Luis is alive and has revealed himself to her, disguised as a traveling merchant, intent on regaining her love. In this involvement Sirena, her maid, acts as Leonor's confidante and go-between in the same way that Manrique, his valet, and Don Juan serve Don Lope.

Don Lope is an impetuous military man, unused to the niceties of courtship, the blandishments of marriage; he feels uneasy, impatient, and estranged in his new role as husband. He senses that he has neglected a more important military duty for a problematic and lesser civil duty; he is clearly not cut out to be a lover or a husband. His personal quandary is immediately magnified into a raging cause of injured honor when Don Luis, invited to the house by Leonor in order to make him stop courting her, is discovered hiding there. Instead of killing the intruder, Don Lope, forewarned by his friend's cautionary example, dissembles his fears and jealousy and helps Don Luis escape. "Secret insult most requires secret vengeance" is the principle which leads the offended man to a delayed and complicated series of ruses before drowning her lover and then burning down the house where he has killed his wife. The king approves the deed which frees Don Lope to join the military campaign. But though he is perversely heroized for committing a double murder, Don Lope is also left exhausted and ready "to end my life" on the battlefield, "if indeed misfortune ever ends."

Don Lope's vehement protests against the tyrannical laws of honor do not prevent his carrying them out. Jealous or not, he is a military man who understands the goads of harsh necessity, the inhumanity which makes of slaughter a social virtue. But a victory on the battlefield is clear-cut while a triumph based on conscientious scruples is only pyrrhic, leaving repercussions that chill the blood, debilitate the soul, and turn glory into a simulacrum. Don Lope is evidently a victim of his own deeds, an implement of the insult–vengeance complex, with its de-humanized rationale of an outmoded justice. For us he is as much a victim as is Kafka's officer when surrendering to the torture machine he charges himself to maintain in *The Penal Colony*. It is finally the authoritarian justice machine to which humanity is sacrificed.

If these are the dramatic consequences of the vengeance-for-insult theme, how are they prepared in the ethos of the play? The answer is, first, through a pattern of persistent and elaborate polarities. The conflict between love and war, peace and duty, is established at the start and is never dropped as an instigative force in Don Lope's behavior. His marriage by proxy that will never be consummated opposes the true passion of love between Leonor and Don Luis. Insult will provoke the cause of honor and vengeance will annihilate the offenders as though they had never existed. The elemental symbols of fire, water, wind, and earth literally and metaphorically influence the course of action. And these in turn are allied with the polarities which enlarge the actions and attributes of all the characters: land and sea, silence and speech, certainty and suspicion, Castile and Portugal, sun and cloud, dissimulation and revelation. In this way Don Lope's personal impasse is given cosmic dimensions, a world larger than the truth or falsity of his emotions, by which to be measured. And in such an environment the moral questions to which his actions give rise are figuratively extended beyond the literal resolution of his problems into the universal problems of order, justice, and renunciation.

A second means of preparing the tragic consequences is evident in the strategy of developing Don Lope's flawed personality. A man who has been traumatically shocked out of his self-esteem, not only by marriage and the loss of his soldierly role but also by the suspicion of sexual incapacity, Don Lope momentarily loses his identity and must do everything he can to regain it. And yet what he does must scrupulously fulfill the law of honor, as though his reputation, his status, his bond to society had not in fact been disturbed. So he must dissemble, play the hypocrite, continually rationalize his doubts, meet duplicity with duplicity, become an underground man living in a state of siege, a "cold war" which he would seem to accept as the normal state of affairs. He must above all safeguard the suprapersonal machine of honor to which his identity is wedded and on which his life depends. Honor is his surrogate, secrecy his escutcheon. From this situation proceed all his dialectical soliloquies, his tortuous, legalistic self-incriminations and defenses, until "the moment is ripe" and he becomes the executioner of honor's law.

A third means of preparation involves the supportive roles of Don Juan, the insulted friend who becomes the mirror and guide of Don Lope's strategy, and Manrique, the servant, whose transforming of his master's problems into comic actions emphasizes their dehumanized absurdity. Without Don Juan's providential appearance at the start and the lengthy sense of outrage he conveys as a man who failed to vindicate his honor because his vengeance revealed and redoubled the insult, Don Lope could not have plotted his own mechanically perfect acts of revenge. And if Don Juan's example instructs and propels him, Manrique defines by exaggerating the basic incongruities, the ironic insubstantiality of his master's plight. Manrique's flirtation with Leonor's maid, Sirena, his zany speeches, his boasting and his fabling on the sick psychology of love reveal the duplicities that his master takes seriously and show them up for being proverbial riddles which are realistically passed off with a wry grin, a vulgar joke. In this way Manrique is as consistent as Don Lope, but because he risks nothing, he is completely invulnerable, as his master is not. Yet grounded though it is in worldly realism so that it balances or relieves Don Lope's intolerable ideality, the servant's view is nevertheless as pitiless as his master's and, finally, as inhuman. We cannot expect to find comfort in him for being so complementary to Don Lope just as we cannot expect anything like a resolution of the dualities and polarities which surcharge the play. The point about such a highly schematized conception of life is that the polarities persist in make-believe, for the sake of the action, as much as they continue to exist in real life, where they are rarely so defined.

The tyranny of honor is mitigated and momentarily transcended in *Devotion to the Cross*. With so harsh a principle to justify, one would expect Calderón to portray, as he does, exemplary subversions against it with scrupulous intensity. What happens here is what must happen in a mercy play: the thaumaturgy of religious faith, upheld by a single individual's belief, succeeds, because it is part of a mightier machine, in toppling the ratiocinative machinery of the insult–vengeance formula. For this victory to occur, the case must be exceptional, and it is —and again, almost absurdly melodramatic, as both miracle and honor plays must be because they enforce the tension between a suprapersonal ideality and a violent renunciation.

Eusebio kills Lisardo, his friend, who goaded him into a duel for daring to court Julia, Lisardo's sister, without the permission of their father Curcio, an impoverished nobleman. Eusebio is presumed to lack the qualifications of nobility, though before killing Lisardo he tells a long story about his miraculous existence as directly influenced by a holy cross, whose symbol was inscribed on his chest at birth. Before Lisardo dies, Eusebio carries him off to be shriven, and before the corpse is brought home Eusebio begs Julia to escape with him instead of entering the convent as her father has ordered her to do. When Lisardo's death is announced, Julia cannot bring herself to hate Eusebio, though, respecting her wish, he agrees to leave her. Eusebio becomes the leader of a brigand gang marauding the mountains and villages, killing and living off the spoils of his victims. One near-victim, the priest Alberto, is saved when a bullet is diverted by a holy book he wears against his chest. Eusebio permits him to go when Alberto agrees to confess him before he dies one day. Curcio, who has denounced Julia for being like her dead mother, now pursues Eusebio in the vicinity of the mountains where once, out of jealousy, he struck at his wife Rosmira, who gave birth to twins at the foot of a cross. One child, Julia, and the mother were miraculously transported home while the other child disappeared. Meanwhile Eusebio breaks into the convent and is about to rape Julia when he discovers that she also bears the sign of the cross on her breast. He flees from her in dread and bewilderment, and she follows behind, though he does not know this. She disguises herself as a man, leads a life of crime and murder, ultimately confronts Eusebio and is disarmed. Curcio's men find Eusebio and stab him, but before dying he is acknowledged by Curcio as Julia's long-lost twin. Alberto the priest returns and Eusebio revives long enough to be shriven. When he dies a second time, Julia reveals herself, confesses her sins, and as she is about to be struck by her father, embraces the cross at the foot of which Eusebio is lying, and both are borne upward to Heaven.

This dry, frenzied morality play, suppurating with immorality and incest, is more notable for the blow it delivers against the nobleman's overweening pride than for any religious exaltation it incidentally dramatizes. The wages of the father's sins are relentlessly visited upon his wife and children until Curcio's survival at the end seems an ironic piece of justice. But we must assume that Curcio's punishment is greater than theirs since he is thus forced to suffer the holocaust of the insult–vengeance complex without any possibility of resolving it. A domestic tragedy, *Devotion to the Cross* shows up the moralistic cannibalism of the honor code in a patriarchal figure who endures like a ruined column standing in the shambles of the proud roof it once supported. In these shambles are the evidence of many hapless falls. Calderonian drama is full of crucial falls; there are half a dozen plays, including *Life Is a Dream* and *The Surgeon of His Honor*, where the action is initiated with a fall from a horse. The action of *Devotion to the Cross* begins with a donkey fallen in a ditch, the first of six such falls involving Lisardo, Rosmira, Alberto, Eusebio, and Julia—not to mention the unspecified number of peasants who fall at the hand of Eusebio. The cause of the cross ascending at the end is obviously intended to answer for them all. All other causes in the play are earthbound, murderously honorbound and incestbound. Eusebio's devotion to the cross saves him from the authoritarian justice of his father, a Jahweh thunder god, and his career despite his crimes (which like Julia's are consequences of original sin) parallels the symbolic career of the fallen Adam become the risen Christ by re-enacting the incestuous crime in the garden (convent) where he seeks to be reunited with Julia—the female Eve, his other self. Otherwise the spectacle of a seducer and his female partner being rewarded instead of punished would be less than meaningless—it would make a mockery of the laws of honor. How far one has come here from the fruitful Moorish conservativism of the harem, the domestic custom underlying the Spanish concept of honor (fear of assault on one's property being equivalent to fear of sexual assault from strangers), we can now judge by witnessing the desolation of an impoverished noble family brought on by the father's fearful pride and exaggerated idealism. Human pride followed to its logical conclusion in a Spanish context invariably leads to a personal *auto da fe*, an act of honorable murder in the name of a suprapersonal faith.

In *The Mayor of Zalamea*, a play based on a historical situation, the strictures of honor are relaxed to allow for an amplification of the code so that its *sui generis* structure may be challenged from within. This happens when the sexual assault on a peasant girl by a nobleman, who is also the captain of a regimental company, alters absolute caste justice and simultaneously elevates peasant justice long enough to incriminate the one and exonerate the other. Another way of putting this would be to say that the act of vengeance receives public and judicial cognizance and is officially sanctioned by the King so that the prestige of honor, though upheld by a peasant, is reaffirmed without seriously victimizing the revenger. Hence the insulted man gains a real and not merely an illusory satisfaction in the end. Something of this satisfaction is even imparted through the play's original title, *El garrote más bien dado* (*The Best Garroting Ever Executed*).

What happens is so forthright that one may easily miss the subversive attack that is being leveled against the autocratic honor principle. Pedro Crespo, a rich farmer, is preparing quarters in his home for the captain, Don Alvaro, when the latter manages to burst in on his daughter Isabel, who has agreeably moved to an upstairs room during the brief stay of the troops in town. The field commander, Don Lope de Figueroa, arrives in time to stop the quarrel between Crespo and the captain. Smitten by the peasant girl he formerly scorned, the captain abducts Isabel after Don Lope has left the house with Crespo's son Juan, now his orderly. When Crespo interferes the captain's men bind him to a tree in the nearby forest where Isabel is raped. Juan meanwhile has wounded the captain, who is returned to town in order to have the wound treated. When Isabel releases Crespo and they return to town, he learns that he has been selected mayor of Zalamea; he then orders the arrest of Don Alvaro and the accomplices. In a private interview, Crespo offers the captain all his wealth and estate if Don Alvaro will marry Isabel and repair the insult. When Don Alvaro refuses, Crespo has him jailed. Don Lope returns to punish the mayor for imprisoning a nobleman, but Crespo refuses to release the captain. A show of force between the troops and the peasants is in progress when the King arrives, hears Crespo's legal defense, is shown the captain garroted in his cell, and concludes the play by honoring the peasant with the permanent mayoralty of Zalamea. Crespo's personal cause, enunciated early in the play ("My life and property I render / to the King; but honor is / the heritage of my soul, / and my soul belongs to God alone.") has been thoroughly vindicated.

But something more than a democratic principle is involved. A humane view of life emerges that is totally different from anything appearing in the conventional honor play. From the beginning the play teems with animation: the expostulations of the braggart soldier Rebolledo and the camp-follower ballad-singer La Chispa; the posturings of the impoverished nobleman Don Mendo and his satiric servant Nuño; the intermingling of soldiers and peasantry; the small-town garden scene on a late August night; and the humorous exchanges between Crespo and the gout-ridden commander Don Lope. From these vital elements rises a pastoral ethic countervailing the austere and darkly marauding incursions of the aristocratic seducer and the exactions of the military caste. The spirit of Zalamea, typified by the bold and independent-minded Crespo, reminds us of the ancient organization of the Roman *municipalia*, the autonomous Spanish town with its own mandates guaranteed by imperial authority. Abetting this qualification is Crespo's diligent husbandry as a cultivator of the land, his concern for the harvest and the small world of the town where his efforts have been rewarded. When pitted against the ephemeral, warbound soldiery who intrude upon it, this small world reveals its own positive and abiding values. These are the values which the King implicitly vindicates at the end by approving Crespo's actions. Ultimately they are the only values which can heal the rift in the divided and conscience-driven agent of the autocratic honor code.

Such ameliorative principles are closely articulated in *The Phantom Lady*, the most charming of Calderón's cape-and-sword comedies. The pastoral ethic which allows for a triumph of bottom dog over top dog in *The Mayor of Zalamea* provides for a much more conclusive victory in the comedy. For here, the romantic heroine, otherwise so dismally sacrificed in the honor plays, invades the scene and by her imaginative stratagems asserts her right to act freely as a woman in love. But her liberty and successful strategy are all the more remarkable when viewed in the context of the honor ideology they oppose. The play becomes a tangle of *enredos*—shadowy complications, mischievous deceptions, appearances turning into realities, matters of fact turning into clinkers and dust. All this is initiated and managed by Doña Angela, the young widow immured in her brothers' house, who maneuvers a mystery by means of a movable glass panel separating her apartment from that of her brother's guest, the gallant Don Manuel.

Closely guarded at home, where she is in effect "wedlocked to a brace of brothers," Angela has slipped out of the house to see the shows at the palace grounds. There she is observed and pursued by her libertine brother Don Luis, who does not recognize her because she is veiled. Appealing for help to a stranger, Don Manuel, she is able to reach home safely while Don Manuel intercepts Don Luis. As they duel, the other brother, Don Juan, appears, recognizes Don Manuel as his friend and guest, and takes him home. A raging libidinal force, Don Luis is doomed to be frustrated at every turn; the more he is frustrated, the more prurient he becomes, turning from his sister to Beatriz, his brother's sweetheart, and back again, unconsciously, to his sister. Like Don Alvaro in *The Mayor*, Lisardo in *Devotion*, and Don Luis and Don Juan in *Secret Vengeance*, he is a type of morose, honorbound intruder who incites the insult–vengeance complex. As the honor spokesman in the play, he thereby masks the strong incestuous drive which Don Manuel, Angela's lover, must thwart. Because he has liberated her imagination, Don Manuel becomes the object of her wakened curiosity: the erotic prince charming (not the bestial male aggressor she fled from in Don Luis) who arrives to rouse her sleeping womanhood. Against the defects of her brother's erotic anarchy are the clearly enumerated virtues in Don Manuel: self-sacrifice, discretion, courage, gentlemanly honor. Believing him to possess these virtues, Angela can feel safe with him, safe from rude assault. In reciprocating, she can feel free to perform her womanly role by using her will and imagination to endow him with the instinctive gifts of love. These are the very gifts which Calderón's honor victims, subdued by rape (Isabel in *The Mayor*), incestuous attack (Julia in *Devotion*), and sterile jealousy and murder (Leonor in *Secret Vengeance*) are unnaturally prevented from bestowing. They are the gifts of a woman's realistic love for a man, framed by the pastoral virtues and unhampered by the paternalistic strictures of the honor code.

Don Manuel and his superstitious servant Cosme are inducted into a mystery created by Angela, in the guise of a phantom lady, whose purpose is to convert the rule of honor into the rule of love. She is the sometimes veiled and hidden priestess of the new rule, accompanied by her servants and Beatriz. Don Manuel is the initiate whose faith must be tested by various trials; these will indicate his fitness to serve and, eventually, marry the lady. Cosme, whose faith is being challenged on a lower level, is also involved, and such involvement is deepened by his close relationship to a master whom he typically serves as an alter ego—as an instigator and guide through the mystery, but also as a threat and a challenge to his rational mind. As the representatives of the rule of honor, the old repressive principle, Don Luis and Don Juan are the antagonists and Doña Angela's keepers within the walls of the house. But Don Juan is distinguished from the rapacious Don Luis on several counts, the most notable being that as Doña Beatriz's favored lover his autocratic rule is tempered significantly by Doña Angela's cause of love. For his part, Don Luis is the unconscious assailant on his sister's honor, the marauder and homicidal force perpetuating the old rule, who must constantly disrupt Angela's love rites. In such a situation the fear of dishonor and the enticements of incest spring up together in the same breast. But one must remember that when his suspicions are aroused, Don Juan himself acts no differently from his brother, and in this sense with regard to Angela ("wedlocked to a brace of brothers") he is also an antagonist of the new rule.

If the developments of the mystery are thus mythotypical, they also parallel the standard devices in Calderón's vengeance plays where the man-with-a-cause is sequestered inside his own consciousness, his movements and strategies swaddled in secrecy, and his growing knowledge and purpose isolate him from all antagonists until he is ready to strike. But since Doña Angela, the principal agent here, is a woman-with-a-cause, and because the ethos she acts in is the social ethos of comedy instead of tragedy, she shares her knowledge and purpose with female accomplices, who help her to penetrate her isolation, go through doors and walls, and light up the darkness. When the play ends, the irrational, in the double form of phantom lady and imaginary devil, has been given its due. The incest threat flickering across the anxious face of honor has been put down, and for once in Calderón, the rites of love have superseded the bleak honor formula that induces the insult–vengeance complex with all its disastrous consequences.

Thus in Calderón's plays where the exigencies of the honor code prevail, the hero's need to find release from a conscientious impasse makes for a temperamental type and a set of attitudes which are at once austere, melancholic, anarchic, conformist, hypocritical, schizophrenic, and dehumanized. The determinism behind the type, which views life as cheap, evanescent, and transitory, perpetuates both the rapacious imperialistic designs of the state and the deathbound consolations of religion. The tragic view of the Calderonian hero subsisting in an all-or-none credo is perfectly represented in those dramas where the motives of church and state coincide. And it is on these grounds, as Albert Camus points out in the preface to his translation of *Devotion to the Cross*, that the opposing precept of the believer's "Grace is everything" and the atheist's "Nothing is just" paradoxically come together. To mitigate if not to resolve the paradox, Calderón presents the intermediate and more humane principle of the freedom of the soul, the right of the individual conscience to choose its own destiny against the dictates of an authoritarian code. And although complete liberation from the strictures of the code seems to be impossible, the conditions for softening its devastating impact and seizures are clearly set forth in the pastoral ethic of *The Mayor of Zalamea* and the imaginative rites of romantic love in *The Phantom Lady*.

IV

For the past century the most respectable versions of Calderón in English were Edward Fitzgerald's prose and blank-verse translations of *Eight Dramas*. Fitzgerald used a stock but modified form of Elizabethan diction, cutting long speeches, altering and adding lines as he saw fit, and generally polishing crude surfaces with his own debonair intelligence. The effect is something like a series of Restoration plays with just a hint of the taste of the Spanish to suggest how much verbal mediocrity had to be applied to reduce the original to innocuousness in English. Fitzgerald's contemporary, the Irish scholar-poet Denis Florence MacCarthy, worked with dogged ingenuity to preserve exactly the whole gamut of verse patterns, if not always the same prose sense, he found in the original. The fourteen plays and three *autos* he translated are plaster-cast relics of unreadability, and Henry W. Wells' latest revisions of six MacCarthy versions have done little to vivify them. Before his recent death, the poet Roy Campbell turned out the most creditable Calderón translations yet available in verse. Less arbitrary than Fitzgerald's but freer than MacCarthy's, his renderings of *The Surgeon of His Honour*, *Life Is a Dream*, and *Love After Death* are accurate, sometimes crude but never embarrassing; they are muscular in their blank verse and in their rhymes, and always readable.

Because rhyme in Spanish is so natural as to be almost inescapable, assonantal patterns are substituted in order to avoid them, particularly in the *romance*, the octosyllabic line which is standard for ballads and dominant for dramatic verse. In translating Golden Age drama into English, where rhyme is rare or simply accidental, the usual solution is to reduce everything to blank verse or to prose that sounds like blank verse. But what is thus normalized in principle is lost in effect to the metronomic rhythms, diction, and inversions of the seventeenth century, which forever fixed dramatic blank verse in English. To skip that pitfall I have adopted a contrivance that will disturb some for its arbitrariness and others for its presumption. But since it seems to work better than any other device, I will stand by it until someone comes up with a more effective one. I use a syllabic line, patterned on the octosyllabic *romance*, but different from its model (which sometimes omits and sometimes adds a syllable) in permitting a regular six-to-nine-syllable limitation. The advantage of such flexibility is that the basic syllabic quantity allows for a fairly regular accentual beat to emerge in a variety of trimeter, tetrameter, and pentameter lines that is not foreign to the English ear, and yet is just strange enough to suggest the Spanish norm. (A few exceptions occur—mainly in the first act of *Secret Vengeance*, where the formality of diction is made to fit into the original Spanish forms, and in the sonnets encountered in this play.) If someone objects that the lines too often read like maladjusted prose, I would point out that there is the same effect in the original when prose diction is cast in verse simply to abide by Golden Age conventions in this regard. It would have been futile to follow such usages when what I was trying mainly to do was reflect the essential poetry of Calderón's language as well as stick to its prose sense. But if, as I hope, these versions of Calderón's plays are dramatically acceptable to readers whom the insipidities of verbal compromise, archaisms, and double-headed anachronisms normally discourage, then I will have succeeded in delivering the substance, and hence some of the strange raw flavor, of the thing in the original.

EDWIN HONIG

# SELECTED BIBLIOGRAPHY

### A. TEXTS OF THE FOUR PLAYS

CALDERÓN DE LA BARCA, PEDRO. *Obras completas, I, Dramas*, ed. Luis Astrana Marin. Madrid, 1951. (*A secreto agravio, secreta venganza*, pp. 295–323; *El alcalde de Zalamea*, pp. 523–53; *La devoción de la cruz*, pp. 975–1004.) (Aguilar)
————. *Obras completas, II, Comedias*, ed. Angel Valbuena Briones. Madrid, 1956. (*La dama duende*, pp. 233–70.) (Aguilar)
————. *A secreto agravio, secreta venganza*, ed. Angel Valbuena Briones. Madrid, 1956. Pp. 1–96. (Clásicos Castellanos)
————. *La devoción de la cruz*, ed. Angel Valbuena. Madrid, 1953. Pp. 1–117. (Clásicos Castellanos)
————. *El alcalde de Zalamea*, ed. Augusto Cortina. Madrid, 1955. Pp. 111–209. (Clásicos Castellanos)
————. *La dama duende*, ed. Angel Valbuena Briones. Madrid, 1954. Pp. 1–110. (Clásicos Castellanos)

### B. ENGLISH TRANSLATIONS OF CALDERÓN'S PLAYS

BIRCH, FRANK and J. B. TREND. *Life Is a Dream*. Cambridge: Heffer, 1925.
CAMPBELL, ROY. In *The Classic Theatre III: Six Spanish Plays*, ed. Eric Bentley. New York: Doubleday (Anchor), 1959. *Love After Death*, pp. 315–405; *Life Is a Dream*, pp. 407–80.
————. *The Surgeon of His Honour*, introd. E. W. Hesse. Madison: University of Wisconsin, 1960.
COLFORD, WILLIAM E. *Life Is a Dream*. New York: Barron, 1958.
————. *The Mayor of Zalamea*. New York: Barron, 1959.
FITZGERALD, EDWARD. *Eight Dramas of Calderón*. New York: Macmillan, 1906; reprinted New York: Dolphin Books, 1961. *The Painter of His Own Dishonour; Keep Your Own Secret; Gil Perez, the Galician; Three Judgments at a Blow; The Mayor of Zalamea; Beware of Smooth Water; The Mighty Magician; Such Stuff as Dreams Are Made of*.
HOLLAND, LORD. *Three Comedies*. London: Hatchard, 1807. Calderón's *Keep Your Own Secret* and *The Fairy Lady*.
JONES, WILLIS KNAPP. *The Feast of Belshazzar*, in *Spanish One Act Plays in English*. Dallas: Tardy, 1934.
MACCARTHY, DENIS FLORENCE. *Dramas I, by Calderón: The Constant Prince; The Physician of His Own Honour; The Secret in Words. Dramas II, by Calderón: Love After Death; The Purgatory of St. Patrick; The Scarf and the Flower*. London: Dolman, 1853.
————. *Calderón's Dramas: Love the Greatest Enchantment; The Sorceries of Sin; The Devotion of the Cross*. London: Longmans, Green, 1861.

————. *Calderón's Dramas: Belshazzar's Feast; The Divine Phi-lothea.* Dublin, 1867.

————. *Calderón's Dramas: The Two Lovers of Heaven; Chyrs-anthus and Daria.* Dublin: Fowler, 1870.

————. *Calderón's Dramas: Life Is a Dream; The Wonder-Working Magician; The Purgatory of St. Francis.* London: King, 1873. (Henry W. Wells has revised and edited six MacCarthy translations in *Calderón de la Barca: Six Plays.* New York: Las Américas, 1961. These include *The Wonder-Working Magician; The Constant Prince; The Devotion of the Cross; Love After Death; Belshazzar's Feast; Life Is a Dream.*)

MORGAN, C. *Life's a Dream.* BBC Great Plays Booklet No. 4; London, 1928.

PAYNE, JOHN HOWARD. *The Last Duel in Spain,* in *America's Lost Plays,* ed. Barrett H. Clark. Princeton: Princeton University Press, 1940.

PIERRA, ADOLFO. *Nobility, or The Mayor of Zalamea.* Philadelphia, 1885.

SHELLEY, PERCY BYSSHE. *The Wonder-Working Magician* (fragments), in *The Classic Theater III: Six Spanish Plays,* ed. Eric Bentley, New York: Doubleday (Anchor), 1959.

SINGLETON, MACK HENDRICKS. *The Great Theatre of the World,* in *Masterpieces of the Spanish Golden Age,* ed. Angel Flores. New York: Rinehart, 1957.

SIPMAN, FRANCIS E. *The Great World-Theatre.* Einsiedeln, Switzerland, 1955.

STIRLING, W. F. *Life Is a Dream.* Havana, 1942.

TRENCH, RICHARD CHENEVIX. *The Great Theatre of the World,* rev. by John Garrett Underhill in *20 Non-Royalty One-Act Popular Classics,* ed. Margaret Mayorga. New York: Greenberg, n.d.

### C. STAGE VERSIONS

ARNOUX, ALEXANDRE. *Calderón: Trois Comédies (La Vie est une Songe; Le Médecin de son Honneur; L'Alcade de Zalamea).* Paris, 1955.

CAMUS, ALBERT. *La Dévotion a la Croix [de Calderón].* Paris: Gallimard, 1953.

### D. BIOGRAPHIES

COTARELO MORI, EMILIO. *Ensayo sobre la vida y obra de don Pedro Calderón de la Barca.* Madrid, 1924.

FRUTOS CORTÉS, EUGENIO. *Calderón de la Barca.* Madrid: Ed. Labor, 1949.

TRENCH, RICHARD CHENEVIX. *Calderon, His Life and Genius, with Specimens of His Plays.* New York: Redfield, 1856.

E. SPANISH DRAMA

CHAYTOR, H. J. *Dramatic Theory in Spain*. Cambridge, 1925.

GOULDSON, KATHLEEN. "Three Studies in Golden Age Drama," in *Spanish Golden Age Poetry and Drama*, I. Liverpool: Institute of Hispanic Studies, 1946.

LEWES, G. H. *The Spanish Drama: Lope de Vega and Calderón*. London, 1846.

PARKER, A. A. "The Approach to the Spanish Drama of the Golden Age," *Diamante* VI, Hispanic and Luso-Brazilian Councils. London, 1957. Reprinted in *The Tulane Drama Review*, IV, 1959.

RENNERT, H. A. *The Spanish Stage in the Time of Lope de Vega*. New York, 1909.

WARDROPPER, BRUCE W. *Introducción al teatro religioso del Siglo de Oro*. Madrid: Revista de Occidente, 1954.

F. CALDERÓN CRITICISM

BRENAN, GERALD. "Calderón and the Late Drama," Chapter XII of *The Literature of the Spanish People*. New York: Meridian, 1957.

CASTRO, AMÉRICO. "Algunas observaciones acerca del concepto del honor en los siglos XVI y XVII." *Revista de Filología Española* (III), 1916, pp. 1–50.

CHAPMAN, W. G. "Las comedias mitológicas de Calderón." *Revista de Literatura* (V), 1954, pp. 34–67.

CONSTANDSE, A. L. *Le Baroque Espagnol et Calderón*. Amsterdam: Plus Ultra, 1951.

CORREA, G. "El doble aspecto de la honra en el teatro del siglo XVII." *Hispanic Review* (XXVI), 1958, pp. 99–107.

COSSÍO, J. J. DE. "La 'secreta venganza' en Lope, Tirso y Calderón." *Fenix*, 1935, pp. 501–15.

DUNN, P. N. "Honour and the Christian Background in Calderón." *Bulletin of Hispanic Studies* (XXXVII), 1960, pp. 75–105.

ENTWISTLE, WILLIAM J. "Calderón et le théatre symbolique." *Bulletin Hispanique* (LII), 1950, pp. 41–54.

————. "Calderón's *La devoción de la cruz*." *Bulletin Hispanique* (L), 1948, pp. 472–82.

JONES, C. A. "Honor in *El alcalde de Zalamea*." *Modern Language Review* (L), 1955, pp. 444–49.

————. "Honor in Spanish Golden-Age Drama." *Bulletin of Hispanic Studies* (XXXV), 1958, pp. 199–210.

MACCOLL, NORMAN. "Introductions" in *Select Plays of Calderón*. London: Macmillan and Co., 1888.

MENÉNDEZ Y PELAYO, M. *Calderón y su teatro*. Madrid, 1881.

OPPENHEIMER, M. "The Baroque Impasse in the Calderonian Drama." *PMLA* (LXV), 1950, pp. 1146–65.

PARKER, A. A. *The Allegorical Drama of Calderón*. Oxford: Dolphin, 1943.

SAUVAGE, MICHELINE. *Calderón: Dramaturge*. Paris: L'Arche, 1959.

SLOMAN, ALBERT E. *The Dramatic Craftsmanship of Calderón*. Oxford: Dolphin, 1958.

VALBUENA BRIONES, ANGEL. "Prólogo General" and "Notas Preliminares," in *Obras completas [de Calderón]*, Tomo II, *Comedias*. Madrid: Aguilar, 1956.

VALBUENA PRAT, ANGEL. *Calderón, su personalidad, su arte dramático, su estilo y sus obras*. Barcelona: Editorial Juventud, 1941.

WARDROPPER, BRUCE W. "The Unconscious Mind in Calderón's *El pintor de su deshonra*." *Hispanic Review* (XVIII), 1950, pp. 285–301.

WIER, L. E. *The Ideas Embodied In the Religious Drama of Calderón*. Lincoln: University of Nebraska Studies, 1940.

WILSON, E. M. "La discreción de Don Lope de Almeida." *Clavileño* (II), 1951, No. 19, pp. 1–10.

———. "The Four Elements in the Imagery of Calderón." *Modern Language Review* (XXXI), 1936, pp. 34–47.

G. CHRONOLOGY AND BIBLIOGRAPHY

HILBORN, HARRY WARREN. *A Chronology of the Plays of D. Pedro Calderón de la Barca*. Toronto: University of Toronto, 1938.

SLOMAN, ALBERT E. "Bibliography: Calderonian Criticism Since 1900," in *The Dramatic Craftsmanship of Calderón*. Oxford: Dolphin, 1958, pp. 309–22.

# SECRET VENGEANCE FOR SECRET INSULT

*(A SECRETO AGRAVIO, SECRETA VENGANZA)*

# DRAMATIS PERSONAE

Don Sebastian, *King of Portugal*
Don Lope de Almeida, *a Portuguese gentleman*
Don Juan de Silva, *his friend*
Don Luis de Benavides, *a Castilian gentleman*
Don Bernardino, *old man*
Duke of Berganza
Doña Leonor, *wife of Don Lope*
Sirena, *her maid*
Celio, *servant to Don Luis*
Manrique, *servant to Don Lope*
*Boatman*
*Retinue*
*Soldiers*

The scene is laid in Lisbon, in the neighborhood of the Galician Quarter, and in other places.

# SECRET VENGEANCE FOR SECRET INSULT

## ACT ONE

*Outside the* KING'S *country house*

*Enter* KING SEBASTIAN, DON LOPE DE ALMEIDA, MANRIQUE,
*and the King's retinue.*

DON LOPE. Once more, great sire, I humbly beg your leave
to add to that consent which once you gave
me, to be married.
Always attentive to your will and word,
in whose grace I thrive, my purpose now
is to acquaint you with my urgent vow,
which is, with your indulgence, to cast away
these arms, as Mars himself yields the victory
to Love when peace begins and must allow
the olive to succeed the laurel bough.
I have served you, and if today I speak
of it my sole intent is but to seek
reward in one word which graciously allows
me to depart at once to greet my spouse.
    *King.* God speed you; your wish is granted.
I am glad to see you married,
and if I were not now about
to wage a war in Africa, I would
hope to stand as your best man.
    *Don Lope.* May the laurel always crown your brow
as loftily as it does now.
    *King.* Don Lope, I value and respect you highly.
                        *[Exeunt the* KING *and retinue*
    *Manrique.* You are happy.
    *Don Lope.*            Such glory
and such bliss would ill
disguise one's happiness.
But I'd be happier still
if I could only fly
away today.
    *Manrique.* Like the wind.
    *Don Lope.* That would not help me much.

3

The wind's a sluggish element.
But if Love would only lend
me wings I'd be borne away
by passion's fire. He who'd use
the wind must go by way
of wind's unsteady wallowings.
But the course that Love would choose
requires fiery wings.
   *Manrique.* Tell me, sir, and relieve
my doubts: why the hurry
to depart at once, supposing you've
a reason for it?
   *Don Lope.*          To marry.
   *Manrique.* But, sir, don't you see it's wrong,
and enough to make the world suspect,
when a man goes rushing headlong
into matrimony? If the day
you are to marry, you elect
to be impatient of the wind,
what's left to do, reflect,
the day you are a widower?

   *Enter* DON JUAN DE SILVA, *in ragged clothes.*

   *Don Juan* [*to himself*]. Oh native land, how differently
I thought of my return
that unhappy day I went away!
Who would not rather stay
with your sweet earth beneath his feet?
But the man who's been disgraced
must always find a place
anywhere but where he's known.
Now these people here have no reason
to see in me the wretch
I take myself to be.
   *Don Lope.* Wait a moment. Incredible!
Can it be or do I dream?
Don Juan!
   *Don Juan.* Don Lope!
   *Don Lope.*         Still doubting
such good fortune, my arms
hang wide and limp; let them
enclose you in a tight embrace.
   *Don Juan.* But wait, and give me time
to justify myself before

one so worthy and so honorable.
For I, who come bereft by fate
and destitute, am ashamed
to rouse your generous heart.
    *Don Lope.* I must condemn your reasoning,
for if fortune grants mankind
all the treasures of the earth,
only Heaven offers one
a friend like you. Now see
what good luck Heaven's brought us!
    *Don Juan.* Though your words encourage me,
there's yet a greater misery.
Consider what my straits must be
if they're far worse than poverty.
If there were any way
to mitigate my grief,
it would begin, Don Lope,
in your attentive audience.
At the famous Conquest
of the Indies, where the tomb
of night and the cradle of the sun
both shared one place of rest,
there, we two were friends—
such close friends, indeed, that
where we fought our two bodies
had one soul, one heart. There
we lusted not for riches
but for honor's sake, and ever
spent our courage probing
with our ships those distant provinces
as yet unknown to science.
Such vessels were entrusted
to the cause of fortune
by Lusitania's noblemen.
Our fleet surpassed in fact
the fleet that Jason only feigned.
The eulogy for that enterprise
and all our nation's valor,
I leave to a much sweeter voice,
the great Luis de Camoens',
who sang the deeds he fought.
Now it happened afterward
that you, Don Lope, were summoned
home upon your father's death,

and I remained behind—
you well know with what acclaim
from friends and others generally,
the sense of which is sharper now
for being wholly lost.
But there's a sort of balm in it
for one who never outraged fortune
and yet lives so utterly
estranged from fortune now.
In Goa there was a lady,
daughter of a man whom wealth
had made greedier for
greater store of enterprise.
Beauty and discretion,
two virtues normally at odds,
were reconciled in her. I wooed
her gallantly enough to be
worthy of her favor.
Yet who that's ever won at first
has not at long last lost?
Who that's ever tasted
happiness has not lived
to see it die? Sport, love,
and fortune are, in this, alike.
Don Manuel de Sosa, son of
the governor of that name,
quite publicly in Goa,
became my rival for the love
of Violante, as she was called
who inspired my unhappiness.
Don Manuel was a man full of
high spirits, civility,
courage, sense, and gallantry.
I do not deny his virtues,
for though I took his life,
I would not take away
his honor. I made light
of his amorous pretensions,
since, as it was, I knew
I was the one she favored,
and perceiving his chagrin
only increased my happiness.
One day the sun arose in all its
glory (if only those rays

had been expunged forever!)
and with that sun rose Violante.
Surrounded by her servants,
she approached the shore where
a throng had rallied to greet
a galley recently arrived
in our harbor. Its arrival
was the occasion both for public
concourse and my own catastrophe.
We were among a group of friends
and soldiers chatting in the crowd
when Violante came by.
She made her way so gracefully
each felt she drew his heart away:
as if her fleet foot were the moving
cause that bore off all imaginings.
One captain cried, "The woman's
beautiful!" to which Don Manuel
replied, "Which reveals her temperament."
And then the other, "She must be cruel."
"It's not on that account I say it,"
Don Manuel replied, "but that
her beauty hides the worst of it."
At this I said, "No one's yet
deserved her love, for there's no one
worthy of it, and if there were,
it would be I." "Liar!" he cried.
I cannot even now proceed:
my voice struck dumb, tongue tied,
my body frozen, one throbbing heart,
my senses mummified, one livid
pain, all singing out the insult.
Fatal error of mankind!
Vile universal law!
That any provocation,
reasonable or not, should stain
a man's proud honor which he spends
a lifetime in acquiring,
and that the ancient name
of honesty should fall prostrate
before the faintest voice!
Oh God, that honor's diamond
should be turned to ash and cinders
by a single puff of breath!

That its purity, more radiant
than the sun, should be clouded
by the merest passing breeze!
I have strayed from my story;
passion carried me away.
Forgive me, I shall return to it.
He had scarcely said the word,
Don Lope, when my sword flitted
from its scabbard to his heart,
to all appearances as if
the insult were the lightning
and my sword the thunder.
Drenched in his own blood,
he fell dead upon the sand.
Then, to protect myself, I ran
for refuge to a church of
the Holy Order of St. Francis.
Since the father of Don Manuel
was governor, I was forced to hide.
In fear and trembling, I lay three
days inside a tomb, alive.
Who would have thought that I,
so far the opposite to death,
should lie as one he'd buried there?
So three days passed until,
favored by the friendship
of the captain of that galley
in our port, who was bound
for Lisbon, I went aboard
one night, and by that token
saved my life. I was hidden
in that vessel under monster
winds and waves. Such is life's impious
deceit! Either his sufferance
should not cast out the man
who bears his own dishonor,
or else, if he revenge himself,
let him be freed of blame.
For it is wrong to let insult
be punished and not let
the punisher be pardoned.
Today I came to Lisbon
in such poverty I dared not
enter it. This is my story,

no longer miserable because
it brings me happily to you.
This hand you take in greeting,
Don Lope, would return
a thousandfold, if one bereft
by fortune were deservant,
the mercy, honor, kindness
which you bestow upon me.

    *Don Lope.* Don Juan de Silva, this is
a grievous tale your burdened heart
has taught your tongue to utter.
I have listened carefully,
and in pondering all you say
conclude there is no argument,
however subtly couched,
to controvert your own.
Which of us can live from birth
untouched by the inclemencies
of fortune and his time?
Who is ever free and who exempt
from negative intention,
a double-purposed heart
rousing the baneful hand
and the tongue's malignancy?
Of these no man is free.
He alone is counted fortunate
who, like you, has cleansed the stain
upon his honor and punished
the transgressor. You're honest:
dark shadows will not tarnish
nor obscure your ancient honor.
In our present friendship
may be seen a virtue like that
of those two herbs, both poison,
so equally opposed that while one
consumes with heat, the other
penetrates with cold, but being
once compounded do achieve
a salutary state both positive
and sound. And so now are we:
you unhappy, I more fortunate:
let's share the difference between us,
and temper my well-being
with your unhappiness, my joy

with your sorrow, my good
with your ill fortune, for none
may hope to do away with
the cause of pleasure or of pain.
I was married in Castile,
by proxy, with the most beautiful
of women . . . (though properly
speaking, beauty is the least
of all her attributes),
noblest, richest, most virtuous
and most wise, a woman of whom
the imagination scarcely
can conceive. Her name is
Doña Leonor de Mendoza,
who, with Don Bernardino
my uncle, arrives today
in the Galician Quarter.
I go there to meet her now
with such glad auspices
as you may witness here. A vessel
gaily decked that waits for her
finds the day too slovenly
adroop in its own light sails,
for good fortune when it tarries
may turn ill when it arrives.
Such is all my happiness,
made happier by the gladness which
your coming adds to it, Don Juan.
Do not let your poverty
give cause for shame or sadness.
I am rich. My house, dear friend,
my table, horses, servants,
all my property, my honor
and my life, they all are yours.
Be comforted that fortune
leaves you one true friend,
and that grim adversity
could not vanquish you; nor
have you lost the spirit
of your valor, the soul
that quickens you, or this arm of mine
that always will defend you.
Do not attempt to answer me:
the finer courtesies between

two friends may be left unsaid.
Come with me now to where you
may privately observe
the happiness awaiting me.
Today my wife arrives in Lisbon,
and these three leagues of sea
(which for me are more like fire)
must be traversed before we meet her,
for she undoubtedly is waiting
on the other side.
  *Don Juan.*  See that your own
nobility is not cast down,
Don Lope, by my ragged state,
since what the world esteems
is fine clothes, not noble breeding.
  *Don Lope.* Then that's the world's illusion
which cannot understand that while gold
may clothe the body, only
nobility can clothe the soul.
Come with me. [*Aside.*] Come, my sighs, inflate
these sails, and steer love's course
through seas inflamed by passion's fire.
       [*Exeunt* Don Lope *and* Don Juan
  *Manrique.* I'll scud away and take the lead
in a common bark they call a scull;
then, being skull-skilled, I'll beg
some token of my new mistress
for the good news her husband comes;
since her wedding day brings
any lady a reward,
for that day ends her maidenhood,
if she is still a maid.
         [*Exit* Manrique


*A field near the Galician Quarter*

*Enter* Don Bernardino, *an old man,* Doña Leonor,
*and* Sirena.

  *Don Bernardino.* Here on this pleasant hillside strewn
   with
flowers, where springtime now comes courting,
here you may rest a while, fair Doña
Leonor, until Don Lope,
your husband, comes for you.

He shall pardon your sweet sorrow,
though I see no cause to wonder
why you must grieve, for having come
to Portugal, you are now compelled
to bid Castile farewell.

    *Doña Leonor.* Venerable Don Bernardino:
my hushed lament is no
sign of ingratitude
for the great honor fate
and fortune have bestowed.
Now as my sweetheart appears,
I feel joy, and yet, as you know,
joy often comes to one with tears.

    *Don Bernardino.* Your excellent discretion
certainly acquits you,
but even though it does,
I shall gladly take the blame.
Meanwhile you shall have time
to overcome your melancholy.
Rest here a while from the rigors
of the sun and its consuming beams.
May Heaven always protect you.

                           [*Exit* DON BERNARDINO

    *Doña Leonor.* Sirena, is he gone now?
    *Sirena.*                           Yes.
    *Doña Leonor.* Will anyone overhear us?
    *Sirena.* I suspect we are alone.
    *Doña Leonor.* Then God relieve me of this burden
of my life, my pent-up breast.
If weeping would only end this
ache that rankles in me, the passion
in my soul that shoots anger
into tears and floods my eyes
and fills my mouth with sighs.
Grant me no peace, no ease,
till they consume my burden,
for all my tears and cries
are kindling points of fire.
May they destroy life's passion
in one torrential flame,
now that my journey's at an end
after miles of sea and wind.
Now my voice is flame and air,

and my tears a sobbing fire.

*Sirena.* What are you saying, madam?
Think of the danger to your honor.

*Doña Leonor.* How can you, who know my sorrow
and my helplessness, offer
lessons in restraint? How can
you turn from my complaints
and tell me to be silent?

*Sirena.* I shall listen to them, though I think
that your complaints are now in vain.

*Doña Leonor.* Sirena, how can you call them vain?
Does the flower not complain
when the quickened breeze has stabbed it
and the senile sun creeps
downward to its jeweled tomb?
The proud hillside complains when
the wild wind has gouged it.
And then there's Echo, vocal nymph,
lamenting her misfortune, who grieves
once more beyond her final accent.
The lovelorn ivy frets, though knowing
how to love, when it has lost
the hard tree trunk it used to cling to.
So too any bird complains,
however gently, of one who claims
it for the gilded cage,
where it seems to soothe itself in song
which, even though ignored
as song, comes through as sorrow's rage.
The sea complains upon the shore,
hurling all its watery tongues
against the rocks' opposing lips.
Fire frets that's locked and whirled
by thunders warring on the world.
Then how can I desist
from quarreling with my pain,
if flower, hillside, stone,
Echo, ivy, bird and sun,
tree trunk, sea and wind and thunderbolt
each has its just complaint?

*Sirena.* Yes, but of what use is your
continual despair
now Don Luis is dead

and you are married? What
is it you seek?
 *Doña Leonor.* Alas,
Sirena dear, to say
that Don Luis is dead is to say
I too am dead. For even
though compelled by Heaven,
I'd still be as you see me now:
calm, benumbed, bereft of soul
and will—yes, a woman dead,
and not a woman married.
Those things which I once learned and loved,
all of them, alas, may be removed
or lost, but not forgotten.
Can I forget the vows I've taken?
Love deceives, else how can so clear
a truth be scorned? Whoever has been
constant once cannot afterward
forget, if he truly loved,
or have loved at all if he forget.
Remember what I felt when they
told me of his death? I forced
myself to marry someone else,
as if only to avenge myself!
Now once for all I take leave
of sorrow. Love, I've walked
with you to the altar steps; I leave
you here. You dare not follow further
to the altar of my honor.

    *Enter* MANRIQUE.

 *Manrique.* How lucky for me to be here first,
how venturesome of me,
oh joy of joys, and doubly
joyous me, to be the first
to press his lips upon your feet
which, overladen with these flowers,
now become the summer's harbingers.
And since I'm quick while others plod,
I'm here to kiss and kiss again,
and kiss as often as I can,
without offending my Lord God.
 *Doña Leonor.* Who are you?
 *Manrique.*       The least of servants

to Don Lope, my master
(though not his least of babblers),
and he has sent me in advance
with news of his arrival.

*Doña Leonor.* Well spoken. I was negligent.
Here, take this, and tell me
how you serve your master.

*Manrique.* As Jack of all trades and humors.
Doesn't such a title tell you that
I'm the nobleman's own gentleman?

*Doña Leonor.* How are you his gentleman?

*Manrique.* As the mouth is to the smile.
Body servant, and as such preferred
for matters of close confidence;
and thus the bawd of all his servants,
to any foot the floor. On guard,
his major-domo; his chamberlain
when I await my master's hand-
me-downs; his dining steward when
I bite into the choicest ham;
his secretary and least friend
in telling his latest secret;
his chief groom consummate
when I'm too bored to walk
and leap upon his horse's back
to exercise it down the street.
When there's anything of such
importance that it's kept from me,
then I spy for him and may become
his teller later, for where there's some
thing to collect, I'll tell anyone.
When pilfering what I require
in the market, I'm his butler,
and keeper of his stores when
I filch from them; his valiant valet
when I have taken to my heels;
the coachman wearing down his wheels
by day, entrusted with his *billets
doux*; and so I clearly argue
that as I serve so variously
I serve him constantly:
each an office, one by one,
and all whispering of him at once.

*Enter* DON BERNARDINO, DON LUIS, *and* CELIO, *his servant;*
*these three remain some distance removed from*
DOÑA LEONOR, SIRENA, *and* MANRIQUE.

Don Luis. I am a merchant and deal in diamonds.
All these now precious flashing stones once
were of the body of the sun, whose burning mine
refined the crudest grain to bright perfection.
In traveling to Lisbon from Castile
I was struck, in this village, by a marvel
most divine, incarnate in the lady
you accompany; the rumor is that she
is married or will very shortly be.
And since the custom is at weddings to display
one's treasure, where jewels and finery
go together, I'll show you these diamonds,
no less aglow than starlight; see if such stones,
the wedding, and your desire may not yield us
some occasion here for roadside commerce.
    Don Bernardino. What you guess and what you hope
        for now strike
home. Your timing's excellent, for you as well
as me. Since the bride is sad, I shall
divert her melancholy with a jewel.
Wait here while I go to tell her.
    Don Luis. Before you go, take this diamond, sir,
as one clear token of my truthfulness; [*Giving it to him.*]
I cannot doubt but that its excellence
and worth, once she has beheld it, will give you
access to her graciousness.
    Don Bernardino.        How strangely pure!
What depths of brilliance in this jewel. Here,
                    [*Approaching her.*]
Leonor, my child, there is
a diamond merchant passing by
whose priceless wares you must inspect.
Lay aside your melancholy.
I shall buy the jewel
that pleases you the most.
This diamond in particular comes
as witness to the rest, a beacon
whose beauty's piercing light
strain the sun's own purity,

as if it were the sun's own child.
Here, take it.                                                    [*Gives it to her.*]
    *Doña Leonor* [*aside*]. My God! What's this I see?
    *Don Bernardino.* Tell me . . .
    *Doña Leonor* [*aside*]. I cannot believe it!
    *Don Bernardino.*   . . . If you wish to see him.
    *Doña Leonor* [*aside*].                                    Alas,
the same, there's no mistaking it. . . .
—Have him come! Sirena!
               [DON BERNARDINO *walks aside.*]
[*Aside.*] Release me, love, from this torment,
this enchantment, this abyss.
—This sun-dipped diamond here
is the one I gave to Don Luis
as my pledge. It is his.
Am I deceived by my own tears?
No, it is his. But I must know
how and why it reappears.
    *Sirena.* Pretend it's nothing. They're coming now.

### *Enter* DON LUIS.

    *Don Luis.* Fair lady, I am . . .
    *Doña Leonor* [*aside*]. My sorrow's cause,
a ghost in flesh and blood.
    *Sirena* [*aside to her*]. I see the reason for
your astonishment. But
conceal it, say nothing yet.
    *Don Luis.* I am one who comes here hoping
to make happy use of a timely
circumstance, so long awaited.
The value of my jewels
is inestimable.
And one among the rest
I know you must esteem
especially, a perfect prize
whose honest beauty I suspect
you'll sense at once when this,
my jewel of steadfastness,
lies fixed upon your breast.
Here's another: Cupid's diamond,
and worth a treasury,
which I've designed in jewels
closely matched, and therefore have
dedicated it to love.

My purpose was to answer those
accusing love of fickleness
with some work made perfect
through my constancy alone.
The heart I bear contains
no counterfeit, no false stone.
Further, among my precious rings
is one aglow with memories. Once
an emerald I had was stolen
from me on the highway, mainly,
I suppose, for its wondrous hue.
It was meant to match this sapphire,
but they took the emerald only,
leaving this blue stone you see.
It was then I shouted in despair,
"How deeply vengeful you must be
to carry off my hope
and leave me to my jealousy!"
If it please your loveliness,
I have more delights in store
that will disclose my memories,
my heart, my love, my constancy.
    *Don Bernardino.* This merchant is most ingenious.
How handsomely his speech awakes
one's curiosity to gaze
upon his glowing jewels.
    *Doña Leonor.* Although the jewels you extol
are all you say they are,
the occasion you have chosen
to display them's inappropriate.
I would have delighted in
such an exhibition
had it been offered earlier.
But as it is, you come too late.
What would they say of me,
a newly married woman,
if, while awaiting the coming
of my noble husband,
I should offer, not regret,
but fullest sympathy,
to that display you call your heart,
your love, your constancy?
Do not show them, for surely
you'd be ill advised to let

such memories, so long
concealed, now be disesteemed.
And take your diamond too,
although I know I lose thereby
the lovely, faithful light
engendered by the sun itself.
Do not blame me for evasiveness,
but blame yourself for coming
out of time and out of place.

[A *noise offstage.*]

    *Manrique* [*looking back*]. Here comes Don Lope, my
        master.
    *Don Luis* [*aside*]. What unhappiness is this
whose edge can cut so fine?
Does any sorrow equal mine?
    *Doña Leonor* [*aside*]. What spite!
    *Don Luis* [*aside*].                What cruelty!
    *Don Bernardino.* We shall go forth to greet him.

[*Exit* DON BERNARDINO

    *Manrique.* Silence, everyone, and listen to
the first stupidity:
the swain, whom his lady pleases,
when he comes to see her, straight away
gambles with stupidities:
what he says and what he does
reveal the gambling cheat.

[*Exit* MANRIQUE

    *Don Luis.* How can you answer me this way,
shameless, fickle, and disloyal
woman, so pliable and vain,
and so like a woman, how
do you propose to justify
your vagrant memory
and your broken pledge?
    *Doña Leonor.* There's a reason for my broken pledge:
I believed you dead; I mourned for you,
though my heart could not forget you.
And if I had not yet been married,
now that I see you are alive,
you would soon discover I'm a woman
neither fickle nor disloyal.
But I've been wed by proxy.
    *Don Luis. By proxy,* yes; that puts it well.
By proxy you've destroyed my fate.

By proxy you've deserted me.
By proxy you've flung my heart away,
and by your proxy I am dead.
This says what you really meant
and not merely what you said.
You've accepted me as dead
is what it comes to; all by proxy.
    *Doña Leonor.* I can't, I cannot, oh misery,
answer you. I am in the presence
of my enemy, not my husband.
Yet since you doubt my loyalty,
the words I must address to him
shall speak to you as well.
                    [DON LUIS *withdraws to one side.*]

    *Enter* DON LOPE, BERNARDINO, MANRIQUE.

    *Don Lope.*

When praise of your rare loveliness was told,
And rumor everywhere reported it,
I loved you on my faith and, thus accepted,
Leonor was idolized in my heart's hold.
    When with astonished heart I now behold
The live Leonor, whose holy image it
Adored, heart blames weak fancy that begot
The copy of the life it had extolled.
    For only you may body forth your beauty.
How fortunate I'd be if I were worthy
Of your love, and more, if so you deemed me.
    Can I offend you or forget you, truly?
I who loved before I met you, surely,
Now I've seen you, loving is no duty.

    *Doña Leonor.*

I signed my troth before I saw you; so
I've lived and died in you alone, because
The object of my love was but your ghost,
Which, being yours, it seemed enough to know.
    How happy I would be if I could love you
As in that copy fancy often wrought!
So life might now redeem the common debt
We owed when I humbly signed my troth.
    I may be pardoned if my love falls short,
When faltering I come to meet your gaze,

Returning less for what's been dearly bought.
   Not I, but you deserve your heart's dispraise,
For though I honor you as spouse, I cannot
Love you as you appeared in former days.

   *Don Lope.* Now, my lord and uncle, give me
your affectionate embrace.
   *Don Bernardino.* These arms are the eternal bonds of
my love and friendship for you.
But come, do not delay:
let us at once make ready
to sail away.
   *Don Lope.* The sea today
salutes another Venus.
   *Manrique.* And as our lover and his lady
depart in married bliss,
I could hope (but do forgive me,
O noble audience),
our story might end with this.
                    [*Exeunt* DON LOPE, DOÑA LEONOR, DON
                         BERNARDINO, MANRIQUE *and* SIRENA
   *Celio.* Sir, now you've been so clearly
disabused, come to your senses,
mend your injuries and
be done with this at last.
For surely there's no other way;
you've no alternative.
   *Don Luis.* Yes, there is one, Celio.
   *Celio.* What can that be?
   *Don Luis.*                That's to die,
the last recourse. It's easy
to die now I've seen her married,
now Leonor has scorned my love
and mocked my hope. What's left
to kill me when only jealousy
keeps me alive? Yet she attempted
to console me, as if to hint
there's still some hope. When she addressed
her husband she was in fact
asking my forgiveness for
her fickle and forgetful heart.
   *Celio.*                What
do you mean—asking your forgiveness?
This is the sheerest madness.

*Don Luis.* I'll repeat her very words.
Notice how they spoke to me.

"I signed my troth before I saw you; so
I've lived and died in you alone, because
The object of my love was but your ghost,
Which, being yours, it seemed enough to know.

How happy I would be if I could love you
As in that copy fancy often wrought!
So life might now redeem the common debt
We owed when I humbly signed my troth.

I may be pardoned if my love falls short,
When faltering I come to meet your gaze,
Returning less for what's been dearly bought.

Not I, but you deserve your heart's dispraise,
For though I honor you as spouse, I cannot
Love you as you appeared in former days."

Well, if this is her apology
for suffering a change of heart,
let my witless hope become
a dagger dipped in poison. For if
I'm to die of sorrow, by Heaven,
I shall do it pleasantly,
and not die for jealousy
but for love. Come, let me boldly
follow up my fate until the end,
and blast all honor, for I must
have Leonor, at any price,
though I pay for her with my life.


# ACT TWO

*A room in* DON LOPE's *house in Lisbon*

*Enter* SIRENA *and* MANRIQUE.

MANRIQUE. Sirena, dearest heart:
you play the very Siren,
which gives me quite a start,
when you bewitch me simply
to deceive me; at least pity me
for suffering your disdain.

Servants, like their masters, may
experience the pain
of unrequited love.
A little token would be enough.
   *Sirena.* What is it I can give you?
   *Manrique.* Oh, a great deal, but now
I want no greater treasure
than that green fillet which you wear
so snugly round the waist,
like any girl who waits
to be untied behind or
like a kitchen wench about
to be divested of her nice
new fleccy woolen girdle.
   *Sirena.* You want my ribbon?
   *Manrique.*               Yes.
   *Sirena.* What strange times we live in when
a gallant can be satisfied
with a ribbon.
   *Manrique.*   That's it,
and if you hand it over I will
squander all my metaphors today
on a hundred thousand sonnets,
just to sing your praise.
   *Sirena.*           I can't resist
the thought of being so well sonneted.
Here, take it now and go.
I see my mistress coming.

                       [*Exit* MANRIQUE

      *Enter* DOÑA LEONOR.

   *Doña Leonor.* I have decided what to do.
I must be absolutely firm,
Sirena, for my life and honor
belong to me no longer
but to my husband, Don Lope.
Go tell Don Luis that as
he's noble, and prizes
his own honor which obliges him,
as a Spaniard and a soldier,
to be courteous, that a lady
(do not say Leonor,
for to any nobleman
simply *lady* should suffice),

that this lady begs him
to banish from his mind
any thought of love for her.
And tell him especially
to consider while he
lingers on a certain street
that the gallantries of Castile
are frowned upon in Portugal.
And tell him that my tears
implore him to go back to Castile
resolved to free me from the fate
of being an unhappy wife.
For Heaven knows, if he does not go
away, he forfeits both our lives.

   *Sirena.* I shall tell him all you say,
if I can only find him.

   *Doña Leonor.* When is he not lingering
somewhere along this street?
But do not speak with him outside.
If you meet, go to the inn instead.

   *Sirena.* Madam, you are very daring.

                                [*Exit* SIRENA

     *Enter* DON LOPE, DON JUAN, *and* MANRIQUE.

   *Don Lope* [*aside*]. Bright honor, how much must
still be done on your account.

   *Manrique.* They say the King's departure
for the wars is now imminent.

   *Don Lope.* There is no courtier or gentleman
in all of Lisbon who will not
think himself most worthy of
the finest panegyric
when he comes to die.

   *Manrique.*            It's true,
though I think otherwise.
For when I come to die
I want no panegyric,
nor tragedy nor interlude,
to be remembered by.

   *Don Lope.* Then you're not thinking of
going off to war in Africa?

   *Manrique.* Possibly I'll go, but if so,
only to have something more
to brag about, but surely

not to kill my fellow man
and vainly break the law of God
by which I live and bind myself.
In Africa there's no difference
I can see in being either
Moor or Christian. Scripture
says *Thou shalt not kill*; I'll
abide by that since I lack the wit
to interpret God's commandments.
    *Don Lope.* Leonor, my dear!
    *Doña Leonor.*               Dear husband!
The time that's passed since last
I saw you! My love complains
of every moment it has lost.
    *Don Lope.* Spoken like the very lady
of Castile you are! Do
put aside the flattery
and fine phrases. Note that
we Portuguese prefer
the feeling to its explanation,
for the lover by his very words
devalues all he feels.
If your love is blind, my love
must be mute.
    *Manrique.* Mine the devil's taken.
    *Don Lope.* Tell me why it is, Manrique,
that when I'm melancholy
you're always so bright and cheerful?
    *Manrique.* First tell me which among
the opposing passions is the better,
happiness or sorrow?
    *Don Lope.* Happiness, of course.
    *Manrique.*                 Then there you are:
would you have me put aside
the better for the worse?
You who choose the worse in feeling sad
would do better to be happy.
It would, at any rate,
be more desirable for me
to go from happiness to sorrow
while you do the opposite.
                           [*Exit* MANRIQUE
    *Doña Leonor.* Are you so sad, my lord?
It must be that my heart owes

you so little or else knows
itself even less, for it feels
nothing of your unhappiness.
   *Don Lope.* The sum of heritage and duty,
long and worthily sustained,
and binding me by laws
both human and divine,
now stirs my blood, cries out
shrilly to my conscience
to awake from this slothful peace
and this forgetfulness
where my proprietary
laurels lie in dusty sleep.
Renowned Sebastian, our King,
who like the phoenix is the heir
of centuries, goes off today
to war in Africa, leaving
no gentleman behind
in Portugal; for none
will lie abed while fame
cries out abroad. I wish, of course,
to join the King, yet since
I am but newly wed, I cannot
offer him my services
until, my dear Leonor,
your own lips grant me leave.
I now must seek that favor of you,
in granting which you honor me
and place me in your debt.
   *Doña Leonor.* You have been most thoughtful,
in following necessity,
to smooth the way with speeches
that inspire and encourage me.
Should you absent yourself, my lord,
through any counsel I may give you,
such an action in effect
would be the same as if
I had sentenced myself to death.
Go without my bidding, and your will
shall not refuse what life itself
bestows on you. And further,
since you see how highly I respect
your gallant inclination, you may
guess if I desire my present guide

to be your courage and not my love.
Join King Sebastian, may Heaven
bless his life; the blood of noblemen
is a monarch's patrimony.
Let no one say that woman's
cowardice deprives her husband
of his valor when reason
urges her to strengthen it.
This my heart advises,
though it be the heart that loves you.
However much the stranger
it may sound in saying so,
its sentiment is yours alone.

[*Exit* Doña Leonor

*Don Lope.* Have you ever seen such courage
in your life?
*Don Juan.* It deserves
to be inscribed and praised
by the pens and tongues of fame.
*Don Lope.* And what would you advise me?
*Don Juan.* Don Lope, I would answer
differently.
*Don Lope.* Tell me how.
*Don Juan.*                    A man
who has already laid aside
the bays of Mars and on his head
now wears the laurels of sweet peace,
what need has he to cleanse
his shields again of all the rust
and grime in which they lie?
I might myself be justified
in serving, were it not that, hidden
and in disgrace, I am as good
as dead. Nor can I volunteer:
the King would frown upon a criminal.
If this excuses me,
he'd surely be excused
whose past soldiery sufficiently
acquitted him. Do not go,
my friend; believe me, though
you are dissuaded by a man
and encouraged by a woman.

[*Exit* Don Juan

*Don Lope.* Heaven help me! Who can prudently

assess his own condition
while someone at the moment
is attempting to advise him?
Who would split himself in two
to find relief in another self?
But that's not it. Rather,
who deliberately would split
his consciousness in two
so that one half may be free
to vent his angry cries,
of which the other half
would continue ignorant?
This way his conscience would never
feel the burden of his voice.
In one breath I might thus become
my own accuser and defender,
yet neither hear nor see
any sign of the proceedings.
Now cowardice, now foolhardiness
have shamed me equally.
How is it one speaks or thinks at all!
For honor has a thousand eyes
to ferret out a fault,
a thousand ears to drink it in,
and only one poor tongue
to articulate its grievances.
What if honor had no eyes or ears
but a thousand tongues instead?
It then would not, as now it must,
being so narrowly regarded,
burst the chest like some exploding mine.
So far so good: I must then
articulate my grievances.
But where shall I begin?
In times of war and peace
my life was always honorable.
Ever loath to mewl complaint,
is it any wonder I never
learned its object or necessity?
No one can prepare for what
he does not fear. Do I dare
permit my tongue to say, *I f . . . ?*
Stay, be dumb, and utter neither
word nor syllable of my disgrace.

If *you* offend me I can punish you
and sentence you to life or death,
for being insult's victim
and offender both in one,
I may suffer insult
as well as punish it.
Do not say I'm jealous . . .
But there, I've said the word,
and cannot stuff it back
into my heart where it has raged.
How can my heart have brought it forth
for lisping on the lip
and not totally consumed my breath—
the facile exhalation
uttering that hateful word
so different from all others?
The effect of other words is felt
proceeding from the lip inward,
toward the heart, while this word flies
straight out from heart to lip.
What asp or serpent ever died
of its own venom bite?
My God, but I am subject
to the very deed when my own
anguish is the venom
I produce to kill myself.
I am jealous, I have said so.
Now, Heaven help me, but who is
that Castilian gentleman
who hangs about my doors,
my railings, and my threshold,
installed there like a living statue?
In the street, the doorway,
and the church, waiting, turning
like some sunflower to my honor
and forever drinking up its light.
God help me, but what can
Leonor have had in mind,
granting me leave to go so lightly;
no, granting it with such
a happy air, and yet, by
the very words she reasoned with,
obliging me to go away
when I may not have planned to go?

Finally, what can Don Juan
have meant by saying one might go
while declaring I should stay?
Would it not have been more reasonable
for my friend to show his reticence,
and my wife, her feelings of concern?
Would it not have been better had they
taken opposite positions:
Don Juan to urge me on,
and Leonor detain me?
Yes, that would have been better,
far better. But since this is
my burden, let me consider
how I may unburden it.
Surely honor can't be twisted
to condemn a man unjustly
by such subtle arguments as these.
Might it not be that Leonor,
so high-minded, resolute
and wise, should answer as she did
because she feared my reputation
would be harmed if I stayed behind?
It may well be that such indeed
is what she meant and felt
in answering as she did.
Might it not be true that Don Juan
really wanted me to stay,
and offered the argument
of my exemption, while only
seeming to cast doubt on Leonor?
Yes, that may be so. And might it not
also be the case that the lurking
gallant is involved elsewhere?
To press that case further:
when he waits and watches,
when he seems to woo some lady,
does he in any way insult me
or offend against my honor?
Being what she is, Leonor's
reputation is sound;
being what I am, my rectitude
is indisputable; nobody can
obliterate these facts.
And yet, alas, it may be said

of the ever-clear, unsullied sun
that the cloud which does not eclipse it
seeks, at any rate, to do so,
and even though it be unstained,
it's dimmed and so, at last, obscured.
Honor, are there further subtleties
to learn, still unpropounded?
More torments and more burdens,
more sorrows and suspicions,
more fears to hound me with,
more insults to drown me in,
more jealousies to confront me with?
There cannot be, and unless
you've greater means at your disposal
to destroy me, I now know how
I must proceed, with silence,
skill, and cunning, forewarned,
and on my guard, solicitous,
even obsequious, until occasion
give me strength to choose between
my life and death: and meanwhile,
come what may, let Heaven be my guide!

[*Exit* DON LOPE

*A street at the door of* DON LOPE'S *house.*

*Enter* SIRENA, *in a cloak;* MANRIQUE, *behind her.*

*Sirena* [*aside*]. Whatever I do, I cannot
escape Manrique, and get inside
the house; he has followed me all day.
What shall I do?
*Manrique.*        Girl in a veil,
hurling your glances about
and gliding so stealthily by, what
skill in the art of battle
your movements convey; your figure
exciting despite the gray goat's-
hair cloth you wear, like a boat
sailing by with the wind in its
poop, your slippers embroidered,
your heavy cloak listing apace:
speak now or unveil your face,
else you'll have me believe it's pimpled
and ugly, as they say of the fools

who go muffled and stealthily by,
though the way you dance past in your mules,
I'd say would give them the lie.
 *Sirena.* You've nothing more to add?
 *Manrique.*          Nothing.
 *Sirena.* And to how many girls have you
spoken this way?
 *Manrique.*   I was
terribly bashful before.
On my word of honor, I spoke
to only five girls all day.
Now I'm immensely reformed.
 *Sirena.* Heaven be praised for a man
so honest and true! I have
no more than nine lovers myself.
 *Manrique.* I believe you, and since you
believe me, I must at least
show you these tokens of love. [*Takes them out.*]
First, a lady's bun: this sinful
bun of hair once-upon-a-time
played its little role, and by way
of curler and switch was martyrized
and shriven. This string of pearls
is false; they are really lice's eggs,
which I admire, for when looked at
from afar they seem to be
a black panache dotted by a stream
of snow-white flies. This slender stick
is actually a whalebone discharged
by a corset; it was my misfortune
to receive it in a cudgeling.
The stick is rich in virtues,
correcting any breast and
the roundest hump, for there's
no figure but plays one false
by virtue of some whalebone.
This little slipper you now
gaze upon in my hand,
was once a house, I'll have you know,
where two midgets dwelt but never
met each other. This is a glove
which was once a nightingale
that undoubtedly was mum-dumb
for a very long time.

Here, sniff it: it oozes goat grease.
This ribbon once belonged
to a high and mighty lady;
but I disdain it.
    *Sirena.*       Why so?
    *Manrique.* Because I know she loves me.
Isn't that reason enough?
    *Sirena.*          Yes.
    *Manrique.* The lady I love must be a liar.
She must deceive and mock me,
make me jealous continually,
abuse me, leave me and, in brief,
must beg to marry me,
which is the thing I feel
most strongly about, for though
this is women's custom anyway,
I'd only take it as my right
to make that pleasant which
must afterwards become
a very grave affliction.
    *Sirena.* And is your lady beautiful?
    *Manrique.* No, but she's filthy.
    *Sirena.*          Then surely
she's a lady of high quality.
    *Manrique.* One eye weeps boiled honey,
and the other olive oil.
    *Sirena.* Is she understanding or prudent?
    *Manrique.* As for understanding herself,
I take it she's prudent; as for
others' understanding her,
quite the contrary; which means
she's prudently misunderstood
or understandably imprudent.
    *Sirena.* To show you I'm sincere and shall
await your loving pleasure,
I'll accept that ribbon from you.
    *Manrique.* Granted, most willingly.
    *Sirena.* Alas, alas!
    *Manrique.*       What's wrong?
    *Sirena.* My husband's coming now.
Begone, quickly; my husband's
the very devil. Disappear
around the corner, quickly,
and meanwhile, sir, when he's passed by,

I'll await you inside this house.

    *Manrique.* What a fine refuge you've discovered;
I live here myself, and shall return
in excellent good time.

                      *[Exit* MANRIQUE

### A *room in* DON LOPE's *house*

#### *Enter* SIRENA.

    *Sirena.* I slipped into the house
without being recognized.
I've tricked him beautifully,
but he's tricked me even more
by shaming and insulting me.
And saying I was ugly!
But that wouldn't trouble me,
even if it were true,
nor his saying I was stupid
and dirty; but to say that
one of my eyes weeps olive oil
and the other boiled honey!
No, by God, no! And even
if my eyes did weep only one
of those things, it wasn't right
of him to say so; the idea
of such a beggar, such an utter knave,
telling me one of my eyes weeps
olive oil and the other, honey!

#### *Enter* DOÑA LEONOR.

    *Doña Leonor.* Sirena.
    *Sirena.*             My lady.
    *Doña Leonor.* How anxiously I've waited for you!
You spoke to him?
    *Sirena.*             Yes, he sends
his answer by this letter
and promises if he may once
speak privately with you,
to go away forever.
    *Doña Leonor.* Now I've greater reason for concern.
Why did you take his letter?
    *Sirena.* To bring it to you.
    *Doña Leonor [aside].*     Alas,

how easily cruel hope steals
into my heart.
    *Sirena.*       Why, what does it
matter if you read the letter?
    *Doña Leonor.* Do you really think me capable
of doing such a thing? Sirena,
only your opinion keeps me now
from tearing it to shreds.
[*Aside.*] Oh, understand me better,
little fool   entreat me further.
I am dying to read it.
    *Sirena.* How can you blame the mere paper
he has written on, my lady,
and vent your anger by
destroying it?
    *Doña Leonor.* Well then,
I'll accept the letter now,
but only to destroy it.
    *Sirena.* Yes, but do read it first.
    *Doña Leonor* [*aside*]. That's it, entreat me further.
—How tiresome you are!
Well, to please you, I'll break the seal
and read it, but only for your sake.
    *Sirena.* Yes, I see; now open it.
    *Doña Leonor.* Well, this is what it says.
                             [*She opens it and reads.*]

"If I could but obey you, Leonor,
That is, forget you and protect my life,
I'd gladly do so; it would be enough
To know that I could never love you more.
    You send me warning of untimely death
If I persist in loving you. Please God
To slay me then, leaving unresolved
My life's endeavor with my passing breath.
    Do you pretend you can forget? Can I
Answer the scorn of such forgetfulness
And yet not feel my lips go numb, and die?
    I'll have you love me, if you'd bind me thus,
And then forget you when I've kissed your smile!
Joy sooner slips the mind than an offense."

    *Sirena.* Does the letter make you cry?
It only speaks of things gone by.
    *Doña Leonor.* I weep because it brings to mind

old memories I thought had died.

*Sirena.* A real love is not soon forgotten.

*Doña Leonor.* I was told the man had died
who now springs back alive,
as though an old wound had freshly
broken out again with blood.
His persistence now only
discredits me; if he does not
go away, I shall soon be dead
or ruined, though death would be a fate
far easier to contemplate.

*Sirena.* But you can make him go away.

*Doña Leonor.* How?

*Sirena.*                By seeing him; as he says,
see him once, and he'll leave Lisbon.

*Doña Leonor.* How can I manage it, Sirena?
If he'd agree to that, I'd venture
the impossible. How would he
come here?

*Sirena.* Listen closely.
The safest time is now, at twilight,
while it is not too early
to receive a male visitor
nor too late to fear the neighbors
will notice that he's here.
My master, as you know,
never comes home so early.
As for Don Luis, I'm sure
he is close by; he can enter
this hallway where you two
may talk, and then you may
speak your mind quite freely.
He will listen to what you say.
Then let fortune do the rest.

*Doña Leonor.* You put it all so neatly,
there seems to be nothing to fear;
even honor cannot doubt it,
when everything is clear.
Go now, find Don Luis.

[*Exit* SIRENA

*Doña Leonor.*          Love,
I have opened up the gate,
yet being what I am,
I can control my passion.

Not levity but honor
is my porter at the gate,
and must be my protector.
But if honor fail, I stand alone,
and if I cannot persevere,
I know well how to die.
I am trembling; each step I hear
I think is Don Lope's.
Was that the wind or he approaching?
Is it listening, has it heard me?
How like fear itself, that sound!
Oh, how can a woman of my
reputation take such a risk?

*Enter* SIRENA *and* DON LUIS, *in the dark.*

  *Sirena.* Leonor awaits you here.
  *Don Luis.*                       God,
how often have I dreamed
of this moment, thinking
it never would come to pass.
  *Doña Leonor.* Now you are in my house, Don Luis.
This is the occasion
you desired; say what you must
quickly, then go away.
I am so frightened of myself,
I feel as though my feet were chained
in ice; my own breathing
points a dagger at my heart,
and a rope around my neck.
  *Don Luis.* Fair Leonor, unless you've chosen
to forget past joys and pleasures,
you must recall how in Toledo
once, our native city,
I loved you dearly, from
the moment I first saw you
one early morning in the meadow,
where your presence adorned
that blossoming field; for the flowers
your hands had plucked, your lovely feet
restored. Now you must recall . . .
  *Doña Leonor.*                       Wait,
I shall be briefer. I recall
the days you used to haunt my street
and, despite my coldness,

sustained your faith and love
until I smiled at you at last.
For who would not succumb to tears
men weep when they truly are in love?
Thus favored, and with the night
as faithful go-between,
as well as with that letter
slipped through my lattice, you spoke
of marriage. But when you learned
that you'd received a captaincy
obliging you to serve the King,
you went away to Flanders.

    *Don Luis.*                    Yes,
and I'll tell you of that now.
I went off to battle
where a certain valiant
gentleman was killed; his name
was Don Luis Benavides,
and he came from Aragon.
Since our names were identical,
I was mistakenly reported
dead. How easily a lie's believed!
Returning to Toledo . . .

    *Doña Leonor.* I can account for that
more simply. Lifeless, shocked,
benumbed, I wept my days away.
Although I might enlarge
upon my feelings then
and name such sorrows one by one,
I must stop here. In brief,
urged and finally convinced
by others, I was married
by proxy in Toledo
to Don Lope.

    *Don Luis.* On the road back home
I learned of this. Intending
to undo the marriage,
I hastened here, disguised
as a merchant, which was when
I saw and spoke to you
so ambiguously.

    *Doña Leonor.* I was already married,
as I then informed you.
Why did you persist in coming here?

*Don Luis.* I came only to discover why
I had been so abused.
And if I can satisfy myself
that you have broken faith,
I shall return to Flanders
where a musket ball will
ultimately make good
a promise long delayed.

    *Sirena.* Someone is coming up the stairs.

    *Doña Leonor.* My God, what can I do?
This hallway is dark; as long
as you remain here all is well.
Since you are alone here
you can slip out, once whoever
it is has come inside.
But do not leave yet for Castile.
There will be occasion later
to finish what you have to say.

    *Sirena.* I shall follow you, my lady.

                   [*Exeunt* Doña Leonor *and* Sirena

    *Don Luis.* My bewilderment is suddenly
as deep as my unhappiness.
The hallway darkens, pulling in
the dismal shadows of the night.
Since I was never here before,
I cannot tell house from doorway.
My heart hangs heavy. Oh, Sirena
and Leonor, your fears
have left me witless in the dark.

   *Enter* Don Juan, *in the dark, who meets* Don Luis,
          *and both draw their swords.*

    *Don Juan.* At this late hour, and nobody's
lit the light? But what is this?
Who's there? You won't answer?

    *Don Luis* [*aside*]. I have found the door. Now I can
get out.

           [*Exit* Don Luis, *groping his way through an-*
              *other door*

    *Don Juan.* Answer me at once or else
my unsheathed sword will answer for you.

    *Enter* Don Lope, *in the dark, and* Manrique.

    *Don Lope.* The sound of clashing swords,
and the room in total darkness!

*Don Juan.* I hear your footsteps now.
*Manrique.* I'll go and get a candle.

[*Exit* MANRIQUE
*Don Lope.* Now there's swordplay in the house,
I have reason to fear the worst.
*Don Juan.* I say it again, who are you?
*Don Lope.* Who dares ask my name?
*Don Juan.*                    Since you ask,
I am one whose sword will slit open
in your breast a thousand mouths.
*Doña Leonor* [*offstage*]. A light, quickly!

*Enter* DOÑA LEONOR *and* SIRENA, *and* MANRIQUE
*with a candle.*

*Don Lope.*                    Don Juan!
*Don Juan.* Don Lope!
*Doña Leonor.*          God preserve us!
*Don Lope.* What does all this mean?
*Don Juan.* As I was going through the hallway,
I saw a man go out that way.
*Doña Leonor.* It must have been a man attempting
to rob the house.
*Don Lope.*          A man?
*Don Juan.* Yes, and when I asked his name,
he did not say a word.
*Don Lope* [*aside*]. I must dissimulate
or else be thought the victim
of the very fear I scorn.
—Upon my word, I might easily
have killed you! It was I
who went out that door, Don Juan.
Since I did not recognize
your voice and thought some stranger
challenged me in my own house,
I was angry, lost patience,
and replied silently, with my sword.
*Sirena.* How close we must have been
to some terrible catastrophe!
*Don Juan.* But how can that have happened?
If the man I say I saw
was actually here,
then he could not have left
this hallway by the door
through which you came in.

*Don Lope.*               I say
I was that man.
    *Don Juan.*   How strange!
    *Don Lope* [*aside*]. How inept, how damaging
an inquisitive friend can be!
The wisest, most prudent man alive
must one day find his conscience
on the very tongue of such a friend.
—Since you take it as a certainty
a stranger's broken in,
I'll have you strictly guard that door
against his leaving, while I
proceed to search the house.
    *Don Juan.* He shall never escape this way.
You may safely search the house.
    *Don Lope.* Be sure to guard it closely.
Do not leave it for any reason.

                         [*Exit* DON JUAN

[*Aside.*] I must now act most cautiously,
and if I find my honor stained,
I'll be so coolly circumspect
that only in my deepest silence
will the world discover
any hint of my revenge.
—Here now, Manrique, light the way
for me.
    *Manrique.* I don't dare; at least
I don't share your fondness for ghosts.

        [DON LOPE *attempts to enter a bedroom, and*
            DOÑA LEONOR *stops him.*]

    *Doña Leonor.* Do not enter this room, my lord.
Trust me; all is safe inside.
    *Don Lope* [*to* MANRIQUE]. Well, what are you afraid
    of?
    *Manrique.* Of everything.
    *Don Lope* [*to* DOÑA LEONOR]. Open it, I say.
[*To* MANRIQUE.] And you now, begone. [*Aside.*] Misfor-
    tune
needs no further witnesses.

        [DON LOPE *takes the light and goes in while*
         MANRIQUE *leaves the other way*

    *Doña Leonor.* Alas, Sirena, how cold
his anger is! Despair
bids me end my life here.

Don Lope will surely find
Don Luis concealed inside.
Don Lope has decided that
whoever left by the hallway door
entered my bedroom and is still there.
But why do I persist in wondering
what has happened? By now
Don Lope's found and spoken with him.
What shall I do? Escape, I cannot:
unhappy fear has chained my feet,
imprisoned me in cowardice.
Wretched, miserable confusion.

*Enter* DON LUIS, *his cloak hiding his face, sword drawn,
and behind him* DON LOPE, *carrying the candle,
his sword drawn.*

   *Don Lope.* Sir, do not conceal yourself.
   *Don Luis.* Then, sir, put down your sword.
Once a man's your prisoner,
there's more harm done than valor shown
in the spilling of his blood.
My home is in Castile;
there, in a field, I killed
a man in fair combat:
the issue was a lady
and my jealousy. I fled
and sought asylum here
in Lisbon, since I was banished
from Castile for that offense.
I learned this morning that
the dead man's brother was lurking
in this neighborhood
where he was seeking, treacherously,
with the help of others,
to take me by surprise.
Thus forewarned, I was passing this house
when three men in your doorway sprang out
and assaulted me. Perceiving
that self-defense against three men
was futile (though one's courage may
sometimes surprise one), I escaped
by climbing up your stairway; and they,
because they saw I'd found
a refuge, or because the change

of circumstance made vengeance
seem more doubtful, in any case,
they did not follow me.
I stayed where I was, behind
the first closed door, waiting
till they departed; then
when I judged they were no longer
in the street and I was about
to venture out, I stumbled into
a man leaving the hallway.
"Who's there?" he shouted at me.
Supposing him to be one
of my assailants, I thought it
safer not to answer,
then fled from one room to another
till I found myself in here.
This, sir, is the reason
you have found me hidden
in your house. Now my life
is in your hands, take it.
For as I've told the truth,
and no one's virtue is at stake,
I can die happily, and sacrifice
my life, heart and soul,
to an honorable sentiment,
not to some infamous revenge.
    *Don Lope* [*aside*]. How can one man harbor in himself
such diverse perplexities?
The substance of one's dread and fears,
the torments and the doubts!
By Heaven, as if it were not
enough already to be plagued
by his presence out of doors,
must I now encounter him
ensconced here in the house?
Suspicions, seal your lips;
and yours too, my agony;
for everything he says
may be quite true, but if not,
the time is not yet ripe
for extremer measures.
—My dear sir, I am glad my house
has served as your asylum
against such treachery.

Because you are a stranger here,
accept my hospitality.
One gentleman must support
another in his difficulties.
I can assure you of my help
on every occasion you
have need of it; my sword
is ready to do you service
against a multitude, and so
you need not turn your back again.
But now, that you may leave
the house quite secretly,
I'll indicate the way
to go, through the garden
and out by a hidden door . . .
I'll open it for you. . . . I must
take proper precautions
so that the servants (who are
one's worst enemies at home)
won't know I found you here.
It will be most important
to satisfy them all on this.
For though surely nobody
would doubt a truth so evident
as yours, and though it convinces me
quite sufficiently, still,
who of us can flee from malice,
and who escape suspicion?
Who is free of rumor's tongue,
and who can defend himself
against malevolence?
For if it once should be believed. . . .
No, what's belief? If I once imagined,
if I once thought that someone
had compromised my honor . . .
no, not even honor—let's say
my reputation, my renown;
and if the hateful syllable
were uttered by my least servant,
a slave, by Heaven, there's
no one's life I'd hesitate
to take, no amount of blood
I would not spill, no quantity
of souls I would not readily

dispatch; and each of them
I'd break in two, bringing
to light the hearts on which
the infamy was written.
Come, I will light the way
ahead of you.
    *Don Luis* [*aside*]. My voice
freezes in my throat. What
a display of Portuguese pride!
                [*Exeunt* Don Lope *and* Don Luis

*Enter* Doña Leonor *and* Sirena.

    *Doña Leonor*. Things have turned out better
than I'd expected, Sirena.
But bad luck may only once
fail to justify one's darkest
expectations. I can speak now,
I can move my frozen feet.
Oh, Sirena, I'm alive again,
and my soul's inside my body.

*Enter* Don Lope.

    *Don Lope*. Leonor.
    *Doña Leonor*.      My lord, what do you
intend to do? Have you discovered
why he came here? Now you know
I was not to blame.
    *Don Lope*.      Would I dare
think otherwise, who love you
and respect you? No, Leonor,
I only wish to ask that we agree
between ourselves now . . .
    *Doña Leonor*.        Did he not
say just now that the reason
he came here from Castile
had to do with someone's death?
Well, I, my lord, knew nothing of that.
    *Don Lope*. You need not defend yourself,
Leonor; understand . . . see how
you mortify me. How, Leonor,
how could you have known of it?
But now let it suffice that he has
given us assurances,
and was not seen leaving here.

And you, Sirena, I would not
have you speak of what's occurred
among the three of us, not to
anyone, not even to Don Juan

*Enter* DON JUAN.

*Don Juan* [*aside*]. Don Lope has delayed so long
I've grown somewhat concerned.
*Don Lope.* By God, Don Juan, that was
a fine idea of yours, urging me
to search the house, though I'm still certain
that the culprit was myself!
Here, take the candelabrum
for a while, and lead the way.
*Don Juan.* But why go on when I'm convinced
I was mistaken? I was wrong,
and I admit it now.
*Don Lope.* Still, we must be thorough;
let's search the house together now.
*Doña Leonor* [*aside*]. What remarkable prudence!
*Don Juan* [*aside*]. What courage and what pride!
*Sirena* [*aside*]. What despair!
*Don Lope* [*aside*].          Thus must he
proceed who seeks revenge until
the moment's ripe: in sufferance,
silence, and dissimulation.


# ACT THREE

*In the courtyard of the* KING's *palace in Lisbon*

*Enter* DON JUAN *and* MANRIQUE.

DON JUAN. Where's Don Lope?
*Manrique.*          When he went
inside the palace, he
left me here.
*Don Juan.* Go find him,
and say that I'm waiting to see him.

[*Exit* MANRIQUE

Now to rehearse alone
the dialogue that must ensue
between us, and the doubtful purpose

I pursue in making it
my duty to discuss the matter
of his reputation with a friend.
I feel I am as closely bound
to him as ever one man
has been to another.
At home, his constant guest,
using his estate as though
it were my own; and what is more,
he trusts me with his life and soul.
How can I ever be ungrateful
for that friendship, loyalty,
and trust? And how can I be silent
while I see his purest honor
trampled down and not give up
my life to aid his vengeance?
How can I coldly countenance
the rumor of that Castilian's
adoration of Leonor,
and while her reputation suffers
for it, plainly see her
encouraging the gallant—
see and hear all this while Don Lope
himself knows nothing of it?
No, that I can't abide.
Don Lope has but to say the word—
I'll shoulder his revenge,
and that Castilian dies today.
Even without such word, I can
dispatch the gentleman
skillfully and silently.
But will slander be avenged
if the arm that strikes it down
is not membered to the body
of the man who suffered it?
My frank advice to Don Lope
will be, "Do not ask the King
to join him, but stay at home.'
But if he asks me why,
how shall I answer him?
This is the sorest point of all;
for to warn another
that his precious honor lies
in jeopardy is but to speak

the word that quits him of that honor.
What must a friend do then?
If I say nothing, I only add
to the offense; if I tell him,
I incarnate the offense; and I
offend him if I avenge it.
If indeed I've served him
as a true reflector of his
conscience, why can't I counsel him?
I see him coming now. He shan't
have reason to complain of me,
for he will now advise himself in
that which I would counsel him to do.

*Enter* DON LOPE *and* MANRIQUE.

*Don Lope.* Manrique, go back and say
that I am going to my
country house and there await
his word when the King is ready
to receive me.
   *Manrique.* There's Don Juan,
who's come to speak with you.

[*Exit* MANRIQUE

   *Don Lope* [*aside*].                Ah,
what new trouble's brought him here?
—Yes, Don Juan, what brings you this way?
[*Aside.*] And so the coward's always
victimized by his own fears.
   *Don Juan.* Dear friend, I've come to ask
for your assistance in clearing up
a disconcerting doubt of mine.
This is in strictest confidence.
   *Don Lope* [*aside*]. I already know it deals
with some misfortune of my own.
—Tell me about it.
   *Don Juan.*            This concerns
a friend who's asked my help.
I seek advice in his behalf.
   *Don Lope.* And the matter?
   *Don Juan.*                    Two gentlemen
were playing cards one day when
some difference arose between them
An argument ensued in the course
of which one man accused

the other of a lie.
In all the hubbub, the man
who was insulted did not catch
the insult, but a friend heard it
and others heard it too.
Because he is a loyal friend,
this doubt assails him now:
is he obliged to tell his friend,
straight out, he has been wronged,
who knows nothing of it?
Or should he stand by and let
the other's reputation suffer
while the insult goes unavenged?
If he conceals it, the wrong increases;
if he discloses it,
he violates the friendship.
What's better: speech or silence?
    *Don Lope.* Let me consider this awhile.
[*Aside.*] Honor outmaneuvers me:
doubt deployed by doubt; this way
madness lies: compelled to speak
about my own condition
as though it were another's.
The question put by Don Juan's friend
clearly is his own, which means
he's seen enough to be aroused.
Shall I tell him? No, I cannot.
I have resolved on silence.
—Don Juan, I imagine I would say,
if my opinion were solicited,
that a man cannot have suffered
insult and not know of it.
The guilt is totally his own
who suffers insult and dissimulates,
because he won't avenge it.
In a case so desperate,
the man at fault is not
the one who knows nothing
of the wrong that's been done him,
but he who knows and, in choosing
to be silent, conceals it.
As for myself, I'd say
that if a friend, like you
(being close as we two are),

came to tell me any such thing,
assuming or imagining
he could do so freely,
he'd be the first I would
avenge myself upon.
It would be too cruel a thing
to speak of face to face.
In fact, I cannot understand
at all how one man would have
the temerity to tell another,
"You have lost your honor."
That one's best friend should bring
such evil tidings—why, I say it
again: as God is my witness,
if I so much as dared tell myself
such a thing, I'd kill myself at once,
I who am myself my oldest friend.

    *Don Juan.* Now I am instructed by you,
I can warn my friend his course
is silence. May God be with you.

                                    [*Exit* DON JUAN

    *Don Lope.* Who would doubt the pass I've reached
      when
an affair involving two calls for
a third to act as mediator?
And so Don Juan suspects that
Leonor intends to ruin me;
sensing what wrong's been done,
he perceives I must avenge it,
and the world perceives this too.
Well, honor, there's an end to it.
I must act at once and not
permit suspicion to yield
to credence, nor apprehension
to the evil it anticipates.
And before her inconstancy
achieves its basely wished-for end,
I'll work out the strategy
by which revenge makes clear
the harsh reward of treachery.

        *Enter the* KING *and his retinue.*

    *King.* Since we intend to spend the night
in what the populace is pleased

to call the King's country house,
tell them we now depart from Lisbon.
Also tell the people to expect
processions where the most brilliantly
arrayed shall pass in full regalia.
Their shining plumes and iridescent hues
everywhere will vie with
flowering April and its sunbeams.
    *Don Lope* [*aside*]. I shrink as I approach the King.
Tormented passion has so far
reduced me that I must imagine
the whole world knows my shame,
my grief, my cowardice.
—Accept my humble salutation, sire.
    *King.* Ah, Don Lope, if only I might have
your stout sword beside me
there in Africa, how swiftly
I'd vanquish the haughtiest of Moors.
    *Don Lope.* Then how can that sword be sheathed,
and I allow it to repose unused,
when yours, great sire, is drawn?
I shall join you in the war.
Sire, what reason can there be
on this occasion to detain me
here in Portugal?
    *King.*            Are you married?
    *Don Lope.* I am, Your Majesty,
but my being married does not alter
the man I was and am.
And formerly my highest honor
thrived only on the highest deeds.
    *King.* Being newly wed, how will your wife
like this?
    *Don Lope.* As a thing most honorable.
She'd feel that she has given you
the soldier in her husband, than whom
none nobler or more manly, great sire,
has ever fought upon your side.
If formerly I lent
my reputation to your cause,
I now offer it both hers and mine.
Being absent from my wife
will not conflict with my desire.
    *King.* I believe you, but I queried you

because it seems to me unjust
you should separate so quickly
in this fashion. Though our present
enterprise is lofty, still, Don
Lope, in making it your cause you
may be leaving things amiss at home.

> [*Exeunt the* KING *and his retinue*

*Don Lope.* Good Lord, what is this shadow passing
over me? Can my heart have rightly
heard the tale my senses tell?
Has some report of wrong done me
already reached the King?
How widely broadcast it must be
if its echoes reach me last.
If so, my misfortune
is immeasurable. My God,
I'd sooner have the punishment
which totally consumes the body
in one lightning stroke while the thunder
rolls insensibly behind me
than suffer the King's grave sentence
implying there is something amiss
at home. For now I suffer more
who must endure a lightning
even more intense, and rise again,
the phoenix of my grief,
from my own ashes. Such
mountains and stone obelisks
hurled down upon my back
now become my monument,
and I lie buried underneath it,
still alive. Yet all this weighs lightly,
far more lightly than the force
of insult that has crushed me down.
Honor, you are greatly in my debt.
Come closer, listen to me.
Why do you complain of me?
Tell me how I have offended you?
To that courage I inherited
have I not brought full measure
of my own, and by it lived my life
and scorned the greatest dangers?
Honor, since I would not subject you
to the slightest risk or fault,

when have I not been courteous
to the humble, friendly
to the gentleman, generous
to the poor, fellow comrade
to my soldiers? And as a husband
now, alas, how have I failed,
and of what am I to blame?
Was not the wife I chose
of noble blood and ancient stock?
Do I not love my wife?
Do I not respect her?
If I have been at fault
in none of these, and if
my conduct has not given rise
to viciousness of any sort,
whether out of ignorance
or malice, why am I exposed
to insult? Why? By what tribunal
must the innocent be so condemned?
Can there be punishment
without a crime, a trial
without an accusation read?
And penalty where there is no guilt?
Oh, the world's insane legalities!
That a man who has ever labored
in the cause of honor cannot know
if he has been insulted!
When the evil consequences
of another's actions
are visited upon me,
then never has the world misprized
virtue more. Again, I ask:
why is goodness less esteemed
than misdemeanor, in whose hands
its proud fortress is surrendered
so supinely, and merely
in response to the blandishments
of appetite? Who put honor
in a glass so fragile,
then, totally inept in physic,
made such crude experiments in
that retort? But let me now be brief.
An injured man will hurl
cries endlessly against

blind custom's cudgelings.
I cannot lessen them a whit,
and this is all men's fate.
I live to avenge, not mend them.
I'll join the King, and then,
returning another way,
when occasion beckons me
I'll strike, and thereby bring about
the world's most overt vengeance.
The King, Don Juan, and everyone
will know of it; then, oh God,
it shall be forever known
to all recorded time and fame
how a Portuguese defends his name.

[*Exit* DON LOPE

### On the seashore

A *clashing of swords offstage; then enter* DON JUAN *and
others fleeing from him, and exeunt.*

*Don Juan.* Cowards, I erased the insult
When I killed the man who uttered it.
  *A Soldier.* Run for your lives! His sword is lightning!

*Enter* DON JUAN *and his antagonists.*

*Don Lope* [*offstage*]. Is that you, Don Juan? I'm coming.

### Enter DON LOPE.

*Another Soldier* [*aside*]. He has killed me.
  *Don Juan* [*returning*].                    With your support,
there is nothing in the world I fear.
  *Don Lope.* They've escaped; tell me what's happened,
unless there's reason to pursue them.
  *Don Juan.* Ah, Don Lope, my wound
gapes wide again; the insult
I once revenged and thought
was stricken out of mind,
now tears at me afresh.
Alas, I was deluded.
For simple vengeance has not served
to bury the offense.
When I left you last, Don Lope,
it was to come here to this

sea-beaten shore, having in mind
your purpose: the transfer
of your household to this country seat
against your imminent departure.
Happily arrived, I saw a group
of men conversing, and in passing
heard one address the others:
"There goes Don Juan de Silva."
Hearing my own name spoken
(the most readily perceived of words),
I soon overheard the rest.
And then another asked, "And who
is this man, Don Juan?" "But
have you never heard of him?"
replied the first. "He's the man
Don Manuel de Sosa
publicly insulted."
But this was intolerable,
and so I drew my sword and said,
"I am the man who killed his enemy
Don Manuel so swiftly, he found
no time for further words
after uttering the insult.
I'm the man who blotted out the wrong,
and not the man who suffered it.
With his blood I cleansed my honor."
On this I closed swords with them all;
they fled, I followed here, and they
escaped. All gossips are cowards;
instead of courage, they show their heels.
This, Don Lope, is my burden.
Would to God my daring equaled
my terrible despair;
I'd hurl myself into those waves
or end my life upon this sword,
and not let injury consume me.
"He is the man," they said,
"Don Manuel insulted," and not
"the man who blotted out the wrong."
Can one ever anticipate
offense? And when it's been redressed,
has one not done enough?
It was not enough to put my life
in jeopardy, preferring

death with honor to life without it.
No, that was not enough.
For however much, however often,
a man of pride and daring
avenge the insult done him,
by so much and so often
does he publicize that insult.
For his vengeance must reveal
what the insult may conceal.

[*Exit* DON JUAN

    *Don Lope.* "For his vengeance must reveal
what the insult may conceal."
And so when I redress the wrong
done me, I broadcast the offense.
Clearly, then, my vengeance will reveal
what the insult may conceal.
And once I have straightforwardly
avenged myself, it must
mistakenly be said of me,
"There goes the man who was insulted,"
not, "the man who blotted out the wrong."
And when this hand of mine today
is bathed in blood, it will bespeak
the insult, since vengeance thus proclaims
what the wrong itself does not.
Then, by Heaven, I must not seek it
publicly, but seal its mouth instead.
Prudent vengeance calls for sufferance,
silence, and dissimulation.
Done secretly, the deed elicits
greater honor, greater praise.
In silence my purpose
refines my instrument;
otherwise my vengeance but reveals
what the insult now conceals.
This happened to Don Juan,
after he regained his honor,
when the soldier said, "There's the man
who was insulted," not, "the man
who blotted out the wrong."
Then let my vengeance be a work
of such skill and forethought that the sun
itself will scarcely see it done.
And whoever now believes me wronged,

let him believe it still.
Meanwhile, until that most secret
of occasions beckons,
oh injured heart, be strong
in sufferance, silence, and
dissimulation. Boatman!

*Enter a* BOATMAN.

*Boatman.*              Sir?
*Don Lope.* Have you a boat at hand?
*Boatman.* I shall surely have one for you, sir.
But at the moment, all the boats
are occupied, coming and going
all afternoon in the train of
King Sebastian (Heaven protect him),
who is moving to his country house.
*Don Lope.* Then see you have one ready for me;
I must be off to my own house.
*Boatman.* Must it be right away?
*Don Lope.*                        At once.
*Boatman.* I'll go to fetch one now.

[*Exit* BOATMAN

*Enter* DON LUIS, *reading a letter.*

*Don Luis* [*to himself*]. I'll re-read this letter
which now commands my fate,
for the pleasure is redoubled
when experienced again.

[*Reads.*] "This evening the King goes to his country
house; disguise yourself among the people in his train,
until occasion grant we meet, you to finish your complaints, and I, my own defense. God keep you.—Leonor"

Now, as luck would have it, there is
no boat to carry me across!
Great God, let fortune aid me now and
I'll never ask another favor.
*Don Lope* [*aside*]. The man reading that letter awaits
my vengeance. He doubtless reads
of my disgrace. How feverish
my honor is: hearing, seeing,
and believing nothing
but the pain that drives me.

*Don Luis* [*aside*]. That fellow is Don Lope.

*Don Lope* [*aside*]. I must give no sign of anger,
but rather smile at fury's prodding
while I suffer and dissimulate,
like the snake that wheedles and cajoles
while it swells its bitter gorge,
then bursts and spits its venom out.
—Sir, I must believe you hold
my offer in very low esteem,
having asked no favor of me yet
who wish so much to serve you.
I was so far taken by
your courtesy, your courage
and discretion, that I've searched
all Lisbon for you since,
hoping to enlist my sword
in your cause against any new
assault by your antagonists,
they who may so easily
encounter and outnumber you,
and while you least expect it,
kill you on this very spot.

*Don Luis.* And I in turn, Don Lope, know
the debt I owe you and am hoping
to repay; but as a stranger
here today, I doubt I'll have
the honor to enlist your aid.
Therefore, good sir, there is no need
to burden you with the affair
against my rivals in which
you would assist me. Aside
from that, I think we two are friends
enough that I may speak
to you quite openly of things.

*Don Lope.* Yes, I hope you may; but first,
be sure you know the risk you take;
for the friendship of a man aggrieved
is not a very stable thing.

*Don Luis.* Quite the contrary: I say,
and feel, once I am your friend,
of whom may I be surer,
unless it be my enemy?

*Don Lope.* The point's debatable, though
you're entitled to believe it

as you do, reasonably or not.
Keep your opinion, I'll keep mine.
But tell me, what brings you
to this place?
    *Don Luis.*  I must find
a boat to take me to the King's
country house.
    *Don Lope.*  You've come in time.
Trust me, I shall help you there.
The boat I've hired will soon be here.
    *Don Luis.* Here the King extends such favor
to the populace, thousands
have crossed over, scarcely
leaving any boat to go by.
I'm eager to be one among
that animated crowd; for
I assume the occasion
is unprecedented.
    *Don Lope.* Then you'll cross with me.
                 [*Aside*]        And speed me
to my own occasion now.
    *Don Luis* [*aside*]. Is there anyone can say
he has better luck than I?
    *Don Lope* [*aside*]. Now he's crept into these hands
in which he soon must die.
    *Don Luis* [*aside*]. And who should bring me on the scene
but her husband, as a go-between!

*Enter the* BOATMAN.

    *Boatman.* The boat's at your disposal.
    *Don Lope* [*to the* BOATMAN]. Board the boat yourself
        while I
wait for my servant here.
No, wait for him here yourself;
you'll know him when he comes.
Tell him we're inside the boat.
    *Boatman.* Don't board her yet; there's no one
at the helm; a single mooring
holds her: she won't be too secure.
    *Don Lope.* Go find my servant, and we'll
both await you in here.
    *Don Luis* [*aside*]. How could I be luckier?
He leads me to the very spot
where I shall try his honor.

*Don Lope* [*aside*]. And so I lead him to the spot
where he shall die at last.

> [*Exeunt* DON LUIS *and* DON LOPE

*Boatman.* I suspect that servant won't
get here for years and years.
But what's this? The boat is gone,
the mooring's broken! They're in the hands
of God; unless He saves them,
they'll surely find their graves,
both of them, beneath the waves.

> [*Exit* BOATMAN

*Another part of the beach, within view of*
DON LOPE's *country house.*

*Enter* MANRIQUE *and* SIRENA.

*Manrique.* Here I stand, Sirena, transfixed
by your glance, enchanted and bewitched.
Perhaps you've wandered this beach
of yours to hear the song
the Siren sings out in the sea?
My sonnet here's most opportune:
heroic, grave, and quite discreet.
Listen, it's not importunate;
simply one of the great hoard
of sonnetry I promised you.

> [MANRIQUE *takes out a sheet of paper and reads.*

"To a Green Ribbon," a sonnet:

"Green ribbon with your neatly tucked-in end,
You could have been the ribbon which that god
(Ruling the fifth planet) steeped in blood
So as to make the goddess Venus pregnant.

Spring dips its brush into your coloring,
For whom I carry through this labyrinth
(As long as that made famous once in Corinth)
My heart, blacker than the blackest ink.

Now let your hope conjoin with my fear,
So love may choose a green or yellow tint,
Guessing which one is phlegm and which is choler.

For since I paint myself in your own color,
It cannot be (harpoons won't make me flinch)
But that my hope is sure to stick much faster."

*Sirena.* Oh, what a beautiful sonnet
you've written! But do show it
to me, the ribbon, I mean—
to see if it's really green.
*Manrique* [*aside*]. I now recall, too well,
what happened to that ribbon.
Let's see: yes!—On a certain
day, Sirena, while strolling
by the Tagus, the idea came
to me: how the sweetness
of the river matched your beauty,
and my happiness as well.
To soothe my fondest hope
I brought the ribbon out;
but seeing it reminded me
of all your fickleness,
and all at once I wept on it,
and kissed it sighingly.
While I stood there thus engaged,
an eagle who had seen me bring
the ribbon to my lips, as though
I'd offered him a bite to eat,
descended from his boulder,
resolutely snatched the ribbon,
and alighted on his perch again.
Giddy with anxiety,
I made as if to scale the boulder
when I recalled I lacked a pot
to serve me as a helmet.
With this event your ribbon
faded out of human history.
That, Sirena, is the story
called "The Green, or Unripe, Ribbon."
*Sirena.* But hear me now recount
that story's epilogue.
Standing in a field one day,
I spied the selfsame eagle
flying by, who deciding
that the ribbon was no
bite to eat, promptly dropped it
not very far away;
I hurried to the spot
to discover what had fallen,

and found this ribbon draped
about the flowers; tell me
if it is the one you lost.

    *Manrique.* What a sweet coincidence!

    *Sirena.* My vengeance will be sweeter.

    *Manrique.* Let's leave that for later; your mistress
is coming through the field.

                      [*Exit* MANRIQUE

Enter DOÑA LEONOR.

    *Doña Leonor.* Sirena.

    *Sirena.*              Madam.

    *Doña Leonor.*                  I am very
much distressed.

    *Sirena.*          Do I know
the reason why?

    *Doña Leonor.*     You do;
but listen to what I say.
Ever since that saddest night,
heaped with such confusions,
while I stood by imagining
the house afire, like another Troy,
I've been absolved by everyone.
Don Juan is deceived still further,
Don Luis gone free, and Don Lope
reassured; since then I've come
to live here in this pleasant
country house, awaiting Don Lope's
departure, while nature
excellently paints this meadow
and adorns the lofty hill,
and never has Don Lope
honored me more. And so, Sirena,
I've come to lose the fear I bore
for my own self-respect.
And since I have emerged so well
from so harrowing a circumstance,
audacity now summons me
to act without restraint.
The danger's past and left
no hint of retribution.
And so it's come to this:
Don Lope is more fond of me
than ever; as if, supposing

he'd suspected some abuse before,
he so enjoys the sense
of being disabused
that he's turned it into love.
How many have loved another
in this fashion, how many
have become love's object
intensified by insult!
The wisest and most learned men
will still succumb to such
mistaken passion, and of all
women, the most judicious
and best loved will not recall
the substance of another's love
for her. Thus when I was loved by
Don Luis, I felt that I
disliked him; when that love
was guiltless, I seemed to fear it.
And now (what utter madness!),
I neither love my being loved
nor fear my guiltiness.
I began to love when I felt
I'd been deserted and offended.
Now my love is guilty,
I become more daring.
And while Don Lope himself
goes off on my behalf today
to join the King, I've written
Don Luis to visit me,
and give my love away at last,
for it belongs to him.

*Enter* DON JUAN.

*Don Juan* [*aside*]. How can a heart that suffers
such continual assaults
stand firm and not finally
succumb to any one of them!
   *Doña Leonor.* What's this, Don Juan: you've come
without Don Lope?
   *Don Juan.*        I could not wait
for him, though he said he'd come shortly,
before the sun sinks in the sea.
   *Doña Leonor.* But now that time seems past;
pallid shadows creep across

the earth, and heavy clouds
hang in the murky sky.
　　*Don Juan.* Sudden irritation seized me.
A man fleeing from himself neither
waits nor cares to look behind.
　　*Don Luis* [*offstage*]. God save me!
　　*Doña Leonor.*　　　　　　　　What pitiful cry
was that upon the wind?
　　*Don Juan.* I see no one here on land.
　　*Doña Leonor.* There against the waves I see
some vague shape moving toward us.
In this trembling twilight,
it is hard to recognize.
　　*Don Juan.* He is desperately attempting
to escape; and now he seems
to lean toward us as if
imploring Heaven's aid.
Quickly, let us go down to him
and give him what support we can.

　　　　　　　　　　　　　　　　[*Exit* DON JUAN

　　*Don Lope* [*offstage*]. Alas, alas.
　　*Don Juan* [*offstage*].　　　　Stretch out your hand!
　　*Don Lope* [*offstage*]. My land, sweet earth of all man-
　　　　kind!

　　　DON JUAN *returns, entering with* DON LOPE,
　　　　*drenched, and with a dagger in his hand.*

　　*Don Juan.* Who's this? Don Lope?
　　*Doña Leonor.*　　　　　　　　Dear husband!
　　*Don Lope.* Merciful fate, that leads to
such a gracious haven as now
you hasten to extend me
in my weariness. Oh Leonor,
my treasure! I should not doubt
that Heaven, with its customary
grace, now showers me with happiness
to make up for so much misery.
My friend!
　　*Don Juan.* What does all this mean?
　　*Don Lope.* This happiness of mine follows
the most pitiful of all events.
　　*Doña Leonor.* Since Heaven has heard my prayers
and brought you back alive,
I would not reproach good fortune,

as tragic custom does.

*Don Lope.* After speaking with the King, I looked
for you, but when I could not
find you, I hired a boat.
The boat was on the point of
moving off when I was hailed
by a gallant gentleman
whose name I scarcely knew,
though I believe it was
a certain Don Luis
de Benavides. He hastened
to explain he was a foreigner,
whose well-meaning boldness
therefore deserved to be excused,
and begged me to forgive
his asking to be taken
with me in the boat, since he
most eagerly desired
to see the populace
join in homage at King
Sebastian's country house. I was thus
obliged to make room for him.
He had scarcely come aboard—
the boat responding to the added
weight, though the boatman had not
yet boarded it—when the mooring,
already strained and rotted
by the sea, broke loose, assaulted by
a wave which rudely claimed it.
I could not ward off the blow,
although I seized the oars.
Then when strength deserted me,
we collapsed inside the boat,
prey to our anxieties
among the blue and thrashing waves:
at one moment raised aloft
the highest salty peaks, and at
the next, buried deep beneath
arched caverns in a sapphire
radiance. We were hurled at last
in this direction when,
just in sight of land lights,
the boat was split and swamped
with sea and sand. I could not save

the gallant gentleman, swept
beyond my reach by the blow that
wrecked us; and since he could not save
himself, he sank into a grave
and watery oblivion.
    *Doña Leonor.* Alas!

                                       *[She faints.]*

    *Don Lope.*         Leonor, my wife,
my treasure, you mar your loveliness.
Merciful God! Look, an icy
pallor slowly moves through
her translucent hands. Oh, Don Juan!
It was not her seeing me engulfed
by peril that mortifies
her soul; the hearts of women
do not succumb so easily
to the telling of sad tales.
Do help carry her to bed.
        *[She is carried off by* DON JUAN *and* SIRENA.]
    *Don Lope.* It well becomes a man
to silence insult, and even
seem to bury his revenge.
This way he comes eventually
to requite his wrongs, who
waits and suffers patiently.
Honor, we have pursued
our course assiduously,
and now silently repay
dissimulated insult
with dissimulated vengeance.
How well I grasped the chance
occasion offered when
I cut away the mooring
and took the oars in hand
to push us farther off
while pretending I meant
to draw us back to shore.
How well my plan succeeded,
for I killed the man (as this
dagger is my witness) intent
on my dishonor and disgrace,
and hurled him, a glassy monument,
upon his raging tomb.
How well I managed when I

crashed the boat against the shore,
for now the act lends credence
to my tale and so dissuades
suspicions of complicity.
Now that I have acted in
conformance with the law of honor
and killed the gallant first,
I must turn next to Leonor.
When the King beholds her blood
staining the sheets of that
still unviolated bed,
he cannot bid me stay behind
for anything amiss at home.
Tonight my vindication ends,
resolved most prudently and wisely.
Leonor, alas! Leonor,
as fair as she is false,
as unhappy as she's lovely,
my honor's fatal ruin.
Leonor, now asleep in sorrow
and subdued by anguish,
as though she had outwitted death
and left it baffled in the hands
of life, Leonor must die.
I shall entrust my secret only
to the elements, since
only they can share my silence.
There, to wind and water,
I have yielded half my vengeance;
and here I now entrust to earth
and fire my sorrow's other half.
Tonight I must boldly burn
my own house down; first the bedroom
will be set afire, and when
the flames start up, in darkest daring
I shall strike Leonor dead—
then let it be surmised the fire
was her bloody executioner.
From that blaze I'll snatch up again
the honor of my former
high renown, purified
of the alloy basely dulling it.
By experiment in such a
crucible, one extracts the gold

to which the lowly metal clung
that dimmed its glow and purity.
And so the sea was first to wash
away the stain of my disgrace;
and now the wind carries it away
where no one shall hear of it again.
Next, the earth must turn away from it,
and fire reduce it all to ashes.
This indeed's the fate of every
mortal breath which dares becloud
the sun; by water cleansed,
by earth interred, by wind borne off,
by fire totally consumed.

*[Exit* DON LOPE.

*Enter the* KING, *the* DUKE OF BERGANZA, *and retinue.*

*Duke.* Because the sea believes it's caught
another sun asleep
within its realm, it gently
etches stars upon the waves.
*King.* Duke, I chose to come by sea,
and though I might have chosen land,
it seemed to offer some delay
and this way is closer.
Besides, the waters seemed so sweetly
beguiling that the sky itself,
a blue Narcissus self-entranced,
lingered fondly, silently above.
I was right to come this way
where so many ships lie anchored,
their beacons like a thousand
burning comets flashing on
a thousand fluttering swans,
suggesting a kind of rivalry
between the ones who'd fly
by using oars and those
who'd row by using wings.
*Duke.* The night's so fresh and still, it
liberates every thing alive.
*King.* This vista is delightful, poised
halfway between the land and sea.
All those country houses
among the trees are so enchanting
they would rouse nymphs out of the sea,

who seem indeed to be approaching
now, obedient, in breathless
quietude. And meanwhile, we appear
to gaze upon a wandering forest
on a moving hill, for as we view
them from the sea, they stir
as if to wave farewell.
Farewell, my sweet beloved land.
I shall return, if my cause is just,
and you shall see me enter
next in victory and laurels
earned triumphantly upon
a thousand bloody fields,
my honor brightened by new fame,
the Church acclaimed by thousands more,
I trust . . .

     [*Shouts offstage of* "Fire! Fire!"]
   Duke, what cries are those I hear?
 *Duke.* They are shouting, Fire; the cries appear
to come from the nearest country house.
If I'm not mistaken, that's Don
Lope's house bursting into flame.
 *King.* I see it now; smoke and fire
gathering in one volcanic roar
spread clouds of spark and ash.
It seems to draw from everywhere,
like some gigantic furnace.
It appears impossible
anyone can be alive inside.
Come, let us go and see
if there is any way to fight it.
 *Duke.* But sire, is this not rash?
 *King.* No, Duke, a simple act of mercy.

    *Enter* DON JUAN, *half naked.*

 *Don Juan.* I must rescue Don Lope,
though I am burnt to ashes.
His bedroom is on fire.
 *King.* Stop that man!
 *Duke.*      Madman, what
can you be thinking of?
 *Don Juan.* Of leaving the world some record
of true friendship. Since the fire
has drawn you here, you should know its cause.

Oh, Your Majesty, no sooner
had we found ourselves inside
than suddenly, without warning,
the fire burst forth, as if
avenging its own violence.
Don Lope and his wife are still
inside; I must save them.

*Enter* MANRIQUE.

*Manrique.* Belching sparks like the devil
in a play, I go flying
from my house. Am I not this Troy's
Aeneas? I must plunge this body
in the sea, though burning
harm me less than drinking water.

*Enter* DON LOPE, *half naked, and bearing* DOÑA LEONOR,
*dead, in his arms.*

*Don Lope.* Forgive me, merciful Heaven,
for though I risked my life,
hers slipped by, eluding me.
Oh, Leonor!
*King.*        Is this Don Lope?
*Don Lope.* Yes, I am Don Lope, sire,
if feeling, rather than this fire,
has left me any trace of life
by which to recognize you
and address you. For now my
heart and soul, plunged in
this hideous catastrophe,
this horror, this tragedy,
lie smoldering in white ashes.
This dead beauty, this flower
frozen by so much fire,
which only it would dare to touch
because it envied her beauty's
radiance, this, sire, was my wife:
a woman noble, proud,
honorable and chaste,
whose praise all the tongues of fame
will sing eternally. This is
the wife I loved so tenderly
that I preferred to lose her,
and never see her more, than find her,

to my great sorrow, as she appeared,
wrapped in heavy smoke and flames,
and who, when all my courage sought
to save her, laid her life
down in these arms. Torment,
bitter agony, catastrophe!
This one consolation's left me:
I may freely serve you now,
my duties at home all ended.
I shall go with you to battle,
and there may end my life,
if indeed misfortune ever ends.
[*Aside to* DON JUAN.]
And you, my valiant friend,
Don Juan, tell him who seeks
advice of you, how a man
must be avenged and not permit
a living soul to know of it;
for vengeance now no more reveals
what the offense no more conceals.
   *King.* This has been a painful tragedy.
   *Don Juan.* May it please Your Majesty
to hear me privately.
It befits the nature of this case
that you alone should know of it.
Wracked by his suspicions,
which soon became realities,
Don Lope prudently resolved
that *secret insult* must be met
by *secret vengeance;* so
he killed the gallant there
at sea, when they came together
in a boat alone. Thereby the secret
perished, first in water, then in fire;
since only he who knew the wrong
he suffered could avenge it.
   *King.* In this most notable
of cases antiquity has known,
we have seen how secret insult
most requires secret vengeance.
   *Don Juan.* This is a true history
of the great Don Lope
de Almeida; in our admiration
this tragicomedy is ended.

# DEVOTION TO THE CROSS

## (*LA DEVOCIÓN DE LA CRUZ*)

## DRAMATIS PERSONAE

Eusebio
Curcio, *an old man*
Lisardo, *his son*
Otavio
Alberto, *a priest*
Celio, *a highwayman*
Ricardo, *a highwayman*
Chilindrina, *a highwayman*
Gil, *a clownish peasant*
Blas, *a peasant*
Tirso, *a peasant*
Toribio, *a peasant*
Julia, *a lady, daughter of Curcio*
Arminda, *her maid*
Menga, *a clownish peasant woman*
*Highwaymen*
*Peasants*
*Soldiers*

The scene is laid in Siena and its surroundings.

# DEVOTION TO THE CROSS

## ACT ONE

*A hilly grove off the main road leading to Siena*

MENGA [*offstage*]. Look out, the donkey's slipping!
   *Gil* [*offstage*]. Ho, you devil! Stop, you stupid ass!
   *Menga* [*offstage*]. Now there, she's stuck; you didn't
      stop her.
Ho! Gee up!
   *Gil* [*offstage*]. The devil take her!
No one to grab her tail, but thousands
like her who should be wearing one!

                     [*They enter.*]

   *Menga*. Gil, a nice mess you've made of it!
   *Gil*. A nice mess *you've* made of it, Menga!
You're the one to blame, you were
riding her—you showed her where
the muck was to get stuck in,
and just to irritate me.
   *Menga*. But I'm the one she threw!
It must be you who told her to.
   *Gil*. Now how are we to get her out?
   *Menga*. You mean you'd leave her in the mud?
   *Gil*. It's no use: all my strength won't budge her.
   *Menga*. Look, I'll pull her by the tail
while you pull her by the ears.
   *Gil*. No, I have a better plan.
I'll just imitate the driver
of the coach that got stuck
in the mud the other day.
Two skinny nags were drawing it,
slinking among the other coaches
like some sort of wretched poor
relation down the street.
It lurched from curb to curb,
if not from door to door, as though
cursed, poor thing, by both its parents,
till it reeled into a wayside ditch
and stuck. Inside, the squire swore;
the coachman lashed his whip.
First by coaxing, then by force,
now by wheedling, now by threats,

they tried to move it out.
But the harder they worked on it,
the tighter it got stuck.
Since nothing would budge it,
a bag of barley was brought out
and placed just out of reach
of the half-starved horses,
who as they strained to reach it
tugged and pulled until at last
they dragged the coach out of the ditch.
Now we'll try this very trick ourselves.

*Menga.* Pooh! All your cock-and-bull stories
aren't worth a single candle.

*Gil.* Menga, I'll have you know I've got
a sharp eye; I'll spot the needle
in the haystack every time.

*Menga.* And because you are so clever
I'm the one must go to town
and see if I can find a neighbor
kind enough to help us now.

*Gil.* There you go, stubborn as ever!

*Menga.* Oh my poor, godforsaken donkey!

[*Exit*

*Gil.* Oh you're the donkey of my heart,
the most respected ass in town.
Scrumptious in your choice of
company, and never one
to gad about, you prefer
the stable joys and a diet
of domesticity
to a life of labor out of doors.
Perhaps you're fickle, well,
even a little vain, but I swear
no one's ever caught you gaping
out the window at some jackass.
You have no tongue for flattery,
plain speaking is your specialty,
as when you say, "My mouth's my own."
And when you've had your fill,
I've often seen you turn
and give away the rest
to some beastly uninvited guest.

[*A noise offstage.*]

But what's that noise I hear?

Ah there, I see two men dismounting
and tying up their horses.
Now they're coming here. My, how pale
they look, and in the open fields
so early in the morning!
I'm sure they must have eaten mud
to look so constipated.
But what if they are highwaymen?
Now wouldn't that be something!
Well, whoever they may be,
I had better disappear.
They're coming very fast; they're here.

[*He withdraws.*]


*Enter* LISARDO *and* EUSEBIO.

*Lisardo.* This is far enough; I find
this spot, hidden by the bushes
from the road, most appropriate
for our present purposes.
Now, Eusebio, draw your sword!
Mine is drawn—no further word
need be wasted on such men as you.
*Eusebio.* Though there's sufficient cause
to bring me to this field, I still
would wish to understand your motives
in this matter. Tell me,
Lisardo, what have you against me?
*Lisardo.* I've more reasons than tongue can utter,
words can tell, or patience suffer,
reasons I would rather silence
and blot completely out of mind—
for an insult that's repeated
is thereby committed once again.
Have you ever seen these papers?
*Eusebio.* Throw them on the ground; I'll pick them up.
*Lisardo.* Here they are; take them. You're surprised.
Why do they disturb you?
*Eusebio.* Ah, the man is cursed, he's cursed indeed,
who confides the secrets
of his heart to pen and paper!
His writing's like a hurtled stone:
the hand that cast it forth is known,
but not on whom it may have fallen.

    *Lisardo.* Then you recognize the letters?
    *Eusebio.* They are all in my handwriting.
I cannot deny that.
    *Lisardo.* Then you should know I am Lisardo,
son of Lisardo Curcio,
from Siena. My father
was a profligate who rapidly
consumed the great estate
his family had left him.
In so doing, he was heedless
of the straitened circumstances
to which his children were reduced.
And yet, although necessity
may beggar one's nobility,
it does not lessen in the least
the obligations one is born with.
Yet it would seem that Julia
(God knows the name is painful
to me now) must either
have ignored them or never
sensed their fullest meaning.
Still, Julia is my sister—
would to God she were another's!
You ought to know it is forbidden
to court a woman of her rank
with *billets doux,* whispered flatteries,
and secret messages conveyed
by some infamous go-between.
But I do not wholly blame you;
I would have done the same,
I must admit, had any lady
given me the liberty.
The reason I do blame you
is that you are my friend,
and on that account are guiltier
for knowing where she was at fault.
As your wife—I surely can't believe
you'd dare to woo her otherwise . . .
and even at that, God knows
I'd sooner see her dead,
murdered by my own two hands,
than married to you—yet, as I say,
if you chose her as your wife,
the proper course would be

to make your wishes known, not to her
but to my father. That would be
the only thing to do.
Then my father would decide
whether you might have her,
though I think he would say no.
For in such a case as this,
an impoverished gentleman
who finds his fortune does not meet
the requirements of his rank
must see to it his maiden daughter,
rather than pollute his blood
by marriage, is taken off
in safety to a convent.
In all this, poverty's the culprit.
Accordingly, tomorrow, my sister
Julia will quickly take the veil,
whether she wishes to or not.
And since it does not suit a novice
to embrace the vestiges
of foolish love and vain desires,
I herewith return these letters
to you, determined not only
to get rid of them but of
their author too. So draw your sword,
for here and now one of us must die:
you, who will be kept from wooing her,
or I, who will not see you do it.
    *Eusebio.* Hold, hold back your sword, Lisardo.
I have listened patiently
to your disparagement of me—
now hear my answer. My discourse
may be protracted beyond
reasonable endurance,
but since we two stand alone
on the point of mortal combat,
which leaves but one survivor,
lest Heaven choose to take my life,
listen to my wondrous story,
the marvels of my life,
which if I die must unhappily
be sealed in eternal silence.
I never knew who my father was,
though I do know that my first cradle

was planted at the foot of a cross,
and that my first pillow was a stone.
My birth was strange—so said the shepherds
who found me lying in a gully
here among these hills.
Three days, they say, they heard me
crying, but they could not reach
the isolated gorge I lay in
because they feared the wild beasts
pacing all around me,
who, yet, neither harmed nor touched me.
That surely must have been because
the cross protected me.
There, at last, a shepherd found me
while searching for a lost lamb
in the mountain fastnesses.
The shepherd carried me to the town
where Eusebio lived, who no doubt
was fated to be living there.
The shepherd told him of
the miracle of my birth,
and with Heaven's aid the tale
aroused his pity. Then
Eusebio had me taken
to his home, where I was reared
as if I were his son.
I am called Eusebio
of the Cross, a name combining
his with that of my first ally
and protector. The pursuit of arms
was my love, books and learning
were my pastime. Then when
Eusebio died, I
inherited his estate.
My destiny has been no less
miraculous than my birth,
hostile and unfriendly
but kind and merciful as well.
While still a babe in arms,
my fierce and savage nature
declared itself against my nurse.
That was when my infant gums,
surely with demonic cruelty,
tore the nipple off the tender breast

that fed me, and the nurse,
desperate with pain and blinded
by fury, threw me deep into
a well, unseen by anyone.
Attracted by the sound of laughter,
my rescuers descended
to the bottom where, they say,
they found me floating on the water
with my infant fingers crossed
softly on my infant lips.
Then again, one day when fire
broke out in our house, fiercely
barred the way, and made escape
impossible, I walked freely
through the flames, emerging
quite unscathed; while doubting
this was due to the fire's clemency,
I later learned that day had been
a holiday—the Day of the Cross.
Again, when I was scarcely
fifteen years of age, while sailing
on a ship to Rome, a heavy storm
drove us floundering toward
a jagged rock, and there the vessel,
split wide open, was splintered
in a thousand pieces. But lo!
I caught a heaving plank, and drifted
safely till I reached the shore.
The plank I'd caught was cruciform.
Then once among these mountains,
while traveling with a friend,
I came upon a cross where the road
divided in two separate ways.
I stopped to pray; my companion
went ahead. Having finished,
I hastened to catch up with him,
only to find him dead,
a bloody victim of the highwaymen.
Another day when I was fighting
in a duel and closely hemmed about,
my opponent struck one blow
which knocked me helpless to the ground.
While all assumed the wound
was mortal, close examination

showed only that the crushing sword
had nicked the cross I wore
around my neck, which thus
had rescued me from death.
Again, while I was hunting
high up in these craggy hills,
the sky grew dark and thickened,
and as though declaring fitful war
against the astonished earth,
hurled down its thunderbolts,
unleashed torrential rain, tilted
like lances, and poured hailstones down
like a barrage of bullet shot.
All sought shelter from the onslaught
under boughs and in the thickest copse.
Then a bolt of lightning struck,
like a dark comet driven
by the wind, and then and there
reduced the two companions
nearest me to heaps of ashes.
Blind and frenzied to distraction,
I turned around and saw a cross—
I believe the very one
that towered over me at birth,
and whose imprint is now pressed
upon my breast. By such means
Heaven has distinguished me
and variously brought to light
the symbol of some secret cause,
unrevealed as yet. Thus,
though I know nothing of
my origin, there is a force
that now impels me, an impulse
that ignites my spirit,
and a courage that informs me
I am worthy of your sister Julia.
Inherited nobility
is not superior to
nobility that's been acquired.
This much I know and have acquired,
and though I understand your cause
and could sufficiently repair
your grievance, a cold passion

blinds me; I cannot tolerate
your manner or your sharp rebuke.
Thus I offer no excuses
for my action nor admit
there's any basis for a quarrel.
And since I wish to marry Julia,
however much you may oppose me,
however high the walls that guard her,
however unapproachable
the convent where you'd hide her,
none shall be an obstacle to me.
And as Julia's held too good
to be my wife, she shall be
my mistress; so far am I impelled
by thwarted love and outraged patience
to punish your contempt and repair
the insult to my honor.

    *Lisardo.* As long as this blade of mine can speak,
Eusebio, further speech is useless.

        [*They draw and fight, and* LISARDO *falls; he tries
        to rise but sinks again to the ground.*]

Alas, I am wounded.

    *Eusebio.*        But not dead?

    *Lisardo.* No, and while there's one breath left
in me, I'll . . . Oh, I cannot even
raise my legs!

    *Eusebio.*    Nor can you raise your voice.

    *Lisardo.* Please, let me be shriven
before I die!

    *Eusebio.* Die, you wretch!

    *Lisardo.* Don't kill me, I beg you not to do it—
by the Cross Christ died on!

    *Eusebio.* That word prevents this final thrust.
Arise, Lisardo. When you cry
for mercy by the Cross,
my arms grow limp, my anger
droops and dies. Up, I say.

    *Lisardo.* I cannot rise. My life's blood
slowly drains away, and I think
my soul would swiftly follow after
if it knew which door, poised before
so many doors, it must go through.

    *Eusebio.* Courage, then—I'll lift you in my arms.

There's a little hermitage nearby
where penitential friars live.
They will give you absolution
if you reach their doors alive.

    *Lisardo.* For the mercy you have shown me,
I give you my word: if I am
worthy to be brought into
the holy fold of God, I shall pray
you do not die unshriven.

        [EUSEBIO *lifts him up and carries him away.* GIL
        *emerges from his hiding place; after him enter*
        TIRSO, BLAS, MENGA, *and* TORIBIO.]

    *Gil.* Have you ever seen the likes of it?
Charity! Sure, it's wonderful,
but excuse me if I say this:
dispatch a chap—like that!—then hoist him
on your back? That's the limit!

    *Toribio.* You say you left him here?

    *Menga.* Yes, waiting with the ass.

    *Tirso.* Look, he's standing there stock-still.

    *Menga.* Gil, what are you gaping at?

    *Gil.* Oh, Menga!

    *Tirso.*          What's up, what happened?

    *Gil.* Oh, Tirso!

    *Toribio.*        What did you see? Speak up!

    *Gil.* Oh, Toribio!

    *Blas.*        Say it, Gil. What's wrong?
Whatever is ailing you?

    *Gil.* Oh, Blas, oh my dear friends!
I'm dumb as that donkey there.
He killed him, picked him up, this way,
on his shoulder, like an animal
he was going off to smoke and cure.

    *Menga.* Who killed who?

    *Gil.*            How should I know?

    *Tirso.* Who was killed?

    *Gil.*          I don't know who it was.

    *Toribio.* Who picked him up?

    *Gil.*          How do I know who?

    *Blas.* Who carried him off?

    *Gil.*         Whoever
you like. But if you'd really like
to know, come, everyone, follow me.

    *Tirso.* Where are you taking us?

*Gil.* I don't know, but come anyway,
they can't be very far away.

[*Exeunt omnes*

A *room in* Curcio's *house in Siena*

*Enter* Julia *and* Arminda.

*Julia.* Let me weep awhile, Arminda.
These are freedom's last few hours, and
while I live there's no end to sorrow.
Have you ever seen a gentle stream
slowly descend to find repose
in a valley? And then, even while
the sweetest blossoms on the banks
are scarcely moved by its downflow,
suddenly the stream erupts, and floods
them all in wildest turbulence.
My grief and pain are such a stream:
pent up so long within my breast,
it now bursts forth in tears. Let me weep
at my father's cruelty.
    *Arminda.* But madam, take care . . .
    *Julia.*                 To die of grief!
What happier fate can I hope for?
The grief that triumphs over life itself
brings one to a glorious end.
The grief that trickles out before
life ends is only pitiful.
    *Arminda.* What can have thrown you into
such despair?
    *Julia.*      Listen, Arminda dear:
every letter of Eusebio's
has been taken by Lisardo
from my writing desk.
    *Arminda.*          How did he know
they were hidden there?
    *Julia.*            It was an
accident—and my unhappy fate.
When I saw him pacing
so despondently about the house,
I thought he might suspect me,
but not that he already knew.
Then he came to me; his face was pale.
With an effort to be calm,

he told me he had lost at cards, Arminda,
and he wished to borrow
a jewel of mine, which might help
turn his luck. Willing as I was
for him to have it immediately,
he could not wait, but snatched the key
impulsively, and angrily
unlocked the drawer, where,
as soon as he had opened it,
he found all Eusebio's letters.
He eyed me once, then locked the drawer.
Without a single word, oh God!
he rushed out to find my father.
Then inside his room behind locked doors,
the two of them spoke loud and long—
to seal my fate, no doubt.
When they emerged and left the house,
they went, as Otavio told me
later, directly to the convent.
Now if everything they spoke of
has been accomplished by my father,
I have good reason for these tears;
what's more, if he means to force me
to forget Eusebio and become
a nun, I shall kill myself at once.

*Enter* EUSEBIO.

*Eusebio* [*aside*]. No one yet has ever dared,
however desperate his
situation, to seek asylum
in his victim's house. Before
she hears about Lisardo's death,
I must speak to Julia, and by some
device disarm fate's tyranny.
While still ignorant of my crime,
she may be swayed by love
to run away with me.
Later, when she learns about
her brother's unhappy end,
she will accept the deed of violence
since she no longer can prevent it.
—My lovely Julia!
    *Julia.*          What's this?
Have you come here?

*Eusebio.*　　　　　My love for you
and my grim misfortune
impel me to take the risk.
　　*Julia.* But how did you get in the house?
What wild notion made you try it?
　　*Eusebio.* Like death itself, I fear no one.
　　*Julia.* But what is it you have in mind?
　　*Eusebio.* Julia, I have come at last
to bind you to me; with your consent,
our love is born anew
and all my hopes are crowned with glory.
I know how much your father
is offended by my suit.
He knows we love each other
and intends to change your state
tomorrow, and so destroy
my hope and joy with one fell stroke.
If I please you and you favor me,
if you ever loved me
and are sure you love me still,
Julia, come away with me!
It's clear that while you stay
you can't oppose your father's will.
Then come with me, and there will be
a thousand ways to cope with him.
Once you've left his house to be
with me, he must bow and make
a virtue of necessity.
I have many houses, and you'll
be safe in every one; I've servants
to defend you, all my wealth
to offer you, and my very soul
to spend adoring you.
If you would have me live, if your love
for me is true, you must be bold
and come away with me, or, to your
grief, see me slain before your eyes.
　　*Julia.* Eusebio, listen . . .
　　*Arminda.*　　　　　　Madam,
I hear my master coming.
　　*Julia.* Heaven help me.
　　*Eusebio.*　　　　　Wherever I turn
misfortune follows me.
　　*Julia.* Can he get out now?

*Arminda.*                    **No,**
that's impossible now; they're
knocking at the door.
*Julia.*                    This is
terrible!
*Eusebio.* Insufferable!
What am I to do?
*Julia.*                    You must hide.
*Eusebio.* But where?
*Julia.*                    Here, inside this corridor.
*Arminda.* Quickly, I hear his footsteps.
          [Eusebio *hides; enter* Curcio, *a venerable old
          man.*]
*Curcio.* Daughter, if you do not yield your heart
and soul to that happiest and most
coveted state that now awaits you,
then you do not deserve
the zealous care I have spent
securing it for you. The matter
is all settled; everything
is ready. You have only
to put on your radiant robe,
and then become the bride of Christ.
Imagine the joyous prospect
as you move along today
towards that holy marriage,
the envy of all your friends.
What do you say?
*Julia* [*aside*]. What can I do?
*Eusebio* [*aside*]. If she says yes to that,
I shall kill myself at once.
*Julia* [*aside*]. I do not know what to say.
—Sir, a father's authority
precedes all others; it dominates
one's life, but not one's liberty
of conscience. Would it not have been
much better, sir, had you made
your wishes clear before,
and also inquired into mine?
*Curcio.* No. Right or wrong, my will
is all you need to know.
*Julia.* The only freedom proper to a child
is the freedom to determine
for himself his state in life.

In this his free will should not be forced
by the dictates of an impious fate.
Give me a moment to decide, sir,
and do not be surprised I ask this
of you: to change one's way of life is
no matter to be taken lightly.

    *Curcio.* My decision will suffice, and that
has been resolved. The matter's closed.

    *Julia.* Since you're determined to live my life,
take the very vows you'd have me take.

    *Curcio.* Rebel, hold your tongue! Are you mad?
I'll twist your braids around your neck,
or else I'll rip that tongue of yours
out of your mouth with my own hands
before it cuts me to the quick again.

    *Julia.* I defend my freedom, sir,
but not my life: take that now and end
my sorrow and your grief together.
The life you gave me I can only
offer back again; but you cannot
take my freedom, which is Heaven's gift.

    *Curcio.* So at last I have the proof
of what I long suspected:
that your mother was dishonorable,
a woman who deceived me.
So you attack your father's honor,
whose luster, birth, nobility
the sun itself can never equal,
with all its radiance and light.

    *Julia.* I do not understand you, sir;
therefore, I cannot reply.

    *Curcio.* Arminda, step outside.

                                  [*Exit* ARMINDA

The secret that has burned within me
these many years, though you may have
seen it lurking in my eyes, blind
passion has torn out of me at last.
To honor my ancient name, the Senate
in Siena once sent me
on a mission of fealty
to His Holiness the Pope
Urban Third. Your mother's
saintly reputation
was a byword both at home

and with all the Roman matrons.
Even now it seems impossible,
my sense of satisfaction in her
being so secure then, I can
utter any word against her.
Your mother stayed behind
while my embassy in Rome
kept me eight months away from home.
The issue was whether to award
Siena to the Pope or not.
The matter still unsettled (which,
may God resolve as He sees fit,
seems of little moment to me now),
I returned to Siena,
and found her . . . words fail me now,
my breath is choked, my spirit falters.
I say I found (I must be brave now!)
your mother nine months pregnant.
Her deceitful letters already
had informed me of this misfortune,
telling how on my departure
the prospect had seemed likely.
Yet I was so certain that
my honor had been stained,
I fell to brooding on the insult
till I imagined my disgrace.
I do not say that I believed it
as an accomplished fact,
though a man of noble blood
need not wait for proof; what he
imagines is sufficient.
Oh, the tyranny of honor
and its laws, the savage edict
of the world! What is the point
of all his misery
if a nobleman has nothing
but want of knowledge to excuse it?
The laws of honor lie, they lie!
How can a man raise mere suspicion
to the certainty of fact who has
no inkling of the truth? What law
proves the innocent is guilty?
And how does mere opinion
prove him culpable? There again

the law is false for calling
mere unhappiness dishonor,
that same law which inflexibly
imposes blame upon the victim
and the thief of honor, both.
And if the world's opinion
weighs against the innocent,
what choice has the guilty one but
to recognize it and be silent?
Wracked by such confusions,
I found no comfort at my table,
no respite on my bed at night.
Divided in myself, my heart
looked coldly down upon me,
my soul tyrannized over me.
And no matter how often
I reviewed the evidence
in your mother's favor and
recognized she might be innocent,
the fear of my disgrace obsessed me.
So, though at bottom realizing
she was chaste, I determined
to revenge myself, not against
your mother's misdemeanors
but against my own presentiments.
To pursue such vengeance in
closest secrecy, I made
arrangements for a fictitious
hunting party. Yes, the greatest
comforts a jealous man can know
are the fictions his mind invents.
We went up into the mountains,
and while the others guilelessly
enjoyed the hunt, I, with honeyed words
(how easily they sweeten
treachery, and delight
a lover's heart!) I led Rosmira,
your mother, off the path
through a winding copse. Amusing her
along the way, I reached
a lonely isolated cave
whose mouth the sun had never touched,
it was so hidden by nature's,
not to say by love's interlacing

thickets, trees, and boughs. And there,
where hardly any other
human foot has ever ventured,
the two of us, alone . . .

*Enter* ARMINDA.

*Arminda.* Sir, if your noble courage and
the fortitude of all your years
would only support you
at this unhappy moment,
such strength will see you through
a very heavy trial.
*Curcio.* What reason have you to force
this interruption on me?
*Arminda.* Sir . . .
*Curcio.*              Say it, quickly. Waiting
is much more painful.
*Julia.*              Why
are you so quiet? Speak!
*Arminda.* I cannot be the voice of sorrow
spelling out misfortune.
*Curcio.* Do not be afraid to say
what I no longer fear to hear.
*Arminda.* Oh, sir, Lisardo, . . .
*Eusebio* [*aside*].              This
will be the end of me.
*Arminda.* . . . . bathed in blood, is being carried here
upon a litter by four shepherds.
He is dead (my God!), killed in a duel.
Ah, here they come. Don't look, sir.
*Curcio.* Merciful Heavens! Are these torments
for my sins? Alas, alas.

*Enter* GIL, MENGA, TIRSO, BLAS, *and* TORIBIO *bearing*
     LISARDO, *his face blood-smeared, on a litter.*

*Julia.* What violent monster spent
its bloody wrath on that poor breast?
What inhuman hand, maddened only
by his innocence, washed itself
in my brother's blood? Alas.
*Arminda.* Oh, mistress, don't . . .
*Blas.*              Better
not look at him.
*Curcio.*      Stand back.

*Tirso.* Sir, don't come any closer.

*Curcio.* Friends, I must. Upon my soul, I must.
Let me gaze upon this cold body,
now the sad repository
of frozen veins, time's ruin,
fate's impious corruption, the last
reliquary of my sorrow.
What tyrannous necessity,
oh my son, raised you like a tragic
monument in sand, only to be
mourned in vain and shrouded round
by my white hair? Oh tell me,
friends, who killed my son, this boy
who was all of life to me?

*Menga.* That, Gil will tell you; he was
hidden in the shrubbery
and saw your son fall wounded there.

*Curcio.* Tell me, then, my friend, who was it
took his life away from me?

*Gil.* I only know the man was called
Eusebio—the one that fought
with him, I mean.

*Curcio.*          Eusebio?
So he has robbed me of my life
and honor both.
[*To* JULIA.]          Daughter, you may
pardon him and say ambition
goaded him to cruel extremes;
or say he dreamed of chastest love
but lacked the means to write of it,
and so he had need to use your blood
to pen his lascivious desires.

*Julia.* Sir . . .

*Curcio.*          Please spare me your customary
insolence, but prepare at once
to take religious vows, or else
prepare to leave your beauty here
and share Lisardo's early tomb.
Both of you at once, though differently,
must be buried now: Lisardo,
though a corpse, shall still live in my
memory; and you, though still alive,
shall be dead to me and all the world.
Prepare, then, for your burial.

You shall not escape; I'll lock this door.
Stay with him and learn that lesson well
which his death teaches you to share.

*[Exeunt* CURCIO *and the others*

JULIA *stands between* LISARDO *and* EUSEBIO, *who
enters from another door.*

*Julia.* Cruel Eusebio, each time
I try to speak, my breath
fails me, my spirit flags,
my voice grows dumb. Oh, I cannot,
I do not know how to speak to you.
All at once my righteous anger
is consumed by some strange sympathy.
Then I want to shut my eyes
to the innocent wet blood,
like pink carnations strewn
so lavishly upon this deathbed
and crying out for vengeance.
And in the tears streaming down your face
I even seem to find some reason
to forgive you. For only wounds
and tears seem true, and melt one's heart.
In the same breath my love rushes
to defend you, and my hate,
to punish you; in the throes
of these perplexities and passions,
I strive to vanquish all compassion,
then slowly sentiment undoes me.
Eusebio, is this the way
you'd bind me to you? Is this the way
you'd woo me, heap cruelties
upon me instead of tenderness?
When I eagerly awaited
my joyous wedding day,
you brought about these obsequies
for me to mourn. When I sought
to seal your happiness
and disobeyed my father,
you caused me to wear mourning
and not my wedding gown.
When I risked my life to make it
possible to marry you,
you offered me a tomb to lie in,

and not the marriage bed.
I proffered this hand, Eusebio,
scorning everyone who whispered
my honor had been lost; in return
you gave your hand, dripping
with my brother's blood. What happiness
can I find in your embrace
when, to reach your arms with all the life
my love embodies, I must first
stumble over this poor body
stilled to death? What will they say of me
who know I am forever wed
not only to the insult
but to the insulter too?
Even if I could forget so much,
each time I found your arms about me
the buried thought would spring to life
again. Then I—yes, I
who cherish you would turn
all love's tenderness and joy
to hateful wrath and cry for vengeance.
How could you bear to have me by you,
a heart in which two instincts clash,
now yearning for your punishment,
now desperate to prevent it?
I have said enough to show
that I forgive you, for I love you.
But you must never hope
to see or speak to me again.
Look, here is the window leading
to the garden; go now, escape.
Escape the peril that awaits you
if my father finds you here.
Go now, Eusebio, and forget me.
From this day forward I am lost to you,
lost forever, which is no more
than you clearly have desired.
Go then, all happiness attend you,
and may your felicity be such
that all its blessings are enjoyed
without forfeiture to sorrow.
I shall make my own life
a narrow prison cell, if not
the sepulcher in which my father

wishes to inter me.
I shall at least be free to mourn
misfortune, the severities
of fate, the bitter turns
now wrought by passion in rebellion,
my star-crossed life, and lament
my shattered love, whose dissembling hand
destroyed me but did not let me die
so that I might relive my every
sorrow, and in each forever die.

    *Eusebio.* If, by chance, your hands
can wreak revenge more cruelly
than your words, I readily
submit myself to them.
My crime has led me here, a captive,
but love for you is my prison cell,
where all my faults are chains,
bonds that shake me to the soul;
conscience is my executioner,
and if your eyes are magistrates,
my doom is sealed, for the sentence
that I read in them is death.
If this be so, then Fame
must subsequently frame
this epitaph: "Here lies one
made victim by his love."
The reason is: my only crime
was loving you. I do not ask
your pardon; there is none
for so gross a deed as mine.
I only ask that you be swift now:
kill me and avenge yourself.
Here, take this dagger: pierce the heart
that so offends you, dispatch the soul
that so adores you, and thereby spill
your own heart's blood with mine.
But if you will not do it,
I'll cry out to let your father know
I'm here inside your chamber,
and let him take his vengeance now.

    *Julia.* Come back! Grant me this last of all
requests I'll ever ask of you.

    *Eusebio.* It is granted.

    *Julia.*              Then go, escape now

while there is time to save yourself.
You have your own estate,
and your servants will protect you.
   *Eusebio.* I would do better staying here
without them, for as I live,
I never shall stop loving you,
nor will you be free of me,
even behind a convent wall.
   *Julia.* Safeguard your own life now,
I can well protect myself.
   *Eusebio.* Shall I come back to see you?
   *Julia.* No.
   *Eusebio.* Then there is no hope for me?
   *Julia.* Do not expect it.
   *Eusebio.*                And all
because you now detest me so?
   *Julia.* I have reason to detest you.
   *Eusebio.* And to forget me too?
   *Julia.* I do not know.
   *Eusebio.*            When shall I see you?
   *Julia.* Never again.
   *Eusebio.*           Then what of the love
we shared together in the past? . . .
   *Julia.* Then what of the bloody corpse
that stares at us this moment? . . .
They're at the door; quickly, go!
   *Eusebio.* I'll go, but only to obey you.
Oh, but how can I and not come back?
   *Julia.* Oh, but how can I let you?
           [*A noise offstage. Exeunt at opposite doors.
           Servants enter and carry off the body.*


# ACT TWO

*Shots are heard; enter* Ricardo, Celio, *and* Eusebio *as
        highwaymen, with harquebuses.*

Ricardo. That ball of lead went straight into
his chest.
   *Celio.* And no shot ever left
a tragic imprint more bloodily
on such a tender flower.

*Eusebio.* Put a cross over him,
and God have mercy on his soul.
    *Ricardo.* Yes, and how's that for honor
and devotion among thieves?

                      [*Exeunt* RICARDO *and* CELIO

    *Eusebio.* Since ignoble fate has forced me
to become the leader
of these highwaymen, my crimes,
like my griefs, grow infinite.
And since I let it be believed
Lisardo's death was caused by
treachery, and not in fairness
by a duel, my country's outrage
knows no bounds and in its fury
adds to my despair so that
I am compelled to take the lives
of many men simply to save my own.
My lands and villas confiscated,
they have pressed so hard I am deprived
even of my daily sustenance,
which is why I must resort to force
and let no traveler pass
these mountain paths, unless
he forfeit his money and his life.

*Enter* RICARDO *and other highwaymen leading in the old
man* ALBERTO *as prisoner.*

    *Ricardo.* I was looking at the fellow's wound
when—believe me, captain,
it's the strangest story.
    *Eusebio.* Well, I'm waiting to be enlightened.
    *Ricardo.* I found the shot embedded
in this book he carried against
his chest, and nothing broken through.
The fellow only fainted, and here
he is again, as sound as ever.
    *Eusebio.* This is astonishing—strange indeed.
Who are you, old man, whom Heaven
so amazingly protects
with such prodigious miracles?
    *Alberto.* Captain, I am the most fortunate,
though not the worthiest of men.
I had the honor to be made
a priest, and in Bologna spent

forty-four years teaching
sacred theology.
To reward my zealous study,
His Holiness offered me
the Bishopric of Trent.
But I was troubled in my heart;
seeing that I could give account
of every soul but mine,
I left behind my titles
and my honors, and shunning all
such worldly blandishments,
came here to seek in solitude
the peace beyond illusion,
and live according to the naked
truth among these rocky wastes.
I was making my way to Rome
to ask the Pope's support in founding
a holy order of hermit monks
when your furious attack all but
cut short my life and destiny.
    *Eusebio.* Tell me, what is this book you carry?
    *Alberto.* The fruit of a lifetime's study.
    *Eusebio.* Then what is it about?
    *Alberto.*                  It concerns
the true history of the Holy
Tree divine on which the dying Christ
in all His Glory triumphed over
death. In short, the book is called
"The Miracles of the Cross."
    *Eusebio.* How well that flaming shot
obeyed your text by turning
stubborn lead softer than wax!
God knows, I could wish my hand burned
to a crisp before it dared fire
any shot against these pure pages.
Keep your money, life, and vestments,
but let me have this book. Friends, see him
safely on his way, then set him free.
    *Alberto.* I shall pray to God for your
enlightenment, that you may see
the error of your ways.
    *Eusebio.* If you wish me well, pray only
that I do not die unshriven.
    *Alberto.* I promise I shall be your

intercessor in that pious hope.
Your clemency has touched my heart,
and now you have my word
that if you call me I shall come
from my hermitage to confess you,
wherever you may be.
I am a priest, my name is Alberto.
    *Eusebio.* Then I really have your promise?
    *Alberto.* Here is my hand.
    *Eusebio.*               I humbly thank you.

    [*Exit* ALBERTO, *accompanied by* RICARDO *and
    the others*

    *Enter* CHILINDRINA, *a highwayman.*

    *Chilindrina.* I have climbed for miles through every
mountain pass to find you.
    *Eusebio.* And what's your news, my friend?
    *Chilindrina.* Two reports—both quite bad.
    *Eusebio.* I fear I know what you will say.
Well, what are they?
    *Chilindrina.*        The first is that—
I wish I did not have to say it—
Lisardo's father has been given . . .
    *Eusebio.* Go ahead, I'm waiting.
    *Chilindrina.* . . . permission by the state
to capture you, alive or dead.
    *Eusebio.* I fear your other news is worse.
The sense of it already drains
my heart and tramples on my soul.
What has happened, tell me.
    *Chilindrina.*           Julia . . .
    *Eusebio.* Then I was right. If you want
to see me turn ill at once,
you'll begin with Julia.
You said Julia, did you not?
Isn't that enough? Oh, how I curse
the fate that made me love her.
Well, then, you said Julia. Go on.
    *Chilindrina.* She's in the convent as a novice.
    *Eusebio.* God, I cannot bear it! To think
that Heaven could exact its vengeance
by such pangs of lost desires,
such mouths full of ashen hopes,
and then that I should come to feel

this jealousy of the very
Heaven she has left me for!
Yet I, who in despair have come to
live by murder and by robbery,
I cannot be worse than I have been.
Then here's to the final leap:
let thought erupt in action
as lightning hurls its thunderbolts.
Call Celio and Ricardo!
[*Aside.*] This love will lead me to my grave!
    *Chilindrina.* I'll call them.            [*Exit*
    *Eusebio.*           And tell them I'm waiting.
I shall scale those convent walls.
The grimmest consequence shan't stop me.
To be lord and master over all
her beauty, I shall force my way,
driven by the tyranny of love,
break into the cloister and
violate those consecrated grounds.
My desperation knows no bounds.
And if love had not forced the issue,
I'd do it simply for the pleasure
of committing every crime at once.

*Enter* GIL *and* MENGA.

    *Menga.* It would be just our luck
to stumble on him here.
    *Gil.* But Menga, can't you see I'm with you?
Forget that bungling bandolero.
But if he comes, don't fuss. I have
this sling and bludgeon handy—see?
    *Menga.* Gil, it's only his mad pranks I fear,
to be caught up in his clutches
like that Sylvia who
went uphill a maiden
and came downhill a matron.
Now that's no trifling matter.
    *Gil.* Well, things might go even worse for me—
because, you know, I'm still a virgin,
and I might end up as a patron.
                    [*They notice* EUSEBIO.]
    *Menga* [*to* EUSEBIO]. Oh, sir, be careful or you're done
        for!
This is Eusebio's territory.

*Gil.* I wouldn't go too far that way, sir.
*Eusebio* [*aside*]. They do not recognize me.
I shall play their little game awhile.
  *Gil.* Would you have that bandit murder you?
  *Eusebio* [*aside*]. They are only peasants.
—How can I repay you for your
good advice?
  *Gil.*            Just run off
and leave the bandit to himself.
  *Menga.* If he catches you, sir,
no matter what his mood may be
or what you do or what you say,
he'll kill you—just like that!
Believe me, sir, and he'll stick
a cross on top of you
and think he's doing you a favor.

*Enter* RICARDO *and* CELIO.

*Ricardo.* Where did you leave him?
*Celio.*                            Here.
*Gil* [*to* EUSEBIO]. Now there's a bandit. Run, I tell you.
*Ricardo.* What is it you wish, Eusebio?
*Gil.* Eusebio? Is that his name?
*Menga.*                          Yes.
*Eusebio.* I am Eusebio. What have you
against me? Have you lost your tongues?
  *Menga.* Gil, where's that sling and bludgeon?
  *Gil.* The devil take them, and you too.
  *Celio.* On a plain that skirts this mountain,
just where it meets the sea, I saw
a band of peasants climbing; they are
fully armed and looking for you,
and will be here any moment now.
They are coming to carry out
Curcio's revenge. Determine
your strategy, call the men
together, and let us leave at once.
  *Eusebio.* Yes, it is time we left this place.
There is much to do tonight.
The two of you come with me; I am
sure I have your strictest confidence.
  *Ricardo.* So you do. In Heaven's name, I would
die at your side, when it comes to that.
  *Eusebio.* Shepherds, your lives are spared solely

to convey a message to
my enemy. Tell Curcio
that together with these brave men
of mine my only wish is
to protect my life and not
deprive him of his own.
Tell him that he has no reason
to pursue me as he does.
It was not by foul means that I killed
Lisardo but in fair combat;
we fought man to man, on equal grounds,
and before he breathed his last
I carried him in my arms
to make sure that he was shriven—
an action worthy of some esteem.
But if Curcio is still bent
on vengeance, I shall know
how to defend myself.
[To the highwaymen.] Now make sure these two do not
     know
which path we take; blindfold them
and tie them to these tree trunks.
What they don't observe they can't report.
    *Ricardo.* Here, I have some rope.
    *Celio.*                        Tie them quickly.
    *Gil.* They've trussed me up like Saint Sebastian.
    *Menga.* And me like Saint Sebastiana.
Just as long as you don't kill me,
you may tie it tighter, if you wish.
    *Gil.* Look here, sir: don't tie me up at all
and I swear I'm a dirty pimp
if I run away. And Menga here,
she'll swear the same thing too.
    *Celio.* Now they're firmly tied.
    *Eusebio.*                   So far,
so good. There'll be no moon tonight
and pitch dark everywhere.
Julia, though Heaven be your guardian,
I must enjoy you totally.
                      *[Exit, with his men*
    *Gil.* Menga, what would they say who saw us
bound and blinkered here but that we are
a pair of thieves going to be
hanged or lynched?

*Menga.* Gil, move a little closer to me.
I cannot budge an inch.

*Gil.* Menga, come here and untie me first,
then I'll free you easily.

*Menga.* Since you're so insistent,
you should be the first to move.

*Gil.* How in the world is it possible
nobody's passing this way?
No muleteer mewling,
no traveler begging bread,
no student munching lunch,
not one pious nun at her beads?
On this great wide open road,
nobody's passing today.
Oh I can see, it's all my fault.

[*A voice is heard offstage.*]

*Voice.* There, I think I heard voices
in that direction. Come quickly!

*Gil.* You come in the nick of time, sir.
Now you can help us unravel
a knotty problem that's tied us down
on this spot for some time.

*Menga.* Sir, if you happen to be searching
these parts for some nice rope,
I have a good supply of it here.

*Gil.* Mine's better and stronger.

*Menga.* Women first! That's only
common courtesy.

*Gil.*                Don't stop
for courtesies; untie me first.

*Enter* CURCIO, BLAS, TIRSO, *and* OTAVIO.

*Tirso.* The voice I heard came from here.

*Gil.* You're getting warm.

*Tirso.*                    Is that you, Gil?

*Gil.* Now you're hot as the devil.
Untie me, Tirso, then I'll tell you
all my troubles.

*Curcio.*      What's this?

*Menga.* Welcome, sir. You've come just in time
to punish a traitor.

*Curcio.* Who tied you up this way?

*Gil.* Who? Why, Eusebio, and in fact
he told us to tell you . . . But what

do I care what he told us!
He just tied us up in one knot
and left us.
    *Tirso.* Well, don't complain.
He seems to have been fairly lenient
with you today.
    *Blas.*        Terribly lenient,
leaving Menga behind for you here!
    *Gil.* Oh, Tirso! I'm not complaining
that he wasn't lenient.
    *Tirso.*           Why then?
    *Gil.* You ask me why? Why, because
he *did* leave her behind.
When he took Anton's wife away,
he kept her for six days,
and when she sallied forth at last,
we had a glorious feast on those
hundred *reales* she brought back.
    *Blas.* Yes, and when Bartolo married
Catalina, wasn't she bearing
a kid before six months were up,
and didn't he strut around
like a peacock crowing,
"Can you beat that? What takes
other women nine months to do,
my little wife does in five!"
    *Tirso.* There's no sense of honor there.
    *Curcio.* Am I condemned to hear about
all that villain's debaucheries?
What a pass I've reached to come to this!
    *Menga.* If you're thinking of putting an end
to him, why even the women
among us would take up arms
against him, if you wish.
    *Gil.* It's clear we're on his trail.
This long procession of crosses, sir,
point to all the men he's killed.
    *Otavio.* We are in the most secluded spot
in the mountain.
    *Curcio* [*aside*]. Heavens, it was here
I witnessed that miraculous proof
of innocence and chastity
in one whose beauty I
so frequently had wronged

with my infamous suspicions.
   *Otavio.* What new thought disturbs you now, sir?
   *Curcio.* The tremors of a soul's disease,
Otavio, a lifetime's grief
and my disgrace, which since
my tongue so stubbornly withholds
can only be revealed
in silent glances. Otavio,
lead my followers away,
for I must be alone a while
to arraign myself and plead my case
to Heaven.
   *Otavio.* All right, men: at ease.
Break ranks!
   *Blas.*     Break what?
   *Tirso.*          What's he saying?
   *Gil.* He says at *ease;* that means it's time
to hunt for lice and fleas.

                          [*Exeunt all but* CURCIO
   *Curcio.* Who has not some time felt the need,
when sorrows weigh him down,
to seek communion with himself
rather than confide in others?
The mind swarms, a dump of thoughts and
notions heaped one upon another.
Sighs and tears flow round them,
like intermittent winds and waters,
where I now stand alone
on this wild crag seeking
my self, my own companion, to lance
the poisoned sac of all my ills with
the scalpel of my sharpened wits.
No bird, no tumbling fountain
even, may hear my tale.
Birds chatter, fountains murmur.
Only these few gnarled trees will be
my witnesses; they are dumb
and pay no heed to passing things.
These very peaks were once the stage
whereon was played the strangest
of moralities which time,
with all its stock of dazzling shows
that echo back to all
antiquity, has yet produced.

It concerned a woman's
innocence and simple truth.
Yes, but who can break the bonds
of his suspicion long enough
to see the truth that lies have stifled?
Jealousy is the death of love.
Neither the humblest nor
the loftiest of souls escape
that fearful consequence.
And as I say, it was on this spot
that Rosmira and I . . . Is it
any wonder now that memory
should clutch my heart and freeze my voice?
Every leaf I see here startles me,
every stone here jars me,
every tree trunk crowds me,
every rock would seem to crush me,
every slope about to hurl me down.
All, all these have been an audience
to my infamous performance.
That time I drew my sword, and she,
so calm and so undaunted—as if
to prove that innocence
does not recoil before
the terrible exposure
of honor held in question—
she said, "Oh wait, wait, my husband,
my life is yours to take;
I cannot refuse to yield
that which is yours already.
I only ask to know the reason I
must die, then beg you to embrace me
as I die." To which I then replied:
"Like a viper you bear the seed
of your destruction in your womb.
The proof is that shameless birth
you now await. If I kill you,
I end your shame, scourging you
and your unborn angel too."
"If, by chance," she said, "husband,
if by any chance you honestly
believe my virtue slack, you are right
to kill me now. But by this Cross
rooted in the ground before me,

I swear I never knowingly
did you wrong or stained your honor,
and I trust the holy power
of the Cross to bear me out." I wish
then that I had thrown myself
at her feet and repented
while her shining eyes bespoke
her innocence of heart.
He who is all intent upon
an act of treachery
would do well to weigh his motives.
For once he openly declares himself,
and specifies his cause,
he must proceed to act upon it,
however much he wishes
to call back his declaration.
And so I raised my hand—
not because I disbelieved
her innocence, but to relieve my
mad and overnourished jealousy—
and slashed the air above her
angrily, as if inflicting
a thousand mortal wounds.
And there, at the Cross's foot,
I left her for dead; but when in my
distraction I fled home
I found her there, lovelier
than the golden dawn that daily
brings the infant sun alive.
There she lay with Julia in her arms,
reflecting Heaven's grace and beauty.
My joy was boundless, for Rosmira
had given birth that very afternoon
at the Cross where I had left her.
And as if to prove the miracle
the work of powerful
divinity, there, for all the world
to see, upon the newborn infant's
breast a tiny cross was etched
in blood and fire. But oh that joy—
when even the child herself
seemed to gurgle with delight—
was tempered by the loss
of another infant left behind.

For as Rosmira later said,
she had felt in the agony
of labor she had borne two children;
then I . . .

Enter OTAVIO.

*Otavio.* A band of highwaymen
are passing through the valley, sir,
and before evening closes in,
it may be wise to overtake them.
Otherwise we'll lose track of them.
They know these mountains better
than we do.
    *Curcio.* Call our men
and let us proceed at once.
There'll be no peace or joy for me
until I have my revenge.

[Exeunt

The outside of a convent

Enter EUSEBIO, CELIO, and RICARDO.

*Ricardo.* Quietly now; come bring the ladder
and stand it here against the wall.
    *Eusebio.* I'll be another Icarus,
though I have no wings, another
Phaëthon, and though I have no fire
I'll scale the sun, if it lend me light,
and climb straight to Heaven's firmament.
Love makes a tyrant of me.
When I have reached the top,
remove the ladder and wait
until I signal to you.
Though I rise only to topple down,
rise I must, and fall when
I am scorned, then burn to ashes.
Yet however grave the fall,
I shall at least have known
the glory of ascent.
    *Ricardo.* What hinders you?
    *Celio.* What obstacle
impedes your proud ascent?
    *Eusebio.* Did you see that livid flame
flashing down on me?

*Ricardo.*          Only
your fancy, sir, born of fear.
     *Eusebio.* What fear?
     *Celio.*          Start up, then.
     *Eusebio.*                    I'm going.
Though a brace of lightning blind me,
I shall penetrate that fire.
The flames of hell won't stop me.

                    [*He climbs up and enters.*]

     *Celio.* Now he's in.
     *Ricardo.*          That must have been
some hallucination come from
a sense of horror at
his own daring.
     *Celio.*     Take the ladder down.
     *Ricardo.* We'll have to wait here until dawn.
     *Celio.* It's a daring thing he's done, all right—
to break into a convent.
As for me, I'd rather spend the night
with my little peasant girl from town.
Well, there'll be time enough for that.

                              [*Exeunt*

JULIA's *cell inside the convent*

*Enter* EUSEBIO.

     *Eusebio.* I have wandered all through this convent,
and so far, unobserved.
My fate has guided me past the narrow
open doorways of a thousand cells,
but Julia is nowhere to be found.
How far my doubtful hopes
have brought me! What stark forbidding
silence now surrounds me!
What a deep and deadly darkness!

                    [*He draws a curtain.*]

Ah, here's a light—another cell,
and Julia is in it. What stops me?
Is my courage now so faint
that words fail me entirely?
What keeps me? Why do I hesitate?
The more I doubt my impulse,
the more my boldness falters
and gives way to cowardice.

She seems lovelier than ever
in that humble robe she wears.
Modesty in women is
their essential beauty.
As her loveliness increases, lewd
desires stir me to possess it,
and with such strange intensity
that while her beauty rouses
all my passion, her modesty
fills me with respectful awe.
Julia! Ah, my Julia!

*Julia.*          Who calls me?
Heavenly God, what is this I see?
Are you the phantom of desire
or the shadow of a dream?

  *Eusebio.* Is the sight of me so appalling?

  *Julia.* Who would not be startled, and wish
only to escape your presence?

  *Eusebio.* No, Julia, stay.

  *Julia*          Why do you
torment me, ghostly image,
specter of the mind which
the eye alone perceives?
Are you the fearful spokesman
of imagination come
to punish me? Are you not
the figure of illusion,
the portrait of some fantasy
transported here on the cold night air?

  *Eusebio.* Julia, listen to me. I am
Eusebio, and quite alive,
who lie here at your feet.
If I were the image of your thought,
I would have been here with you always.

  *Julia.* I only deceive myself again
by listening to you, and I know
that in the shame of my dishonor
I would prefer the false and ghostly
to the true and living Eusebio.
Here where every day I die
again in torments of a living death,
you come to me. What do you want?
I can scarcely breathe! What is
your purpose now? I am dying!

What object can you have?
I am afraid to hear of it!
Whatever fatal plan you have,
I do not want to know of it.
How can you have found me here?
    *Eusebio.* The turbulence of love prevailed
against my own despair
and your severity.
Until you took the veil,
fond hopes still sustained me.
But once you passed inside these walls,
I kicked aside religious scruples
and the convent's sacred law.
Whether justified or not, I say
you are my accomplice in this act.
Spurred by passion and necessity,
I have forced my way in here.
But in the sight of Heaven,
I plead my cause is just.
Before you took religious vows,
you swore to be my wife.
Now you cannot pledge yourself
to both such lives at once.
    *Julia.* I do not deny the bonds of love
which happily united us,
nor that sweet urgency
which prompted me to call you
my beloved spouse; all this,
I must admit, is true.
But in this holy sanctuary,
prompted by a higher law,
I have given both my word and hand
to be the bride of Christ.
I am His; what more have I
to do with you? Go, and leave me now,
you who cast a pall upon the world
by murder and by rape.
Go now, Eusebio, and forget me.
Your love is hopeless and insane.
Remember where you are, this holy place,
and let it fill your heart with horror.
    *Eusebio.* The more you contradict me,
the more you kindle my desire.
Now that I have scaled these walls

and found you, some darker cause than love
goads me on. Submit to me
or I shall say you called me here
and have kept me hidden in your cell
these many days. I cannot bear it,
I am desperate, I'll shout: "Hear me! . . ."
    *Julia.* No, be silent! Oh, Eusebio . . .
My God, listen to me. . . .
I hear footsteps, the nuns
are on their way to chapel.
Heavens! What can I do now?
Shut the cell door, bar it.
Stay here now: one fear feeds
another, and the danger spreads.
    *Eusebio.* How huge and heavy is my love!
    *Julia.* How implacable is my fate!

### Outside the convent

#### Enter RICARDO *and* CELIO.

    *Ricardo.* Three o'clock. What's keeping him?
    *Celio.* The lover sunken in his bliss,
Ricardo, is no night watchman
waiting for the sunrise.
I'll wager he thinks the dawn never
came so soon—today especially.
    *Ricardo.* Yes, it always comes too soon
when passion's kindled, and too late
when it's been consummated.
    *Celio.* Well, at any rate, I don't think
he's inside now yearning for the dawn.
    *Ricardo.* But he's been in there two hours.
    *Celio.* It wouldn't seem that much to him.
    *Ricardo.* Yes, it's true: the hours of
your impatience set against
the hours of his pleasure.
    *Celio.* Do you know, Ricardo, I suspect
that it was Julia after all
who summoned him to come.
    *Ricardo.* Yes, I agree; otherwise, who'd have
the gall to break into a convent?
    *Celio.* Ricardo, did you hear voices now?
    *Ricardo.* Yes.
    *Celio.*        Well, bring the ladder here.

*Enter* JULIA *and* EUSEBIO *above.*

*Eusebio.* Woman, go back.
*Julia.*                          How can I?
I submitted to your desires.
You entreated me, your anguish
moved me, I relented.
Now I have flaunted Heaven twice:
first by disobeying God, then
by disobeying Him, my spouse.
Now you tear yourself away
and leave me, made hopeless
by your disdain, and by your scorn,
still waiting to be your wife.
Where are you going?
*Eusebio.*                  Woman,
what do you want of me? Leave me.
I tore myself away because in your
embrace I felt the presence
of some strange divinity.
What it was I cannot say.
Your eyes were two fiery jets,
your sighs blew scorching flame.
Each word you spoke was a volcano,
each hair jagged as a lightning flash.
Each phrase you uttered sentenced me
to death; each caress tore
open the gates of hell.
All these omens rocked my brain
when I spied the livid cross
upon your breast. That sacred symbol
has been Heaven's prodigy,
which I cannot fail to venerate
despite my sinfulness.
For if hereafter I let it be
the witness of all my villainies,
how can I shamelessly
invoke it in moments of distress?
Stay here, Julia, in your cloistered
cell; I do not scorn you.
I adore you more than ever.
  *Julia.* Oh, listen to me! Wait, Eusebio!
  *Eusebio.* Here's the ladder.
  *Julia.*                          No, stay!

Or take me with you.
    *Eusebio.*          I cannot.
                           *[He descends.]*
I must leave you here, and leave behind
all the joys I have so long awaited.
God help me, I am falling!
                       *[He falls.]*
    *Ricardo.* What's happened?
    *Eusebio.*               There, there!
Don't you see that ball of fire with bolts
of lightning in its bloody fist?
Don't you see that lowering
red sky rolling toward me?
Where can I find refuge now
that Heaven rages over me?
Oh Cross Divine, this I promise you
and take this solemn vow
with strict attention to each word:
wheresoever I may find you,
I shall fall upon my knees
and pray devoutly, with all my heart.
      *[He rises; exeunt* EUSEBIO, CELIO, *and* RICARDO.
      *The ladder is left behind.*

      JULIA, *alone, at a window*

    *Julia.* I am alone, in my confusion
and perplexity. Ingrate, are these
your promises to me? Is this
the sum of what you called your love's mad
passion, or is it my love's madness?
How you persisted in your suit—
now by threats, now by promises,
now as lover, now as tyrant,
till I at last submitted to you.
But no sooner had you become
master of your pleasure
and my sorrow than you fled
before you had possessed me.
Now in escaping you have
vanquished me entirely.
Merciful Heaven, I am lost
and dead! Why does nature provide
the world with poisons when the venom
of contempt can kill so swiftly?

So his contempt will kill me,
since to make the torment worse
I must follow him who scorns me.
When has love been so perverse before?
When Eusebio wooed me, pled
with me and wept, I scorned him.
But now that he scorns me,
I am impelled to seek his favor.
Such is woman's nature that
against her inclination
she withholds that pleasure
which she most delights to give.
And he does not love her well
who would overvalue her;
for when she's loved at such a rate,
she scorns him, and when she herself
is scorned, her love for him is strongest.
I would not care if he had ceased
to love me; it is his leaving me
which hurts. This is where he fell; then I
must fall there too and follow him.
But what is this? His ladder?
Yes, of course. But what can I
be thinking? Oh no, the dreadful
thought's too overwhelming.
Stop! Does not my creed tell me
that once I give assent in thought
I thereby commit the crime?
Did not Eusebio scale
these convent walls for me?
And did I not feel pleased
to see him run such risks
for my sake? Then why am I afraid?
What scruple holds me back?
If I leave now I do the very thing
Eusebio did when he entered;
and just as I was pleased with him,
he'll be pleased to see me too,
considering the risks I've taken
for his sake. Now I have assented,
I must take the blame. And if
the sin itself be so tremendous,
will enjoying it be any
less so? Since I have assented

and am fallen from the hand of God,
it is useless to suppose
I may be pardoned for committing
such a heinous crime. Then why wait?

[*She descends the ladder.*]

Now as I turn my hooded eyes
blindly on this dark immensity,
I find that my esteem for mankind,
honor, and my God is nothing
but an arid waste. Like an angel
flung from Heaven in my demonic
fall, I feel no stirring of
repentance. To return is hopeless.
I have left my sanctuary.
The night is dark and silent
and I am wrapped in fright.
I stumble down this murky path
as though headed toward the pitfall
of my crime. Where now? Where can I turn?
What must I do? The silence deepens,
horrors swarm about me; my blood
is frozen, my hair stands on end.
Conscience traces ghostly figures
on the air, and every echo
booms out my heavy doom.
The crime which briefly fed
my bloated pride now stalls
and shackles me in cowardice,
till I can scarcely drag
my heavy feet another step.
My back is sunken, as though
weighted with tremendous loads,
and I am stiff with cold.
No, I'll not go any farther.
There's the convent, I'll go back,
confess my sin, and pray
to be forgiven; faith teaches
there is nothing which the clemency
of Heaven cannot touch or reach:
all the sparkling constellations,
all the sands of all the oceans,
every atom, every mote upon
the air, and all these joined together,
are as nothing to the sins

which the good Lord God can pardon.
I hear footsteps! I'll hide back here
until they pass; then, unobserved,
I'll climb inside again.

[*She hides.*]

*Enter* RICARDO *and* CELIO

*Ricardo.* The ladder was forgotten in
Eusebio's fright; I've come in time
to take it so that it won't be seen
at dawn leaning against this wall.

[*Exeunt, carrying the ladder between them*

*Julia.* They're gone, at last. Now I can climb
inside unobserved. But where is it?
Isn't this the wall it stood against?
No, but surely it's over there.
No, it's not here either. Good Lord!
How am I to get inside?
Ah, but I begin to understand
the depths of my misfortune.
This is a sign my way is barred,
and thus when I would strive
to creep back, a penitent,
I am shown my cause is hopeless.
Mercy is refused me.
Now a woman doubly scorned,
I shall perpetrate such
desperate deeds even Heaven
will be astounded, and the world
will shudder at them till
my perfidy outrages all time
to come, and the deepest pits
of hell shall stand agape
with horror at my crimes.

# ACT THREE

## *On the mountain*

*Enter* GIL, *covered with crosses; a very large one is sewn
on his breast.*

GIL. Here I go, at Menga's bidding,
scouring the mountainside for firewood,

and for my own protection
I've concocted this stratagem.
They say Eusebio loves crosses.
Well, here I am, armed from head to foot
with them. Oh, Lord—don't tell me!
No sooner speak of the devil than
there he is! I'm so frightened now,
I can't budge an inch. Where do I hide?
He hasn't seen me yet;
maybe I can slip off there and freeze
until he goes away. But what's this
I'm stuck to now? A bramble bush!
Oh, forget it, forget it. God,
these little thorns are prickly!
From the frying pan into the fire!
This is worse than a woman's
tongue-lashing, or a public
confession, or envying
the village idiot.

*Enter* Eusebio.

*Eusebio.* Where can I turn to now?
Life is burdensome and tedious,
but death never seems to come
to one who wearies of life.
Julia, how long ago it was
when marriage seemed so imminent, and
in your happy arms' embrace I dreamed
our sweet love's consummation.
Yet I turned away and left that joy
behind untouched, untasted.
It was not my fault. I was driven
by the impulse of a higher power
whose cause prevailed against my will,
forbidding me to trespass on
the Cross—the Cross that I respect—
inscribed upon your breast,
and identically inscribed on mine.
Oh Julia, the two of us were born
subject to that sign, and thus I fear
the portents of a mystery
which only God can understand.

*Gil* [*aside*]. I can't stand it any longer;
I'm stung all over!

    *Eusebio.*        There is
someone in the bushes. Who's there?
    *Gil* [*aside*]. Well, here's where I get tangled
in my snare.
    *Eusebio* [*aside*]. A man tied to a tree,
and wearing a cross on his breast!
I must be true to my word and kneel.
    *Gil.* Why do you kneel, Eusebio?
Are you saying your prayers, or what?
First you tie me up, then you pray
to me. I don't understand.
    *Eusebio.* Who are you?
    *Gil.*               Gil. Don't you remember?
Ever since you tied me up here
with that message, I've been yelling out
my lungs but, just my luck,
nobody's yet come by to free me.
    *Eusebio.* But this is not the place
I left you.
    *Gil.*    That's true, sir.
The fact is, when I realized that
no one was passing by, I moved on,
still tied, from one tree to the next
until I reached this spot.
And that's the only reason
why it seems so strange to you. [EUSEBIO *frees him.*]
    *Eusebio* [*aside*]. This simpleton may be of use
to me in my misfortune.
—Gil, I took a liking to you
when we met the other time.
So now let us be friends.
    *Gil.*             Fair enough,
and since we're friends, I'll never
go back home but follow you instead,
and we'll be highwaymen together.
They say the life's ideal—not a stitch
of work from one year to the next.
    *Eusebio.* Good. You'll join me then.

*Enter* RICARDO *and highwaymen leading* JULIA *in; she is
    dressed as a man, and her face is muffled.*

    *Ricardo.*                 We caught
the prisoner at the crossroads
down below, and I thought

this one would amuse you.

*Eusebio.* Yes, that's fine, but first, look here:
we have a new recruit.

*Ricardo.*                    Who's he?

*Gil.* I'm Gil. Can't you see?

*Eusebio.*                    Though he may not
look it, this peasant knows every
landmark in these hills and plains,
and he will serve us as a guide.
What's more, he'll go down among
the enemy and be our trusty spy.
You may give him an harquebus
and a uniform meanwhile.

*Celio.*                    This way.

*Gil* [*aside*]. Oh, pity me! What do
I know of brigandry?

*Eusebio.* Who is this gentleman whose face
is muffled?

*Ricardo.* He refuses to tell
his name or where he comes from except
in the presence of our captain.

*Eusebio.* Then it is time to reveal them;
you are in his presence now.

*Julia.* Are you the captain?

*Eusebio.*                    Yes.

*Julia* [*aside*].                    My God!

*Eusebio.* Speak. Who are you, and why
have you come here?

*Julia.*          I shall answer that
in private only.

*Eusebio.*     Leave us a while.

[*Exeunt all but
Eusebio and Julia*

*Eusebio.* Now we are alone where only
silent trees and flowers eavesdrop
on your words. Remove the cloth
that hides your face and tell me—
who are you? Where do you come from?
What is your purpose here? Speak.

*Julia* [*drawing her sword*]. So you may know me and my
                    purpose
both at once, draw your sword.
This is the only way to tell you
I am one who comes to take your life.

*Eusebio.* I shall draw, but only
to defend myself against
your rashness and my own suspicions.
Your voice is gentler than you pretend.

*Julia.* Coward, fight! Lift your sword,
and you will see how quickly death
relieves you of suspicions.

*Eusebio.* I'll fight, but not to injure you,
for I must protect myself
as well as you; otherwise,
if I kill you or you kill me,
I shall never know the reason
for this duel. Therefore, I beg you,
show your face.

*Julia.*        Your point's well taken.
One's honor would not be
completely satisfied
unless the offender recognized
the vengeful hand which struck him down.

[*She reveals herself.*]

Do you know me now? What startles you?
Why do you stare at me?

*Eusebio.*        Because
I still can only half believe
that you are standing here, and because
I cannot doubt that it is you,
your presence now appalls me.

*Julia.* Then you have surely recognized me.

*Eusebio.* Indeed, and as I look at you
I feel new confusions heaped
upon dismay. A moment ago
I would have given both my eyes away
to catch a glimpse of you.
Now I'd gladly pluck them out
not to see you here. You, Julia,
wandering through these mountains?
And dressed in men's clothing?
You commit a double sacrilege.
How did you come here all alone?
What prompted you?

*Julia.*        Your scorn
and my despair prompted me.
You have yet to learn that a woman's
burning passion is swifter

than an arrow sprung from its bow,
more fiery than a shot of lead,
more sudden than a lightning bolt,
which is why I gloried in the crimes
I have committed until now—
and what is more, I would be glad
to do them all again.
I left the convent, fled into
the mountains, and there, because
a shepherd told me I had been
ill advised to take the path
I came by, and because I panicked
foolishly, I quickly reassured
him by stabbing him to death.
I killed him with the knife
he carried in his belt. That knife,
which proved so fine a
minister of death, I used again.
To relieve me in my weariness,
a traveler kindly made room
behind him on his horse.
I went along until we reached
the outskirts of a village;
and because he wished to lodge there
when my purpose was to flee again,
I killed him for his kindness
on the spot. Three days and nights
I wandered in the wilderness,
with nothing but wild roots and herbs
to eat and cold boulders for my bed
at night. When at last I came upon
a humble cottage, I remember
thinking how the thatched roof glistened
like a gold pavilion
to my quickened senses.
There, a shepherd and his wife
showered me with hospitality.
Their fare, though crude, was plentiful;
their simple board was good and clean.
Soon they dispelled my weariness
and hunger. And yet, on leaving them,
I resolved that they would never live
to tell pursuers, "Yes, she was
our guest." So I killed the gentle

shepherd when he came along
to guide me through the mountain;
then I returned and killed his wife.
But knowing that the dress I wore
would be incriminating, I now
concluded I must find a suit
of clothes. These, together with his sword,
were furnished by a hunter
whom I killed, along the way,
as he was sleeping. After
many such encounters,
surmounting every obstacle,
scorning every danger, and wreaking
havoc everywhere I went,
I came here at length to find you.

    *Eusebio.* I listen to you, fascinated,
enchanted by your voice,
bewitched by everything you say,
although the sight of you
fills me with dread. Julia, please—
it is not that I despise you
but that I fear Heaven's
retribution looming over me.
This is why I turn away, and beg you
to go back now to your convent.
I live in such horror of that Cross,
I must avoid you.—What's that noise?

        *Enter the highwaymen.*

    *Ricardo.* Sir, prepare for their attack.
Curcio and his men have crossed
the highway and are climbing
toward you up the mountain.
All the villagers are roused
against you; more and more
are joining him—old men, women,
even children. They are coming
to avenge the murder of
Lisardo, and they swear to seize
and punish you for all the lives
you've taken, and then to bring you
as a prisoner, alive or dead,
to justice in Siena.

*Eusebio.* Julia, we'll speak together later.
Cover your face now, and come with me.
You must not be taken
by your father and your enemy.
Men, show your strength and courage now!
Remember, if you fail, they come
prepared to wipe us out
or take us prisoners.
Once we're captured, we'll find ourselves
in prison, our honor lost
and hounded by disgrace.
Knowing this, which of us would fear
to take the greater risk—
for honor and dear life?
Do not let them think we hesitate.
Forward, to the attack!
Fortune smiles upon audacity.

*Ricardo.* There's no need to get at them;
they're coming at us now.

*Eusebio.* Take up your arms, stand firm!
And, by Heaven, if I see
one of you retreat or run,
my sword will find that coward's heart
before it nicks the enemy.

*Curcio [offstage].* I can see that wretch Eusebio
taking cover there among the crags,
but he cannot long defend
himself behind those boulders.

*Voices.* There they are! We see them now
from here, through the foliage.

*Julia.* To the attack!                               [*Exit*

*Eusebio.*                    Miserable
peasants! As Heaven is my witness,
it won't be long before your blood,
which stains these fields, will flow in torrents.

*Ricardo.* They're nothing but a pack of cowards!

*Curcio [offstage].* Where are you hiding, Eusebio?

*Eusebio.* Hiding? I'm coming after you!

                                        [*Exeunt omnes*
               [*Shots are fired offstage.*]

*Another part of the mountain; a stone cross*

*Offstage shouts; enter* JULIA.

*Julia.* Coming down the mountain,
I had scarcely set foot in the fields
when the air was torn with
agonizing cries, the clash
of companies of men in battle.
The echoing guns choked my hearing;
the glittering swords blinded my sight.
But now—what is this I see?
His troops dispersed and driven back,
and Eusebio left to face
the enemy alone. I'll go back,
bring his men together, and try
to rally them again in his
defense. If I succeed,
I shall grow monumental
by his side, become the terror
of the world, the cutting shears of Fate,
the fiery executioner
of all their lives, the symbol
of terrifying vengeance,
the wonder of our age
and all ages yet to come!

                                              [*Exit*

                *Enter* Gil, *as a highwayman.*

*Gil.* To save my skin, I became
a novice highwayman.
I'd scarcely done so when I found
a bandit's life is full of danger.
When I was a laborer,
laborers were always being drubbed.
Now that I'm a highwayman,
I'm still stuck on the losing side.
Far from being miserly,
I'm loaded down with misery.
I am so unlucky
that this has often struck me:
If I turned Jew, I'd be the reason
why all Jews are oppressed.

        *Enter* Menga, Blas, Tirso, *and other peasants.*

*Menga.* After them, they're running off!
*Blas.* Catch them, and don't let any one
escape alive.

*Menga.*     Look, there's one
who's crawled away to hide.
     *Blas.* Kill the thief!
     *Gil.*                    Oh, can't you
tell it's me?
     *Menga.*     He's a highwayman—
I can tell it by his clothes.
     *Gil.* Then my clothing is a liar
for deceiving you about me.
     *Menga.* Thump him good and hard!
     *Blas.*                         Paste him down,
I say!
     *Gil.* I've been thumped and pasted down
enough; remember now . . .
     *Tirso.*                    All we need
remember is that you're a brigand!
     *Gil.* Look, for Heaven's sake, I'm Gil!
     *Menga.* Gil? Well, why not say so
in the first place?
     *Tirso.*          Yes, Gil,
why not tell us sooner?
     *Gil.* First place! Sooner! When I said it's me,
that should have told you to begin with.
     *Menga.* What are you doing here?
     *Gil.*                         Can't you see?
Just breaking the Fifth Commandment,
killing off more souls than a doctor
and a summer plague put together.
     *Menga.* Where did you get that uniform?
     *Gil.* It's the devil's; I killed one
and dressed up in his clothes.
     *Menga.* But if you killed him in it,
how come the uniform's not bloody?
     *Gil.* That's easy. The answer is
he died of fright.
     *Menga.*          Come along now,
we're running all those brigands down.
They're nothing but a pack of cowards.
     *Gil.* Now good riddance to this uniform,
though I catch my death of cold.

                              [*Exeunt omnes*

          *Enter* EUSEBIO *and* CURCIO, *fighting.*

     *Curcio.* We are alone at last. Heaven be

praised for granting me the power
to avenge myself upon you,
for not permitting someone else
to do the deed for me, or me
to see you slain by another's sword.
    *Eusebio.* This time, Curcio, Heaven has not
frowned upon our meeting, so that if
you come in anger, you will return
in anger, punished for your pains.
I do not know what reverence
the sight of you instills in me,
but I know your suffering awes me
more than your sword; though your courage
might well daunt me, I confess it is
your white hairs alone which so
appall me that I fear
I have grown cowardly.
    *Curcio.* Eusebio, I grant that
your appearance tempers overmuch
the grievous wrath I feel.
But I'll not have you so mistaken
as to think you fear these poor white hairs
while there's any valor left in me.
Come, lift up your sword and fight!
No lucky star or other omen
will suffice to turn me now
from the vengeance which I seek.
Lift up your sword!
    *Eusebio.*        I, afraid?
It would be rash of you to call that
fear which is simple reverence;
and truth to tell, the only
victory I seek is to fall
upon my knees and beg you
to forgive me; here at your feet
I lay this sword which has struck
so many hearts with fear.
    *Curcio.* Eusebio, I will not
have you think that I could kill you
by taking such unfair advantage.
There's my sword.
               [*Aside.*] And so I miss
the chance of killing him.

—Come, fight with your bare hands.

[*They close and struggle.*]

*Eusebio.* I do not know what influence
you cast upon my heart,
disabling wrath and vengeance
as tears well up in my eyes,
and I am so unnerved
I can only beg you
to revenge yourself and take my life.
Take it, sir, for I am vanquished.
I lay my life down at your feet.

*Curcio.* However just his cause, a nobleman
does not stain his sword upon
a vanquished enemy.
The better part of glory's gone
when victory is tinged
by such a victim's blood.

*Voices* [*offstage*]. They went this way.

*Curcio.*                          My men are looking
for me. They have won the day, while yours
have fled the field in panic.
I want to spare your life: go now,
escape. I cannot stay the anger
of a vengeful peasant mob. Alone,
you cannot possibly survive.

*Eusebio.* I have never fled from any show
of force except your own,
which I truly fear. But once
this sword is in my fist again,
you will find that all the valor
which you paralyzed in me
will more than serve against your men.

*Enter* Otavio *and all the peasants.*

*Otavio.* From the deepest valley
to the highest crag, not a soul
among them's left alive except
Eusebio, who escaped.
I saw him running off at night . . .

*Eusebio.* Liar! Eusebio never
runs away.

*Otavio.* Is this Eusebio?
Kill him!

*Eusebio.* Come on, peasants, try it!

*Curcio.* Hold on, Otavio, wait!

*Otavio.* What is this, sir? You rallied us
before, and now you'd stop us?

*Blas.* And defend the man whose sword
destroyed your honor and good name?

*Gil.* And such a man—who coolly goes
about ravaging the countryside,
enjoying every maid and melon
on his way, and killing all the rest—
how can you defend him now?

*Otavio.*                                  Sir, what
do you say? What can you be thinking?

*Curcio.* Wait, listen to me (oh bitter day!).
Would it not be better now
to take him to Siena?
Eusebio, if you surrender,
I promise, on my honor as a
nobleman, to help you all I can.
Even against my interests, I'll be
your advocate before the law.

*Eusebio.* I yield to Curcio, but not
to any court of law. Respect
for him would prompt me to surrender,
but to the law, only fear.
And there is nothing that I fear.

*Otavio.* Death to Eusebio!

*Curcio.*                                  No, wait . . .

*Otavio.* Would you still defend him, and be
a traitor to your country too?

*Curcio.* I, a traitor? No—Eusebio,
forgive me, for if I am
suspected and insulted,
I am afraid that I shall have
to be the first to see you dead.

*Eusebio.* Stand aside, sir; otherwise
your presence will unnerve me,
and then your men, I know,
will use you as a shield against me.

          [*Exeunt all the peasants and* EUSEBIO, *fighting*

*Curcio.* They are swarming after him.
No one can save you now,
Eusebio, even if
he shields you with his life.

There he goes, stumbling up that crag,
the victim of a thousand
bloody wounds. He is stepping back.
Oh, he has fallen down the valley.
I must run: his chilling blood cries out
to me so timidly. And if
his blood were not my own in part,
it would not beckon me,
nor would I hear it cry.

[*Exit* CURCIO

*Having fallen headlong from the cliff,* EUSEBIO *is seen,
lying at the foot of the Cross.*

   *Eusebio.* Fallen from the highest cliff, I see
my fitful life must here ebb away
where there is no earth to bury me.
Guilt pricks at me and goads my soul,
yet not remorsefully
for this departing life of mine,
but only for some way
I may atone for all my crimes
with something more than this,
my one small life. Soon the vengeful mob
will come to take me, but since they'll
never take me while I'm still alive,
I must die fighting. Though I would
rather crawl away and pray for
Heaven's mercy, this Cross towering
in my path would seem to urge
that my pursuers only seek
my instant death while it
offers me eternal life.
Oh Tree, where Heaven chose to hang
the one true fruit to ransom man
for his first forbidden mouthful!
Oh flower of paradise regained!
Rainbow light that spanned the Flood
and thus pledged peace to all mankind!
Oh fruitful vine; the harp of yet
another David; and the tablets
of another Moses:
Here I am, a sinner seeking grace.
What was given you to do
must be rendered to me too.

Had I been the only sinner
in the world, God would have died
for me alone. You are my own Cross,
for God never would have suffered death
upon you were it not
for all my crimes. Oh Holy Cross,
from the very first my most ardent
prayer has ever been that never
would you let me die unshriven.
I shall not be the first thief
who by your grace, within your arms,
was taken unto God. Now I,
the second thief, who lie repenting
in your arms, I beg you to bestow
on me that redemption
granted to a former thief.
You too, Lisardo, whom I held
dying in my arms, though I could
have killed you instantly—
I saw to your confession
in good time, before the mortal coils
unbound you. And now, with my own
dying breath I summon you
and that old man, and beg you both,
take pity on me. See, Lisardo,
I am dying! Alberto, listen,
I am calling to you.

*Enter* CURCIO.

*Curcio.* He must have fallen here somewhere.
    *Eusebio.* If you have come to take my life,
there is very little left of it,
and that no longer in my keeping.
    *Curcio.* Oh, the sight of so much blood
would blanch a statue made of bronze.
Give up your sword, Eusebio.
    *Eusebio.* To whom?
    *Curcio.*            To Curcio.
    *Eusebio.*                            Here it is,
                        [*Giving it to him.*]
and I yield myself to you as well;
forgive me for the injury
of that first crime against you . . .
I cannot speak, for I've a wound

that swallows up the breath of life
and floods my soul with dread and fear.
    *Curcio.* What can I do? Is there
no human remedy for this?
    *Eusebio.* My sick soul needs the medicine
of God, I think.
    *Curcio.*        Where is your wound?
    *Eusebio.* Here, in my chest.
    *Curcio.*             Let me place
my hand there and see if I can feel
your breathing. Alas, I fear the worst!
        *[He uncovers the wound and sees the Cross.]*
What is this sign, so fair and so
divine, which stirs me to the roots
of my whole being?
    *Eusebio.*        The escutcheon
I inherited from this Cross,
at whose foot I was born.
That is all I know about
my origin. I do not blame
my father for denying me
a cradle. He must have sensed
the evil that was in me.
Yes, I was born here.
    *Curcio.*         And here
is where grief contends with joy,
pleasure locks with pain, twin
burdens of a fate both glad
and impious. Oh, my son!
The pride and pain of finding you!
You are indeed my son,
Eusebio. All these signs
have proved it and justly overwhelm
my heart to mourn you on your deathbed.
Every word you say confirms
my premonitions. On this very
spot where I found you, your mother
once abandoned you; and here,
where I once sinned against her,
Heaven's wrath descends upon me.
More and more this place brings
confirmation of my guilt.
Yet what stronger proof is there
when I find the Cross inscribed

upon your breast the same as Julia's?
By this sign Heaven wrought
a mystery that was sealed
upon the two of you here at birth.
    *Eusebio.* My breath is failing, father.
Farewell! An icy shroud numbs
my body; death flies swiftly down
to choke the words of my reply,
the life to greet you with,
the heart that would obey you.
There, the heavy stroke is fallen,
the last rigor seizes me.
Alberto!
    *Curcio.* How I hated him
alive; now how I grieve his death!
    *Eusebio.* Alberto, come!
    *Curcio.*               How cruel
his struggle, and how futile!
    *Eusebio.* Alberto! Alberto!

                                *[He dies.]*

    *Curcio.* That terrible convulsion
snuffed out his final breath.
Let me begin to count each grief
by these white hairs.

                         *[He tears his hair.]*

### Enter BLAS.

    *Blas.*            Sir, it is useless
to complain. Your courage has always
been equal to the worst misfortune.
    *Curcio.* It was never tried so much
as it is now. The fury of
my scalding tears would burn
this mountain down. Heavenly God,
I cannot bear this bitter grief!

### Enter OTAVIO.

    *Otavio.* Curcio, fate pummels you today
with the cruelest blows of all.
Heaven knows how sad I am
to tell you this.
    *Curcio.*     What is it?

*Otavio.* Julia has fled the convent.

*Curcio.* In my wildest dreams, could I ever
frame so horrible a sentence or
imagine this stroke of pain it brings?
No, it goes beyond belief.
This poor cold corpse, Otavio,
this thing you see was once my son.
Consider, should not any one
of these adversities suffice
to kill me? Heavens, let me be
patient, or else crush out this
savagely tormented life of mine!

*Enter* GIL *and peasants.*

*Gil.* Sir!

*Curcio.* What new sorrow do you bring?

*Gil.* The bandits we routed
now rally to attack again,
led on by some fighting devil
out of hell—a man who keeps his name
and face a secret, even from them.

*Curcio.* Now my griefs are legion,
the worst seem little more than jests.
Take up this broken body
of Eusebio's, and lay it
mournfully aside till there is time
to build an honorable
sepulcher from which his ashen gaze
may contemplate my tears.

*Tirso.* What? How can you think of burying
a man in holy ground who died
beyond the pale of Church and God?

*Blas.* For anyone like that, a grave here
in the wilderness is good enough.

*Curcio.* Oh, villainous revenge!
Are you still so outraged
you must strike at him beyond the grave?

[*Exit* CURCIO, *weeping*

*Blas.* He was a fiend. Let wild beasts
and carrion be his grave.

*Voice.* That's too good for him. Let's throw him
off the cliff and watch him land
in pieces.

*Tirso.* No, we'd better move him
now and cover him with branches.
> [*They place the body of* EUSEBIO *under the
> branches.*]
But night is falling in its murky
shroud; so Gil, you stay here and guard
the body on this height since yours
is the only voice loud enough to
reach us when the bandits climb uphill.
> [*Exeunt omnes, except* GIL
*Gil.* They're very calm about it all!
They put Eusebio away
and leave me here alone
to watch him overnight.
Eusebio, sir, remember please
how you and I were such good friends.
What was that? Am I dreaming
or is that an army down there
coming up to get me?

### *Enter* ALBERTO.

*Alberto.* Returning now from Rome,
I find I have lost my way again,
here beneath the silent twilit sky.
This is where Eusebio spared
my life, and I fear the peril
of encountering his men.
*Eusebio.* Alberto!
*Alberto.*          Whose breathless voice
is this I hear quavering out
the syllables of my name?
*Eusebio.* Alberto!
*Alberto.*          Again it calls me.
It seemed to come from here; now I must
find it.
*Gil.* God Almighty!
It's Eusebio. I think
my hair's standing on its end.
*Eusebio.* Alberto!
*Alberto.*          That sounds closer.
Whose voice repeats my name
upon the fleeting wind? Tell me,
who are you?

*Eusebio.* I am Eusebio.
Come closer here, Alberto,
and remove these branches
that cover me. Do not fear me.
*Alberto.* I am not afraid.

[*Uncovering him.*]

*Gil.* But I am.
*Alberto.* Now I have uncovered you,
tell me, in the Name of God,
what is it you wish me to do?
*Eusebio.* Through Him, Alberto, my faith
summoned you to hear my
confessional before I die.
I have been dead some while,
but my spirit, severed from this
useless body by the savage stroke
of death, remained within my corpse.

[*He rises.*]

Come close, Alberto, let me confess
my sins, more numerous than all
the grains of sand beneath the sea
and all the atoms of the sun.
Yet still more powerful than all
of these in Heaven is
my devotion to the Cross!
*Alberto.* Every penance I have given
sinners till this day, I offer you.
May they somewhat assuage
the heavy burdens of your conscience.

[*Exeunt* ALBERTO *and* EUSEBIO

*Enter* JULIA *and the highwaymen from the other side.*

*Gil.* Almighty God, there he goes,
walking off! And to make this plain as
day, the sun shoots down its last few rays.
I am bursting to tell the news!
*Julia.* Now that victory and sleep
have put them off their guard,
we can take them by surprise.
A *Highwayman.* If you want to ambush them, we must
lie in wait in here, for they
are coming now this way.

*Enter* CURCIO *and the peasants.*

*Curcio.* Grief has not yet put an end to me
and my adversities; it must be
I am made, past endurance,
to bear them all forever.
      *Gil.* People stream in from everywhere . . .
Let me be the first to tell you all
the most amazing miracle
this world has ever seen.
Where only now Eusebio
lay dead, a corpse, he suddenly
arose, calling loudly for a priest.
But why bother putting into words
what all of you can plainly see?
There, look at how devoutly
he is praying on his knees.
            [EUSEBIO *is shown kneeling before* ALBERTO,
                  *who is confessing him.*]
      *Curcio.* My son! Oh Lord Divine,
what a miracle you have wrought!
      *Julia.* Who has ever seen a more
astounding sight?
      *Curcio.*          Look, just as
that saintly elder made the sign
of absolution over him,
Eusebio fell dead at his feet,
a corpse again.
                        [ALBERTO *approaches.*]
      *Alberto.* Of all the wonders of this world,
let my voice extol the greatest
it will ever know: Heaven kept
Eusebio's soul in his
dead body till he could confess
his sins. By this sign the Lord
reveals how much He esteems
devotion to the Cross.
      *Curcio.* My dearest son! You were not
so wretched or forsaken
after all, when in your tragic death
you merit so much glory.
Now if only Julia
would recognize her crime.
      *Julia.* God help me! What is this I hear,

what ominous revelation?
Can it be that I who was
Eusebio's lover
was his sister too? Then let
my father and the whole wide world,
let everybody know about
my crimes. My perversions hound
and overwhelm me, but I shall be
the first to shout them out.
Let every man alive be told
that I am Julia, Julia
the criminal, and of all
the infamous women ever born,
the worst. Henceforth my penances
will be as public as the sins
I have confessed. I go now to beg
forgiveness of the world for the vile
example I have given it,
and pray that God forgive
the crime of all my life.
    *Curcio.* Monster of every wickedness,
I shall kill you with my own two hands,
and have you die as violently
as you have lived.
    *Julia.*            Oh Cross Divine,
save me now. I pledge my word to you
I shall atone beneath your sign
and be born again to a new life.
Farewell!

> [*As* Curcio *is about to strike her, she embraces
> the Cross, which is* Eusebio's *sepulcher, and
> it rises heavenward.*]

    *Alberto.* Another miracle!
    *Curcio.* And with this wondrous close,
the author happily concludes
*Devotion to the Cross.*

# THE MAYOR OF ZALAMEA

## (*EL ALCALDE DE ZALAMEA*)

# DRAMATIS PERSONAE

PHILIP II, *King of Spain*
DON LOPE DE FIGUEROA, *commander in chief*
DON ÁLVARO DE ATAIDE, *captain*
A SERGEANT
LA CHISPA, *a camp-follower*
REBOLLEDO, *a soldier, her sweetheart*
PEDRO CRESPO, *an old farmer, later the Mayor*
JUAN, *his son*
ISABEL, *Pedro Crespo's daughter*
INÉS, *her cousin*
DON MENDO, *an hidalgo*
NUÑO, *his servant*
A CLERK
*Soldiers, a Drummer, Farmers, Attendants*

The scene is laid in ZALAMEA and its outskirts.

# THE MAYOR OF ZALAMEA

## ACT ONE

### A *field near Zalamea*

*Enter* REBOLLEDO, LA CHISPA, *and Soldiers.*

REBOLLEDO. I say, damn his bloody hide
for forcing us to march
this way from town to town
without a break!
    *All.*           Hear, hear!
    *Rebolledo.* What are we now, a pack
of wandering gypsies? Must we
traipse around to hell and gone
behind a wrapped-up flag,
thanking our lucky stars
if the drum's . . .
    *1st Soldier.* He's off again!
    *Robolledo.* . . . stopped banging for a while just be-
                cause
it hasn't split our heads yet?
    *2nd Soldier.* Don't let it get you down.
You'll forget your aching back, I guess,
soon as we get to town.
    *Rebolledo.* To town? I'm dead beat now!
Even if I get there half alive,
God knows if we'll have billets.
Suddenly the Mayor's Council
will pop up to reassure
the Commissary they'll give us
everything we need—if we move on.
First he'll tell them, "No, impossible!
The men are all fagged out."
But if the Council slip
a little something in his pocket,
he'll add, "Men, we can't stop here.
I've got orders we must push on now."
Then we poor foot-slogging fools obey,
snap to the order, making him
rich as any cloistered monk, and me
as poor as any begging friar.
Well! I swear to God, when we get

143

to Zalamea this afternoon
and they make us march straight through
on some damn excuse, they'll go
without me. I'll put it to you straight:
it won't be the first time in my life
I've turned and gone—over the hill.

   *1st Soldier.* No, and you won't be the first wretched
common soldier to pay for it
with his life; especially now
that Don Lope de Figueroa
commands the regiment.
Though he's praised and famous
for his valor in the field,
he's also the most ruthless
and hardest-swearing man alive.
He'd sentence his best friend
to death without bothering
to give him a fair trial.

   *Rebolledo.* You've all heard what he said?
Well, I'm still game: I'll desert.

   *2nd Soldier.* How can any soldier boast of it?

   *Rebolledo.* It's all the same to me, and if
it weren't for this poor wench here
who shadows me . . .

   *La Chispa.*       As for me,
Sir Rebolledo, don't give it
another thought; as you know,
I was born with hair on my chest,
so to speak—so your qualms about me
are insulting. I'm here to serve for
honor's sake, and suffer for it too.
Otherwise it's clear I wouldn't
for the world have left that Magistrate
and his groaning board, where at the end
of every month a thousand gifts
pour in, since he's one of those
who hold a monthly open house.
But as I'd rather march and suffer
right along with Rebolledo,
and never burden him, what's this
he says about his having
qualms and doubts about me?

   *Rebolledo.* In Heaven's name, my girl,
you're the crown of womankind!

*2nd Soldier.* It's true, she is. Three cheers for Chispa!

*Rebolledo.* And three cheers again, if she'll
take the curse off this march,
up the hill and down again,
with a rousing song or ballad.

*La Chispa.* Here are the castanets
to answer that summons, sir.

*Rebolledo.* I'll be a party to it,
if every chap here will agree
to pass judgment on this trial.

    *1st Soldier.* That's well said, by Heaven!

             [REBOLLEDO *and* LA CHISPA *sing.*]

    *La Chispa. Ti-teeri-ti-teeri-ti-teers,*
*I'm queen of the balladeers.*

    *Rebolledo. Ti-tari-ti-turri-ti-teevs,*
*I'm king of the thugs and thieves.*

    *La Chispa. Let officers go overseas,*
*And fight the war on their knees.*

    *Rebolledo. And kill all the Arabs they please,*
*Who aren't my enemies.*

    *La Chispa. Just fill up the oven with meat,*
*And make sure I've plenty to eat.*

    *Rebolledo. Kill a chicken or two, yessiree,*
*But keep mutton away from me.*

    *1st Soldier.* Wait! I'm sorry to stop the singing
and the happy din it makes
as we go along, but I've just
caught sight of that tower,
which must be where we halt.

*Rebolledo.* Then that's Zalamea?

*La Chispa.* The belfry says so, plain enough.
Our song must end, but don't be sad:
there'll be many a chance
to pick it up again.
I love to sing, and where
other women burst into tears
over any little trifle,
I myself burst into song.
So I've hundreds yet to sing.

*Rebolledo.* Let's stop right here now and wait
until the sergeant brings the order:
we either enter in formation
or else break ranks.

*1st Soldier.*            That's him coming now
alone; and the captain's
waiting right behind him.

*Enter the* CAPTAIN *and the* SERGEANT.

*Captain.* Men, I have good news: we stay here now
in billets until Don Lope
and his troops arrive from Llerena.
The order of the day's come up
to wait in readiness
and not take up the march
to Guadalupe till
the regiment is reunited.
Then Don Lope joins us here.
Meanwhile you all can have
several days of well-earned rest.
      *Rebolledo.* That's good news, all right!
      *All.* Three cheers for the captain!
      *Captain.* Your quarters are all arranged.
Soon as he gets the word,
the Commissary will assign you
each a billet.
      *La Chispa.* I swear to God,
before the day is over
I'll find out for myself
why that gang of thugs ended with:

      *Kill a chicken or two, yessiree,*
      *But keep mutton away from me.*

                                    [*Exeunt omnes*


*A street in Zalamea*

*The* CAPTAIN, *the* SERGEANT.

*Captain.* Sergeant, have you found my billet?
You know where I'm to stay?
      *Sergeant.* Yes, sir.
      *Captain.*            And where is it?
      *Sergeant.* It's at a farmer's house,
the richest man in town.
They say he's proud as a peacock,
vain and full of pomp and circumstance,
like the royal prince of old León.
      *Captain.* Well, if he's a wealthy peasant

he's entitled to be vain.

*Sergeant.* And they say he's got the finest house
in town, though I must confess
the reason why I chose it for you
has little to do with that,
but much more with another fact:
there's not a girl in Zalamea
lovelier than . . .

    *Captain.*        Go on.

    *Sergeant.*            . . . his daughter.

    *Captain.* Well, whatever pride and beauty
she may have, she'd still be
nothing more to me than a peasant
with her dirty hands and feet.

    *Sergeant.* Then you'd be the only man alive
to say so.

    *Captain.* And your reason, fool?

    *Sergeant.* Do you know a better way
to pass the time of day—I mean,
if you happen not to be in love
and simply wanting some diversion—
than to woo a simple farmer's
daughter, and she so dumb
she can't tell yes from no?

    *Captain.* There's something I never could abide—
no, not even for a moment:
unless the woman's neat and trim
and has the wit to bring it off
in the way she dresses,
she's not for me.

    *Sergeant.*        As for me, sir,
any woman's right who comes my way.
Suppose we go now—by God, I mean
to have a turn or two at her.

    *Captain.* Now do you really want to know
which of us is right? Say the beauty
I adore goes by. What do I say?
"There goes my lady love!" Of course.
Not "There goes my peasant love!"
So if the beauty I would call
"my lady love" is nothing but
a peasant girl, it follows that I
take the name of lady quite in vain.
Now what's that noise?

*Sergeant.*                    Why, some chap
just dismounted at the corner
from a scrawny nag that looks
like Rocinante. The chap himself's
so stiff and spare you'd think
he were another Don Quixote—
the one Cervantes wrote about.

*Captain.* Look at that amazing face!

*Sergeant.* Sir, it's time we were on our way.

*Captain.* Sergeant, first bring my clothing
to the house; then come back
and let me know you've done so.

[*Exeunt*

### Enter DON MENDO *and* NUÑO.

*Don Mendo.* How's my dapple-gray steed?

*Nuño.* He's so fagged out, he can't raise a hoof.

*Don Mendo.* Come, come, did you tell the groom
to walk him up and down a bit?

*Nuño.* Without feed? Hm, that's food for thought.

*Don Mendo.* There's nothing like a little walk
to freshen up a tired horse.

*Nuño.* I'd say a little barley'd do it.

*Don Mendo.* And what about the hounds?
Are you sure they're all unleashed?

*Nuño.* Yes, and they're delighted,
though I know the butcher isn't.

*Don Mendo.* That's enough! It's three o'clock;
I'll have my toothpick and my gloves.

*Nuño.* What if someone guesses
your toothpick's just a ruse?

*Don Mendo.* If anyone should dare suspect
I haven't lunched on pheasant,
I'd say he lied in his throat
and I'd cut him down right here—
or anywhere else.

*Nuño.*                    I'd rather see
you cut my hunger down
than bother with a stranger.
I'm your servant, after all.

*Don Mendo.* That's a lot of nonsense!
Tell me now: did the soldiers
come to town this afternoon?

*Nuño.* Yes, sir.

*Don Mendo.* I pity the poor peasants.
They were expecting paying guests.

*Nuño.* There are others I pity more
for expecting no guests at all.

*Don Mendo.* Who?

*Nuño.* The gentle folk. But
don't let that worry you.
No one would think of lodging soldiers
in the home of some hidalgo.
And do you know the reason why?

*Don Mendo.* No, why?

*Nuño.* Because they'd starve to death.

*Don Mendo.* Heaven rest my father's soul,
my good sire who, at his going hence,
left me his mighty patent
of nobility, blazoned o'er
in bluc and gold, attesting
to my ancient lineage.

*Nuño.* Heavens, if he'd only put
something of that gold aside!

*Don Mendo.* Yet, when I consider it—
and now I must speak honestly—
there is no need to thank him
for my noble birth. I would never
have allowed anyone but
a nobleman to beget me
in my mother's womb, however much
another might insist.

*Nuño.* Quite a job to draw the line there.

*Don Mendo.* On the contrary: quite simple.

*Nuño.* How, sir?

*Don Mendo.* Knowing nothing
of philosophy, you miss
the first principles, of course.

*Nuño.* That's right, I do, sir; and since
I eat with you, I miss desserts
together with first courses.
In fact, your table at the moment
smacks a bit of Heaven,
having no beginning, middle,
or final course whatever.

*Don Mendo.* That's not the sense in which
I used the word; but you should know
that when we're born our substance

is the food which our parents ate.

*Nuño.* You mean to say your parents ate?
That trait was lost in you.

*Don Mendo.* The food they ate becomes
our very flesh and blood.
And so if my father
had been eating onions,
the instant the odor struck me
I would have cried out, "Stop!
You've no right to make me
out of slops like that!"

*Nuño.*                Well,
now I see it's true . . .

*Don Mendo.*          What's true?

*Nuño.* . . . that hunger sharpens wit.

*Don Mendo.* Rogue, how dare you say I'm hungry!

*Nuño.* Don't be angry, sir, because if
you aren't hungry, you might well be.
After all, it's three o'clock,
and we've enough saliva,
you and I, to wash away the stains
of fuller's earth in potter's clay.

*Don Mendo.* What of it? And besides,
is that a reason why I should be
hungry? Let peasants be hungry!
I'm different. A nobleman
has no need of food.

*Nuño.*              Ah,
if I were only a nobleman!

*Don Mendo.* And now, no more of this.
We're on the street where Isabel lives.

*Nuño.* If you're so wrapped up in devotion,
why not ask her father
for her hand in marriage?
That way you'd kill two birds with one stone:
you'd get three meals a day
and he'd have noblemen for grandsons.

*Don Mendo.* Nuño, let's have no more of that.
Am I to get down on my hands
and knees for a bit of cash and let
a man of common stock
become my father-in-law?

*Nuño.* Well, I used to think it was

important to have a simple
commoner for one's father-in-law,
though it's often said such men are traps
to gobble up a son-in-law.
But if you do not mean to marry her,
why go through the motions of
professing your undying love?

    *Don Mendo.* Aren't there nunneries enough
where I can drop her if she bores me,
without my marrying the girl?
Now go see if you can find her.

    *Nuño.* But if Pedro Crespo happens
to see me, I'm afraid . . .

    *Don Mendo.* You're my servant—how can anyone
possibly harm you? Therefore,
follow your master's orders.

    *Nuño.* That I will, although I never sit
at table with him.

    *Don Mendo.*       Proverbs!
What else does one expect of servants?

    *Nuño.* Ah, now you'll owe me something
for the news: she's coming to
the window with Inés, her cousin.

    *Don Mendo.* Go tell her she's the sun
come forth, diamond-crowned, again,
from an early morning sky
now dawning in the afternoon.

    Isabel *and* Inés *at the window*

    *Inés.* Good Lord, cousin: do come and look
out the window, and see the soldiers
marching into town.

    *Isabel.*         Don't ask me
to stand at the window
while that man is on the street.
Inés, you know how much
the sight of him annoys me.

    *Inés.* But think of all the trouble that
he takes to woo and honor you.

    *Isabel.* I'm no happier on that account.

    *Inés.* I think you're wrong to take it sadly.

    *Isabel.* How would you have me take it?

    *Inés.*                Lightly.

*Isabel.* Take my own displeasure lightly?
*Don Mendo* [*approaching the window*].
    As I am a gentleman, I swear
(and my oath's unbreakable)
there was no dawn today until
this moment. But why should I wonder
at it, or even that the day
should dawn again to greet in you
its dazzling twin aurora?
    *Isabel.* Now I've told you many times,
Don Mendo, all the pretty speeches
and fine frenzied lover's compliments
you deliver here, day after day
at my window, are simply wasted.
    *Don Mendo.* If lovely women only knew
how much anger, cruelty, and
sheer disdain enhanced their beauty,
they'd waste no time applying
any paint but indignation.
I swear you're beautiful.
Come, come, pile on your anger,
for I'll have more of it.
    *Isabel.* Since anger won't convince you,
Don Mendo, this will. Inés, come in
and shut the window in his face.

                                          [*Exit*

    *Inés.* Sir Knight Errant, thou who must
forever champion thyself in jousts
of self-defense since thou canst not
easily endure a rival,
may thy love itself suffice thee.

                                          [*Exit*

    *Don Mendo.* Inés . . . So, Nuño, beauty must
always win the day.
    *Nuño.*            And may I add,
born beggars are born losers.

    *Enter* PEDRO CRESPO, *and then* JUAN CRESPO.

    *Crespo* [*aside*]. I can never walk up or down
this street of mine without spotting
that little country squire taking
the breeze—always with a face so long!
    *Nuño* [*aside to his master*]. Here's Pedro Crespo com-
        ing.

*Don Mendo.* Let's turn the other way;
he's such a mean-mouthed commoner.

### Enter JUAN CRESPO.

*Juan [aside].* I never come here without
finding this phantom in the doorway,
in plumes and gloves, and bold as brass!

    *Nuño [aside to his master].* Now here comes Crespo's
    son.

    *Don Mendo.* Don't let it worry or upset you.

    *Crespo [aside].* Now here's Juanito.

    *Juan [aside].*                              And there's father.

    *Don Mendo [aside to Nuño].* Pretend.

        [*To* CRESPO.] Pedro Crespo, my good man.
God be with you.

    *Crespo.* And with you.

                [*Exeunt* DON MENDO *and* NUÑO

### PEDRO CRESPO *and* JUAN

*Crespo [aside].* The fellow persists too much;
one day I'll see to it
he feels it where it really hurts.

    *Juan [aside].* Some day he'll really get me mad.
Greetings, father; where have you been?

    *Crespo.* At the threshing floors. This afternoon
I went to see the fields all richly
heaped in piles with sheaves of grain.
They looked like mounds of purest gold
as I approached them, and the grain
so precious it could only be
assayed in Heaven. The breeze
flows gently over them, the fork lifts
grain to one side while chaff falls
to the other; even here it seems
the meek make way before the strong.
I pray God grant me leave
to bring it safely to the granary
before a squall flings it far away
or a whirlwind lays it all to waste.
And you, what have you been doing?

    *Juan.* I don't know how to say it
without annoying you.
This afternoon I placed two bets
at bowls and lost them both.

    *Crespo.* There's nothing wrong, if you covered them.
    *Juan.* But I didn't; I had no money.
So I was just coming
to ask you, sir . . .
    *Crespo.*             Well, listen to me
before you speak. There are two things
you must never do: promise what
you can't accomplish, and bet more
than what you have on hand.
Then if by chance you lose
you don't lose your reputation too.
    *Juan.* Advice that fits you to a *T*.
Let me, out of filial piety,
offer this: never give a man
advice who's just run out of cash.
    *Crespo.* Excellent, you won that round!

                                 *[Exeunt*

*The courtyard and entrance of* PEDRO CRESPO's house

*Enter* CRESPO, JUAN, *and the* SERGEANT.

    *Sergeant.* Does Pedro Crespo live here?
    *Crespo.* Is there something you would have him do?
    *Sergeant.* Take these clothes belonging to
Don Álvaro de Ataide,
the captain of the company that's
just arrived this afternoon
to bivouac in Zalamea.
    *Crespo.* Enough, that's all I need to know.
My home and all I own are God's; next,
the King's and all his officers.
And while the captain's room is readied,
you may leave his clothing here,
then go and tell him everything
awaits his pleasure and his coming.
    *Sergeant.* Then he will come at once.

                                      *[Exit*

CRESPO *and* JUAN

    *Juan.* You're a wealthy man—how can you
subject yourself to playing host
to guests like these?
    *Crespo.*           Well, how
can I avoid it or beg off?

*Juan.* By purchasing a patent
of nobility.
    *Crespo.* Tell me,
but truly now, is there anyone
who doesn't know, however pure
my ancestry, that I'm a simple
commoner? No, of course not!
Well then, what use is there
in purchasing a patent from the King
if I cannot buy the noble blood
to go with it? Would I be taken
for a better man than I am now?
That's ridiculous. Then what would
they say of me? That I've become
a gentleman by virtue of five
or six thousand silver pieces.
Well, that's money for you, not honor.
No one can ever purchase honor.
Here's the plainest little story
to illustrate my point.
Suppose a man's been bald for ages,
then finally gets himself a wig.
According to his neighbors,
has he stopped being bald?
Not at all. When they see it they say,
"The old so-and-so looks good
in that new wig!" But what's he gained?
Though they cannot see his bald spot,
everyone knows he still has it.
    *Juan.* He's got rid of certain nuisances,
improved his situation,
and repaired the ravages
of wind and frost and sun.
    *Crespo.* I can do without such wiggish
honor which only calls attention
to what I lack by hiding it.
My parents and theirs before them
all were peasants; I trust my children
accept their lot.—Now call your sister.
    *Juan.* Here she comes.

*Enter* Isabel *and* Inés.

    *Crespo.* Daughter, the King our sovergin lord
(may God protect him all his life),

is on his way to Lisbon, there
to claim the crown which properly
belongs to him. This is why
the troops and the artillery
are moving forward now, and with them
the famous Flanders Regiment
under Don Lope, a man they call
the Spanish Mars. Soldiers
will soon arrive to stay here.
It is essential that they do not
sce you here. And so, my dear,
you will go at once and occupy
the attic rooms in which
I used to stay.
    *Isabel.*        I was on my way
just now to ask for your permission
to do that very thing. I know
that staying here below
would only mean listening
to a stream of endless nonsense.
When Inés and I withdraw
into the attic, nobody,
not even the sun itself,
will know our whereabouts today.
    *Crespo.* God bless you. Meanwhile, Juanito,
stay here to receive our guests
while I rummage through the house for
the wherewithal to entertain them.

                                [*Exit*

    *Isabel.* Come, Inés.
    *Inés.*              Yes, cousin, let us go.
But I think it just absurd to put
a woman under lock and key when
safe's the last thing she wants to be.

                  [*Exeunt* ISABEL *and* INÉS

       *Enter the* CAPTAIN *and the* SERGEANT.

    *Sergeant.* This is the house, sir.
    *Captain.*               Well,
see to it my things are brought up
from the bivouac at once.
    *Sergeant* [*aside to the* CAPTAIN].
             I want to be the first to have
a go at the peasant girl.

                                [*Exit*

*Juan.* Welcome to our house, sir. It is
our great good fortune to have
a noble gentleman like you
honor it. [*Aside.*] How bold and trim he looks!
What I wouldn't give to wear
that uniform!

    *Captain.*   My compliments.

    *Juan.* Forgive these makeshift arrangements.
My father would wish this house
had been a castle for your sake.
He has gone to look after
your supper, something quite special.
Meanwhile I shall see to it
your room is ready.

    *Captain.*      I
appreciate your kind attention.

    Juan. You have only to command me.

                              [*Exit*

### The CAPTAIN *and the* SERGEANT

    Captain. Well now, sergeant, have you seen
your peasant girl?

    *Sergeant.*      By Heaven,
I've looked everywhere—in the kitchen,
in the bedroom—but I've still
to find out where she is.

    *Captain.* That country bumpkin must have stowed her
off somewhere.

    *Sergeant.*     I did ask the maid
about her, and she said
the girl's father locked her
in an attic room with strict orders
not to show herself at all down here.
It seems he's quite suspicious.

    *Captain.* Show me a commoner who isn't.
Now perhaps if she were here
and quite available,
I wouldn't care two pins about her.
But just because the old man's
locked her up, so help me, he's made me
want to force my way up there.

    *Sergeant.* But what excuse have we
to get inside, sir, without
arousing their suspicion?

*Captain.* By sheer doggedness I'll find
some pretext to dig her out.

*Sergeant.* It doesn't have to be
a clever pretext; that won't
matter much as long as it succeeds.
And that might make it all the more
appreciated.

*Captain.* I have it now.
Listen.

*Sergeant.* Fine, what is it?

*Captain.* Now, you'll pretend . . . No, that won't do.
[*He sees* REBOLLEDO *coming.*] Now here's that soldier;
He's cleverer and a better blind
for the little plan I have in mind.

### Enter REBOLLEDO *and* LA CHISPA.

*Rebolledo* [*to* LA CHISPA]. That's the reason why I've
        come
to see the captain—to find out
if I've any luck left.

*La Chispa.*          Well, then,
ingratiate yourself with him.
After all, the idea is not
completely mad or scatterbrained.

*Rebolledo.* Lend me a bit of sanity
and wit.

*La Chispa.* You're welcome to
the long and short of it.

*Rebolledo.* Wait here for me while I speak to him.
[*Advancing.*] I've come, sir, to beg of you . . .

*Captain.* By Heaven, I've grown to like
this Rebolledo; he's full of bounce
and wit. I'll help him all I can.

*Sergeant.* Yes, he's a fine soldier.

*Captain.*                    Well,
how are things? What can I do for you?

*Rebolledo.* Sir, I've lost whatever money
I have, have had, and will have,
and hereby take the pauper's oath
to cover present, past, and future.
So may it please you, sir, to ask
the ensign to advance me a little
something over and beyond my pay
to defray the costs of running . . .

*Captain.* Say it—of running what?

*Rebolledo.* A little table game of bowls.
I am a man burdened by debt,
but still a man of honor.

*Captain.* Your point's well taken. The ensign
will know my pleasure in this matter.

*La Chispa* [*aside*]. Hurrah for the captain!
Oh, I can't wait till everyone
calls me Mistress of the Bowling Game!

*Rebolledo.* I'm off to give him that message.

*Captain.* Wait, a word before you go.
I shall need your help to carry out
a little plan I have in mind,
and so, I hope, relieve myself
of certain doubts.

*Rebolledo.*        But what's
all the hesitation?
No sooner said than done!

*Captain.* Now listen to me. I plan
to go up to that attic room
and see if there's a certain person
living there who has been trying
to escape detection.

*Rebolledo.*        Well, then,
why not go up at once?

*Captain.* I'd rather not attempt it
without a good excuse.
There now, let's pretend we're quarreling,
and you're forced to flee upstairs.
I'm angry, then; I draw my sword.
You're so frightened that you burst in
upon the hidden person
I am looking for up there.

*Rebolledo.* Fine! Now I know the score.

*La Chispa* [*aside*]. Rebolledo and the captain
are getting on so famously,
I'm sure to be the Mistress
of the Bowling Game.

*Rebolledo* [*raising his voice*]. By God!
Am I to be denied
the same allowance freely given
to a thief, a sniveling coward
and a scoundrel? And I, a man
of honor, get nothing for my pains?

*La Chispa* [*aside*]. The deal was sealed, and now
he opens up his trap!

*Captain.* What, are you addressing me this way?

*Rebolledo.* Since I'm right, can't I get angry?

*Captain.* No, and don't you dare speak of it
to me. Just be grateful now
that I've forgiven you.

*Rebolledo.* Sir, you're captain here, so mum's the word,
I guess. And yet, by God,
if I were captain for a while . . .

*Captain* [*grasping his sword*].
Yes, what would you have done to me?

*La Chispa.* Stop, Sir! [*Aside.*] I'm sure he'll kill him now.

*Rebolledo.* I'd have you mend your speech a bit.

*Captain.* What's kept me from killing
this cheeky beggar on the spot?          [*Draws his sword*]

*Rebolledo.* I withdraw, in deference to your rank.

*Captain.* That won't help; you're a dead man now.

*La Chispa.* What a mess he's made of it!

*Sergeant.* Easy, sir!

*La Chispa.*                Stop!

*Sergeant.*                         Wait, hold on!

*La Chispa.* Good-by Mistress of the Bowling Game.

> [*The* CAPTAIN *runs off after* REBOLLEDO, *and the*
> SERGEANT, *behind the* CAPTAIN; *enter* JUAN,
> *with drawn sword, followed by his father.*

### JUAN, CRESPO, *and* LA CHISPA

*Juan.* To the rescue, everybody!

*Crespo.* What's going on here?

*Juan.*                          How did it
get started?

*La Chispa.* The captain drew his sword
against a soldier, then bounded
up those stairs behind him.

*Crespo.* Of all the nasty tricks of fate!

*La Chispa.* After him, everyone!

*Juan* [*aside*]. It was a pointless gesture,
hiding my cousin and my sister.


### *A room upstairs in the same house*

> REBOLLEDO, *fleeing, meets* ISABEL *and* INÉS; *the*
> CAPTAIN *and the* SERGEANT *follow.*

*Rebolledo.* Fairest ladies, since a temple
has always been a place of refuge,

let this, which is love's shrine,
now become my sanctuary.
   *Isabel.* Who forces you to flee this way?
   *Inés.* And what's your excuse for entering?
   *Isabel.* Who is it that's coming after you?

*Enter the* CAPTAIN *and the* SERGEANT.

   *Captain.* It's I, by God, who mean to kill
that beggar, if he thinks . . .
   *Isabel.* Sir, control yourself, if only
for the reason that he came
to beg for refuge here.
Gentlemen like yourself
are duty-bound to honor
womankind, if not because
they're individuals,
then because they're women.
As a gentleman, let that
suffice you now.
   *Captain.*      Your beauty
is the only sanctuary
through which he may escape my wrath.
In consequence, I spare his life.
But consider how ill-advised
you'd be in such a case as this
to take a human life yourself
while you'd have me refrain.
   *Isabel.* If, sir, your courtesy
has now indebted us to you
for life, do not move so quickly
to endanger such a mortal balance.
I beg of you to spare this man,
but do not seek to claim of me
that debt for which I am obliged.
   *Captain.* The rare perfection of your beauty
is twin to your intelligence.
And I discern how now in you
both grace and wit conjoin
to pledge their single troth.

*Enter* CRESPO *and* JUAN *with drawn swords;* LA CHISPA
*is behind them.*

   *Crespo.* What's this, sir? Expecting in my fear
to find you killing a man,

I find you're . . .
   *Isabel* [*aside*]. Heaven help me!
   *Crespo*. . . . simply flirting with a woman.
You're a nobleman, no doubt of that:
you quickly forget your anger.
   *Captain*. A man whose birth saddles him
with obligations must uphold them.
Because of my esteem for this lady,
I overcame my wrath.
   *Crespo*. Sir, my daughter Isabel's
a peasant girl, not a lady.
   *Juan* [*aside*]. By Heaven, all this was nothing
but a trick to get inside!
It discomfits me no end
that they should think they've hoodwinked me.
This can't go on. [*Aloud*.] Captain,
had you considered this,
you might have better understood
how much my father wished to serve you,
and prevented this affront to him.
   *Crespo*. Boy, who's asked you to meddle here?
And what affront's there been?
If the soldier angered him,
was the captain not obliged
to follow him? My daughter deeply
appreciates the favor shown
in pardoning the man, and I
the esteem which he has shown her.
   *Captain*. There clearly could have been
no other issue, and so be
more careful of the words you use.
   *Juan*. I have been most careful.
   *Crespo*. How is it you speak to him that way?
   *Captain*. Since you are present, I shan't
chastise the boy again.
   *Crespo*. Hold on, captain. Chastising
my son's my own affair, not yours.
   *Juan*. And I'll take it from my father,
but from no one else.
   *Captain*.         What
would you do about it?
   *Juan*. I'd stake my life on my good name.
   *Captain*. And what can a good name mean
to a peasant?

*Juan.*        As much as it does
to you, who wouldn't be a captain
if there were no peasants.
    *Captain.* By God, this insolence
is insufferable!
    *Crespo.*        Look here,
to get at him you go through me.

                    [*They strike swords.*]
    *Rebolledo.* In God's name, Chispa, there's going
to be a brawl!
    *La Chispa* [*shouting*]. Guards, this way!
    *Rebolledo.* Don Lope! [*Aside.*] Here's trouble coming!

*Enter* DON LOPE, *in an elegant uniform and carrying his
        baton;* SOLDIERS *and a* DRUMMER.

    *Don Lope.* What's all this about? I've just arrived,
and must the first thing I come up
against be a squabble?
    *Captain* [*aside*].        And what a rotten time
for him to come!
    *Crespo* [*aside*]. That shaveling of mine,
by Jove, held his own against them all!
    *Don Lope.* What's up here? What happened?
Now, speak up, by God, or I'll throw
the whole pack of you, man, woman, and child,
out the window! Did I have to
drag myself up here, game leg and all
(the devil take it!), and still
not hear a word from anyone
to tell me why?
    *Crespo.*        It's nothing
at all, sir.
    *Don Lope.* Speak up now, the truth!
    *Captain.* Well, the fact is I'm billeted
in this house, and one of the soldiers . . .
    *Don Lope.* Go on.
    *Captain.*        . . . forced me to draw my sword.
I chased him up here, and followed
when he entered the room
these peasant girls were in.
Then their father and brother,
or whatever they are, were riled
because I'd broken in.
    *Don Lope.* Then I've come in the nick of time

to settle everything. Now tell me,
who was the soldier who forced
his captain to draw his sword?
    *Rebolledo* [*aside*]. Am I supposed to take
the brunt of this for all of them?
    *Isabel.* This was the man who first broke in.
    *Don Lope.* Give him the rope treatment, twice.
    *Rebolledo.* Treatment? How will I be treated, sir?
    *Don Lope.* With a rope, like that.
    *Rebolledo.*                I'm not a man
who's used to being treated so.
    *La Chispa* [*aside*]. Now they're sure to cripple him for
      me.
    *Captain* [*aside*]. Keep your mouth shut, Rebolledo.
I'll see you get off scot-free.
    *Rebolledo* [*aside to the* CAPTAIN].
How can I? If I keep still
they'll tie my arms behind
and treat me like a criminal.
[*Aloud.*] The captain ordered me
to sham a quarrel so he'd have
a good excuse to break in here.
    *Crespo.* Now you can see that we were
justified.
    *Don Lope.* But not enough
to warrant exposing this town
to the danger of being razed.
All right now, sound the drum,
and let the guard round up all troops.
Everyone today's confined
to quarters, on penalty of death.
As for you, Captain, I discharge you
from your duties here, and likewise
you, sir, from further discomfiture.
And to satisfy you both meanwhile,
Captain, find other lodgings.
I'll set up quarters in this house
myself, and stop here till we march
to Guadalupe to meet the King.
    *Captain.* Sir, your wishes are my strictest
orders.

        [*Exeunt the* CAPTAIN, SOLDIERS, *and* LA CHISPA
    *Crespo.* You may leave us, now.
               [*Exeunt* ISABEL, INÉS, *and* JUAN

### CRESPO *and* DON LOPE

*Crespo.* Sir, I thank you heartily
for your gracious intervention.
It has saved me from the consequence
of suffering a fatal loss.

*Don Lope.* How do you mean—suffering
a fatal loss?

*Crespo.*    The result
of killing a man against whom
I bore no grudge at all.

*Don Lope.* In God's name, you know that
he's a captain, don't you?

*Crespo.* In God's name, yes, and even if
he were a general, I'd kill
the man who sullied my good name.

*Don Lope.* Sullied or not, should anyone
so much as touch the cuff
of the lowest soldier here,
I'd hang him, as Heaven is my judge!

*Crespo.* Should anyone so much as breathe
a syllable against my honor,
I'd hang him too, as Heaven
is my judge!

*Don Lope.* Don't you know
you're duty-bound, because of who
you are, to lend your services?

*Crespo.* Of my estate, but not my honor.
My life and property I render
to the King; but honor is
the heritage of my soul,
and my soul belongs to God alone.

*Don Lope.* By Heaven, there seems to be
some truth in what you're saying!

*Crespo.* Yes, by Heaven, and I've always
said so.

*Don Lope.* I'm very tired,
and this devilish leg of mine
cries out it needs some rest.

*Crespo.* Well, and who'd say no to that?
Here's this devilish bed of mine
all ready for you.

*Don Lope.*    And did you
get it from the devil all made up?

*Crespo.* Of course.
*Don Lope.*          Then I'll unmake it now.
I'm worn out enough, by God.
  *Crespo.* Use it then, by God.
  *Don Lope* [*aside*].          This chap's
a stubborn one, all right,
and maybe he'll outswear me.
  *Crespo* [*aside*]. Don Lope's hard as nails:
we won't get on at all.


# ACT TWO

## A *street*

### *Enter* DON MENDO *and* NUÑO.

DON MENDO. Who told you all this?
  *Nuño.*                    Ginesa,
her maid—she told me everything.
  *Don Mendo.* So the upshot of the quarrel
in her house, whether sham
or genuine, is that the Captain
has begun to court my Isabel!
  *Nuño.* It turns out he stays at home
just about as little as we do.
They say he sticks to her door
all day long, and every hour
on the dot he sends in a note.
His messenger's a wretched little
private who trots in and out with them.
  *Don Mendo.* Enough! That's more poison,
far more poison, than one heart
can imbibe.
  *Nuño.*       Especially when
one's resistance is so low
he has no stomach for it.
  *Don Mendo.* Nuño, let's be serious
a moment.
  *Nuño.*    Ah, God help me,
if I could only joke about this!
  *Don Mendo.* And how does she take to him?
  *Nuño.* Just as she takes to you,
for Isabel's a goddess in her way:
aloof and beautiful she shines on high,

unmoved by vaporings profane.
    *Don Mendo.* God bring you better news!
[*With this exclamation, he slaps* Nuño *across the face*]
    *Nuño.* And you a beak of broken teeth!
You've knocked out two of mine.
Go on, knock them all out, if you like.
They're not much use, they've nothing
now to chew on anyhow. Here comes
the Captain.
    *Don Mendo.* If I thought less of
Isabel and her reputation,
by Heaven, I'd kill him on the spot!
    *Nuño* [*aside*]. Less of your own head, you mean.
    *Don Mendo.* I'll get behind here, and listen in.
Come on, get in here with me.

    *Enter the* CAPTAIN, *the* SERGEANT, *and* REBOLLEDO.

    *Captain.* This fire and passion which I feel
are not the pangs of love alone
but a fixed idea, a madness,
a raging inner fury.
    *Rebolledo.*          Oh, sir!
You should never have set eyes
on that lovely peasant girl.
She's driven you to distraction!
    *Captain.* What did the servant tell you?
    *Rebolledo.* Don't you know it well enough by now?
    *Don Mendo* [*aside to* Nuño].
I must act at once! Now while night
begins to cast its darkling shade,
and before discretion bids me
take a tamer course, go and bring
my arms.
    *Nuño.* Come now, what other arms
do you possess, sir, than those
portrayed in your escutcheon
on the tile that's framed above your door?
    *Don Mendo.* For purposes such as this,
I imagine there are some pieces
in my ancestral armory
which I can don.
    *Nuño.*          Let us go then,
before the Captain hears us.
                                                    [*Exeunt*

*The* CAPTAIN, *the* SERGEANT, *and* REBOLLEDO

*Captain.* Not even the slightest word
of recognition from her!
How can a mere peasant girl presume
to stand upon her virtue
as though she were a lady!

*Sergeant.* Such girls aren't smitten, sir,
with gentlemen like you.
It would take some bumpkin
of her own class, wooing her
accordingly, to make her
turn her head. Besides, your courtship's
not very opportune. Since you leave
tomorrow, how can you expect
a woman to respond and give herself
to you within a single day?

*Captain.* Within a day the sun sheds light
and fades away; kingdoms fall and rise
within a day. In one day,
the proudest building lies in ruin;
in a day a losing battle's won.
An ocean storms and stills within a day;
in a day a man is born and dies.
And so within a day my love,
like a planet, may come to know
both dark and light, and like an empire,
pain and joy; like a forest,
men and beasts; like an ocean,
peace and storm; as in a battle,
victory and defeat; and as
master of all my faculties
and senses, know life and death.
And so, having come to know within
one day an age of love's torment,
why may it not still grant me time
to know its bliss? Is joy so much
more sluggish to be born than pain?

*Sergeant.* But you've seen her only once.
Is this the pass it's brought you to?

*Captain.* Having seen her once, what better
reason is there for seeing her
again? The slightest spark will
all at once burst into flame;

a sulphurous abyss will all at once
heave up a furious volcano.
All at once a bolt of lightning
consumes whatever's in its way;
and all at once the sleeping cannon
spews forth its deadly horrors.
Is it any wonder then that love,
a fire four times more intense,
containing flame and cannon shot,
volcano and the lightning bolt,
should terrify and scorch,
wound and lay one low, all at once?

    *Sergeant.* Weren't you the one who said peasant
girls can never be attractive?

    *Captain.* Overconfidence was precisely
my undoing. The man aware
of danger finds protection
in forewarning; the man who runs
a risk is the man who's all cocksure:
danger takes him by surprise.
The girl I thought would be another
peasant wench turned out to be
a goddess. Does it not follow then
that danger overcame me
through my very inadvertency?
In all my life I've never seen
such perfect beauty, such utter
loveliness. Ah, Rebolledo,
there is nothing I would not do
to get another glimpse of her!

    *Rebolledo.* There's a soldier in our company
who can sing superbly;
then there's La Chispa, keeper
of my bowling game, and she
can dance and bawl out ballads
like no one else alive.
Look now, suppose we have a revel, sir,
and serenade your Isabel
beneath her window; in that way,
Captain, you can see her,
even speak to her as well.

    *Captain.* But there's Don Lope; I wouldn't like
to wake him.

    *Rebolledo.* Don Lope? With that leg

of his, when does he ever sleep?
Besides, Captain, if you went along
disguised among the troops,
and any question rose,
we'd take the blame, not you.

    *Captain.* Though this lead to worse complexity,
love's anguish must endure it all.
We'll all meet here tonight;
meanwhile let no one know
I've anything to do with it.
Ah, Isabel, my love for you
grows costlier and hazardous.

*[Exeunt the* CAPTAIN
*and the* SERGEANT

## LA CHISPA *and* REBOLLEDO.

    *La Chispa* [*offstage*]. Take that!
    *Rebolledo.*                La Chispa, what's going on?
    *La Chispa.* There, the wretch has got his face slashed
for his pains.
    *Rebolledo.* What was all the row
about?
    *La Chispa.* He had the gall to try
and cheat me of my due; he kept me
watching odd and even numbers
for an hour and a half
while he maneuvered. I got sick
of it and cut him up with this.   [*She shows the dagger.*]
While he's getting stitched up
at the barber's, let's go
to the guard room and I'll tell you
all about it.
    *Rebolledo.* A fine time to have
a row when I've come about
a revel!
    *La Chispa.* Well, what's one got to do
with the other? My castanets, sir—
here! Now what is it we sing?
    *Rebolledo.* Not till tonight, and then the music's
got to be more formal. Come now,
don't straggle, we're off to the guard room.
    *La Chispa.* My name is made, ah worldly fame!
La Chispa's Mistress of the Bowling Game.

*[Exeunt*

*A downstairs room in* Crespo's *house, with a view and
an exit on the garden. A window on one side.*

### Don Lope *and* Crespo

*Crespo* [*offstage*]. Set the table for Don Lope
in this veranda; it's cooler here.
—You'll find dinner here much more
enjoyable. After all,
there's not much in the way
of recompense for August days
except the evenings.
    *Don Lope.*       Indeed,
this bower's most pleasant now.
    *Crespo.* It's just a bit of garden which
my daughter finds agreeable.
Sit down, sir. Here the tender breeze
that stirs the gentle leaves
within the trellised bower
murmurs in a crowd of voices
to the cadence of the fountain,
a zither silvery and pearled,
with pebbly strings where chords are struck
across its golden frets.
Pardon us, sir, if our music
is simply instrumental,
unaccompanied by singers
and their song for your further pleasure.
Our sole performers here are
warbling birds who will not sing at night,
nor may I force them to.
But do sit down and let the scene
divert you from your pain.
    *Don Lope.* Nothing will—it nags and nags,
and makes relaxing quite
impossible. God help me!
    *Crespo.* Indeed, sir, I hope He will.
    *Don Lope.* And give me patience to endure it.
Sit down, Crespo.
    *Crespo.*       Thank you, I am fine.
    *Don Lope.* Do sit down.
    *Crespo.*            Since you give me leave,
I shall obey you, sir—
but excuse the liberty

I take in doing so.     [*He sits down.*]
    *Don Lope.* Do you know what I've been thinking?
That yesterday you must have let
your temper get the best of you.
    *Crespo.* No, it never gets the best of me.
    *Don Lope.* Then how was it that yesterday
you sat down without waiting
to be asked by me, and even took
the finest chair?
    *Crespo.*        Because you didn't
ask me to. And today, because
you did, I preferred not to.
Courtesy nods to courtesy.
    *Don Lope.* Yesterday you were full of hissing
oaths, b'gods and b'heavenses.
Today you're pleasant, gentler,
and much more circumspect.
    *Crespo.* Sir, I always answer as I'm
spoken to; yesterday I was
compelled to use the tone
which you applied to me. I take it
as a prudent policy
to pray with him who prays,
and swear at him who swears at me.
I am all things to all men.
And so it happened that all last night
I could not sleep a wink for thinking
of your lame leg. When I arose
this morning both my legs were lame.
Not knowing which it was that pained you,
the right one or the left, I managed
to ache in both of mine. I wish
you'd tell me which it is
so that I may reduce
the pain to only one.
    *Don Lope.* I've good reason to complain.
Do you know, in thirty years
of wartime service out in Flanders,
through winter frost and scorching
summer heat, I've never taken leave
nor have I known what it is to be
a single hour without pain?
    *Crespo.* May the good Lord give you patience!
    *Don Lope.* What would I do with it?

*Crespo.* Then do without it.

*Don Lope.*                         Let it steer clear
of me, or let a pack of devils
come and make away with me
and patience altogether!

*Crespo.* If you say so. But if they don't,
it will be because they're not inclined
to do good deeds.

*Don Lope.*          Oh, God!
God Almighty! God!

*Crespo.*                    May He
keep you in His grace—and me.

*Don Lope.* Good Lord, it's killing me!

*Crespo.* Good Lord, I'm sorry for you!

*Enter* JUAN, *bringing in the table.*

*Juan.* Here's the table for you.

*Don Lope.* How is it my own servants
are not waiting on us?

*Crespo.* I beg your pardon, sir,
but my instructions were
they need not bring provisions
nor wait upon you here.
Thank God, I am sure you won't lack
for anything while you are my guest.

*Don Lope.* Well, since my servants aren't here,
please ask your daughter to come
and dine with me.

*Crespo.*              Juan, go and call
your sister in at once.

                                        [*Exit* JUAN

*Don Lope.* On that score, my ailment
places me above suspicion.

*Crespo.* Even if your health were as sound
as I could wish it, I would not be
suspicious of you. You belittle
my affection for you; nothing of
the sort disturbs me. The reason
I'd kept my daughter from coming down
here was simply to protect her
from being subject to crude,
impertinent remarks. If all
soldiers were gentlemen like yourself,
she'd have been the first to wait on you.

*Don Lope* [*aside*]. What a wily chap this peasant is,
or else he's naturally astute!

Enter JUAN, INÉS, *and* ISABEL.

*Isabel.* Sir, what is it you'd have me do?
*Crespo.* Don Lope wishes to honor us.
It's he who's called you in.
*Isabel.* Your humble servant, sir.
*Don Lope.* But I wish to serve you.
[*Aside.*] What remarkable beauty!
—I should like you to dine with me.
*Isabel.* It would be better if we two
served you your dinner.
*Don Lope.*          Be seated.
*Crespo.* Sit down. Do as Don Lope says.
*Isabel.* There's virtue in obedience.
          [*They are seated. Guitar music from offstage.*]
*Don Lope.* What's that?
*Crespo.*                    They're playing and singing
outside—some of your soldiers
strolling along the street.
*Don Lope.* War's a pretty grim business—
hard to put up with without
a little relaxation.
Yes, a soldier's life is rather strict;
he's got to have some time off
to loosen up a bit.
*Juan.* Still, it's a wonderful life.
*Don Lope.* You'd take to it quite willingly?
*Juan.* I would, sir, if I could spend it
at the side of Your Excellency.

Sounds of REBOLLEDO *and* SOLDIERS *offstage.*

*A Soldier* [*offstage*]. We'd do better singing right here.
*Rebelledo* [*offstage*]. Sing some lines for Isabel.
To make sure that she's awake,
throw a pebble at her window.
                    [*Sound of a pebble against a window.*]
*Crespo.* The music's aimed at someone's window;
let's wait and see.
*A Voice* [*offstage*].

> *Rosemary buds, so blue today,*
>      *Isabel, my dear,*

*Tomorrow will be turned to honey,*
*Just like you, my dear.*


*Don Lope [aside].* Ah, the music's fine, but throwing
      stones
another matter, and then pitching
these ditties at the house
where I am staying! . . . Well,
I'll let it pass for Crespo's
and the girl's sake. —What nonsense!
   *Crespo.* Just boys, boys. [*Aside.*] If it weren't for
Don Lope, I'd see to it that they . . .
   *Juan [aside].* If I could get that old buckler down
that hangs in Don Lope's room . . .

                                    [*Starting to leave.*]
   *Crespo.* Where are you off to, young man?
   *Juan.* To see to it they bring the dinner.
   *Crespo.* There are servants there to see to that.
   *Soldiers [singing offstage].* Oh Isabel, wake up, wake up!
   *Isabel [aside].* Good Lord, what have I done
to deserve this?
   *Don Lope.*     This wretched thing's
intolerable—I won't stand for it!

                              [*He knocks over the table.*]
   *Crespo.* I'll say it's intolerable!

                              [*He knocks over his chair.*]
   *Don Lope [aside].* My impatience carried me away
—tell me, isn't it incredible
how much one leg can ache?
   *Crespo.* That's exactly what I meant.
   *Don Lope.* When you knocked the chair over,
I thought you'd something else in mind . . .
   *Crespo.* I had nothing closer to knock down
when you upset the table . . .
[*Aside.*] Oh honor, let me endure this!
   *Don Lope [aside].* If I were on that street right now!
—Well, I don't want any dinner now.
Leave me.
   *Crespo.* As you wish, sir.
   *Don Lope.* God be with you, madam.
   *Isabel.* And with you, sir.
   *Don Lope [aside].*          My room's right off
the front door, isn't it? And isn't
there some sort of buckler in it?

*Crespo* [*aside*]. Can't I take my trusty sword
and go out the back way?
    *Don Lope.* Good night.
    *Crespo.*                    Good night to you, sir.
[*Aside.*] First I'll lock the children in.
    *Don Lope* [*aside*]. I'll wait till the house is quiet.
    *Isabel* [*aside*]. Heavens, how badly the two of them
conceal the thing that troubles them!
    *Inés* [*aside*]. Each pretends so poorly
for one another's sake!
    *Crespo.* See here, young man! . . .
    *Juan.*                    Yes, father?
    *Crespo.* Your bedroom's over there.

                                          [*Exeunt*


### The street outside

*The* CAPTAIN, *the* SERGEANT, LA CHISPA, *and* REBOLLEDO
        *with guitars, and the* SOLDIERS.

    *Rebolledo.* We're better off right here.
This spot's more convenient.
Now, everyone to his place.
    *La Chispa.* Now the music again?
    *Rebolledo.*                    Yes.
    *La Chispa.* Ah, this is right down my alley.
    *Captain.* But she's not even left
one window ajar!
    *Rebolledo.*     They'll hear it
pretty well inside anyhow.
    *La Chispa.* Wait!
    *Rebolledo.* I suppose I'll pay for this!
Let's wait and see who's coming.
    *La Chispa.* What's the matter? Don't you see
it's just that little knight in armor?

    *Enter* DON MENDO *with an old shield, and* NUÑO.

    *Don Mendo* [*aside to* NUÑO]. Can you make out what's
            going on?
    *Nuño.* Not much, though I can hear it clearly.
    *Don Mendo.* Oh God, who can possibly
endure this?
    *Nuño.*     I can.
    *Don Mendo.*     Perhaps
Isabel will open her window.

*Nuño.* Well, perhaps she will.
*Don Mendo.*                    No, she won't, fool!
*Nuño.* Well, then she won't.
*Don Mendo.*                    Ah, my jealous heart,
cruel pain! I could easily slash
and scatter them all right now,
but I must hide my grief
until it's clear what part she's played
in all this perfidy.
*Nuño.*              Well, then,
let's sit down a while.
*Don Mendo.*          Good,
from here I shan't be recognized.
*Rebolledo.* Well, now the chap is sitting down,
unless he means to crawl about and groan
like some poor soul in limbo suffering
the blows he caught behind his shield.
[*To* LA CHISPA.] Open up and sing!
*La Chispa.*                          It's coming
to me now.
*Rebolledo.* Let's have a song so fresh
it makes the blood run cold.
*La Chispa.*                  Yes, indeed!

DON LOPE *and* CRESPO *enter armed from opposite sides
of the stage.*

*La Chispa* [*singing*].

> There once was a certain Sampayo,
>   As natty a chap as you'll find,
> Bursting with gypsy bravado
>   To melt you and rob you blind.
> He found his sweetheart Chillona
>   One day, the day was . . .

*Rebolledo.*  Let's not mention
the day of the week; everyone knows
it was on a blue Monday
when the moon shows lovers its horns.
*La Chispa.*

> He came, as I say, on Chillona,
>   With the sun sinking fast out of sight.
> She was drinking a pint with that fella
>   Named Garlo—both looking quite tight.

> *Garlo's sword was like greased lightning*
> *    When he decided to fight.*
> *So he whisked off his cloak, and whipping*
> *    The thing to his left and his right . . .*

*Crespo.* You mean like this!
*Don Lope.*                    Like this, no doubt!
> [DON LOPE *and* CRESPO *thrust at the* SOLDIERS,
>     *at* DON MENDO *and* NUÑO, *and rout them all;*
>     DON LOPE *returns.*]
They've all scampered away,
except for that one over there.

>                              [CRESPO *returns.*]
*Crespo* [*aside*]. Here's someone who's left behind.
No doubt a soldier.
*Don Lope* [*aside*]. And this one won't get off
until his blood flows like wine.
*Crespo* [*aside*]. And I won't let up on this one
until I drive him up the street.
*Don Lope.* Now get going, like the others!
*Crespo.* Try it yourself, you're better at it!

>                              [*They fight.*]
*Don Lope* [*aside*]. By God, the chap's handy with that
    blade!
*Crespo* [*aside*]. This chap fights well, by God!

> *Enter* JUAN, *with a drawn sword.*

*Juan* [*aside*]. Now, by Heaven, let me get at him!
—I'm here, sir, at your side.
*Don Lope.* Is that you, Pedro Crespo?
*Crespo.* Yes, it's me. Is that Don Lope?
*Don Lope.* Yes, indeed. But didn't you say
you weren't going outside? What's
the meaning of your little exploit?
*Crespo.* My excuse and my reply must be:
I've done exactly what you've done.
*Don Lope.* But this was my affair, not yours.
*Crespo.* Well, I won't keep it a secret:
I left the house to join the fight,
and to keep you company.

> *Enter the* SOLDIERS *and the* CAPTAIN.

*Soldier* [*offstage*]. Let's join ranks and mop up these
    peasants.
Look there!                    [*Appearing onstage.*]

*Don Lope.* Where are you off to? Halt!
What's this uproar all about?

*Captain.* The men were strolling in the street,
strumming along a bit and singing
(not really making a commotion),
when they got into an argument,
and I've come to put a stop to it.

*Don Lope.* Don Álvaro, I know you've shown
good sense. The town's been in
a fairly nasty mood today;
and I'd like to keep from using
any stricter measures.
Now the dawn's come up, my orders are
to take your company out
of Zalamea, and keep them out
of town all day so there won't be
any further trouble here.
Once that's done, I don't want to hear
of things like this again,
and if I do, by God, I'll settle
their hash personally,
with the end of this blade!

*Captain.* I give you my word: the company
will be out of town this morning.
[*Aside.*] My lovely Isabel,
you shall be the death of me!

*Crespo* [*aside*]. Don Lope's hard as nails:
we'll get on together after all.

*Don Lope.* Come along with me now; don't let me
catch you wandering off alone.

[*Exeunt*

*Enter* Don Mendo, *and* Nuño *wounded.*

*Don Mendo.* Well, Nuño, how is your wound?

*Nuño.* If it were slighter than it is,
I'd still say it's most unwelcome
and might have spared me its company.

*Don Mendo.* I have never felt such pain
or anguish in all my days.

*Nuño.* Me either.

*Don Mendo.*        Now I've a right
to be angry. He gave you
quite an ugly blow there on the head,
did he not?

*Nuño.*    It throbs down to my toes.

                    [*Drumbeats offstage.*]

*Don Mendo.* What's that?

*Nuño.*                    The troops are going off now.

*Don Mendo.* That's music to my ears: I won't be
jealous of the Captain any more.

*Nuño.* He'll be gone, at least all day.

*On one side of the stage, the* CAPTAIN *and the* SERGEANT;
*on the other,* DON MENDO *and* NUÑO.

*Captain.* Sergeant, keep the troops marching
until nightfall; and then,
as the gleaming beacon's quenched
in the cold spindrift of our Spanish
ocean sea, I'll await you
on that hill, and from there today
proceed to find my life and love
when death engulfs the sun.

   *Sergeant* [*aside to the* CAPTAIN]. Shhh! There goes that
     town character.

   *Don Mendo* [*aside to* NUÑO]. Courage, Nuño; don't be
     so thin-skinned!

   *Nuño.* Is there a choice, then? Could I be stout?

                    [*Exeunt* DON MENDO *and* NUÑO

*The* CAPTAIN *and the* SERGEANT

*Captain.* I must steal back to town.
I've already bribed her maid,
and so, with luck perhaps,
I may yet speak to her again,
my fatal enchantress. I hope
my gifts will pave the way.

   *Sergeant.* Well, sir, if you must go back,
be sure to take a good escort.
You can't trust those peasants now.

   *Captain.* Right. Go pick some men to come along
with me.

   *Sergeant.* I'll do anything you wish.
But what if you happen to meet
Don Lope on the way? . . .

   *Captain.* Love has vanquished fear, in this
and every other way.
On leaving Don Lope before,

I discovered he is due
in Guadalupe to inspect
the Regiment today,
because the King, who's on his way,
is expected momentarily.

    *Sergeant.* Your orders shall be carried out
at once, sir.

                                   [*Exit*

    *Captain.* Remember now,
my life hangs on a thread.

        *Enter* REBOLLEDO *and* LA CHISPA.

    *Rebolledo.* Sir, I've good news for you.
    *Captain.* To what effect, Rebolledo?
    *Rebolledo.* Oh, I think it's very good.
Wait until you hear this . . .
    *Captain.* I'm waiting.
    *Rebolledo.*          Well, simply this:
you've one enemy less to be
concerned about.
    *Captain.*      Who's that? Be quick now.
    *Rebolledo.* That chap, Isabel's brother.
Don Lope asked his father for him;
the father has agreed to it, and now
the chap's to serve with Don Lope.
I came across him in the street:
all got up so fine and dashing,
the farmboy manner not rubbed off yet,
and the soldier in him
just breaking into bud.
Well, now we've just the old man
to worry about.
    *Captain.*    So far so good,
and even better if her maid
comes through who's fed my hope
I'll speak with Isabel tonight.
    *Rebolledo.* And I'm sure you will, sir.
    *Captain.* I'll be going back along this road;
meanwhile my duty's to attend
the troops just marching off.
You two will be my escort; stand by.

                                   [*Exit*

    *Rebolledo.* We two? That's a mighty skimpy
escort; even if there were four

of us, or six or eight, God knows
that would still be few enough.

    *La Chispa.* Talk about *your* having to go back!
Now what about me? What am I
to do, and how safe will I be
if I meet that chap whose face I slashed?

    *Rebolledo.* But what am I to do with you?
Are you ready to come along?

    *La Chispa.* Yes, indeed! Ready, willing, and able!

    *Rebolledo.* Fine. Then there'll be a uniform
for you—the extra one
the captain's page was using
and left behind here.

    *La Chispa.*        Well, then
I'll step into it and take his place.

    *Rebolledo.* Come on, there's the color guard.

    *La Chispa.* Now it dawns on me! How's that song go
I've been singing all along?

    "A soldier's love lasts but an hour."

                            *[Exeunt*

      *Enter* DON LOPE, CRESPO, *and* JUAN.

    *Don Lope.* My deepest gratitude to you
for many things, but above all
for giving up your son today
to join me as a soldier. Accept
my heartfelt thanks and my esteem.

    *Crespo.* I give him up to you
to be your orderly.

    *Don Lope.* I take him with me as a friend.
I'm partial to his energy
and spirit, and to his feeling
for the military life.

    *Juan.* I shall be your faithful servant,
*always.* You'll see, sir. And I shall do
my best to heed every word you say.

    *Crespo.* But I beg you, sir, to make
allowance if he doesn't quite
come up to snuff. In this crude
academy of country life,
where our best books are plow and harrow,
shovel, hoe, and pitchfork,
he's learned nothing of those fine manners
and age-old civilities

which only living in
great mansions can teach one.

*Don Lope.* Now the heat of the sun's somewhat
abated, I'll take my leave.

*Juan.* Sir, let me see to your litter first.

[*Exit*

*Enter* ISABEL *and* INÉS.

*Isabel.* Are you going, sir, without
bidding farewell to one
who's wished so much to serve you?

*Don Lope.* I would never leave before
I'd kissed your hand, nor before
I'd begged your pardon for my boldness
in presenting you with something
meriting your forgiveness.
In this the gift is nothing,
the giving everything.
I hope you will accept this poor
medallion; though set in richest
diamonds, it grows dull in your hands.
Yet wear it round your neck, I beg you,
as a souvenir from me.

*Isabel.* I'd be very sorry if you thought
this most generous of gifts
were a payment for your stay here.
For that honor we are in debt
to you, and not you to us.

*Don Lope.*                    No,
not as payment but as a token
of my affection.

*Isabel.*          Only
then, sir, do I accept it.
Let me commend my brother to you;
he is fortunate indeed to merit
service as your orderly.

*Don Lope.* I assure you once again: do not
concern yourself about his safety.
He shall be close to me, my dear.

*Enter* JUAN.

*Juan.* Your litter is ready, sir.
*Don Lope.* God keep you all.
*Crespo.*                    And you too, sir.

*Don Lope.* Ah, Pedro Crespo, you're a fine chap!
*Crespo.* Ah, Don Lope, and you're a brave one!
*Don Lope.* Who'd have thought that first day
we spotted one another here
that we'd become such bosom friends?
*Crespo.* I would, sir, if I'd known then,
when I first heard you speak,
that you were . . . [*while* DON LOPE *is leaving*]
*Don Lope.*          Well, out with it now!
*Crespo.* . . . such a fine, warmhearted old bully!
[*Exit* DON LOPE

CRESPO, JUAN, ISABEL, *and* INÉS

*Crespo.* While Don Lope is getting ready,
listen, Juan, to what I have
to tell you, in the presence of
your cousin and your sister.
By the grace of God, my son,
your lineage is as pure
as golden sunlight, though
you come of peasant stock.
Remember both these things:
the first, so that you won't
allow your natural pride,
through lack of confidence,
to stifle prudent judgment
by which you may aspire
to make something more of yourself;
nor forget the second, so that
you won't be so puffed up
you become something less
than what you are. Be equally
aware of both endowments:
employ them with all humility.
Being humble, you'll be more likely
to conform with right opinion,
whereby you'll find yourself forgiven
where prouder men are soon accused.
Think how many men succeed
in erasing some personal
defect through their humility;
then think how many, having
no defects whatever, acquire
them because they lack humility.

Be courteous in every way,
be generous and good-natured.
A hand that's quick to doff a cap
and offer cash makes many friends,
but all the gold the sun observes
heaved up in the Indies
and wafted hither overseas
is less precious than the general
esteem a man is held in by
his fellows. Don't speak ill of women;
even the most abject of them
is worthy, I assure you,
of all possible respect.
Were we not all born of women?
Fight only when you have just cause.
Now when I see those in our towns
who teach the use of foils, I often
tell myself: "Their schools leave
something wanting, it seems to me.
The chap they teach to duel with so much
fervor, skill, and gallantry
should be instructed first
as to why—not how—he fights.
And I believe if there were only
one fencing master prepared
to teach the why and wherefore
of the duel, we'd all entrust
our sons to such a man."
To this advice I add the money
to defray expenses for your journey
and to buy your several uniforms
when you reach your quarters.
Now with Don Lope's benefactions
and my blessings, I pray God
I shall see you soon again.
Farewell, my son. Words fail me.
    *Juan.* I shall take every word you say to
heart, and remember them forever.
Father, your hand—and sister,
your embrace. Now I must be off
to catch up with Don Lope, my lord.
    *Isabel.* If my arms could only hold you back!
    *Juan.* Cousin, farewell.
    *Inés.*                    My tears

can only speak for me.
Farewell.
    *Crespo.* Go now, quickly.
Your presence only makes me wish
to keep you here. Remember
all I've told you.
    *Juan.*         God bless you.
    *Crespo.* God keep you and protect you.

                          [*Exit* JUAN

CRESPO, ISABEL, *and* INÉS

    *Isabel.* How cruel of you to let him go!
    *Crespo* [*aside*]. Now he's no longer here,
words come more easily again.
—What would I have done with him at home?
He'd be a lazy good-for-nothing
all his life. Let him serve his King.
    *Isabel.* I'm so sorry he had to leave
at night.
    *Crespo.* In summertime
traveling at night's a pleasure,
no job at all. Besides,
he's due to catch up with Don Lope
as soon as possible.
[*Aside.*] Ah, the boy's leaving is hard to take;
outwardly I must be braver.
    *Isabel.* Come, father, let us go indoors.
    *Inés.* Now the soldiers have gone away,
why not stay a little longer
in the doorway and enjoy the breeze
that's just sprung up. Soon the neighbors
will be passing by here.
    *Crespo* [*aside*]. It's true, I can't go in now.
Out here at least I can imagine
Juan is that white speck I see
far down the road. —Inés, bring out
a chair for me, here beside the door.
    *Inés.* Here's a little bench.
    *Isabel.*                They say
this afternoon the town
elected new officials.
    *Crespo.*        Yes,
that's customary here in August.

                          [*He sits down.*]

*Enter the* CAPTAIN, *the* SERGEANT, REBOLLEDO, LA CHISPA, *and the* SOLDIERS, *their faces muffled in their capes.*

*Captain* [*aside to his men*]. Quietly, quietly now.
You, Rebolledo, go on
ahead and tell the maid
I'm waiting outside in the street.
*Rebolledo.* I'm going. But what's this I see—
there are people in the doorway!
*Sergeant.* One of them is Isabel, I think:
see, the one whose face is now
reflected in the moonlight.
*Captain.* Yes, it's she! I know it
instinctively, without the moonlight.
We've come in good time. Now that we're here,
we must be absolutely fearless;
then everything will turn out
as we planned.
*Sergeant.*          Can you still
take a word of advice?
*Captain.*                    No.
*Sergeant.* Well, then, don't; go right ahead
and do what you wish.
*Captain.*                    I must get
to her there, and then boldly
carry her off. Meanwhile,
use your swords to keep them back.
*Sergeant.* We've come this far with you;
we'll do exactly as you say, sir.
*Captain.* And remember our rendezvous
is in the woods nearby, just off
the road to the right.
*Rebolledo.*               La Chispa?
*La Chispa.* Yes?
*Rebolledo.*          Hold on to these capes.
*La Chispa.*                                             Oh, well.
In fighting you're safest, I suppose,
if you stand guard on the clothes.
Though this is said about swimming.
*Captain.* I must get there first.
*Crespo.*                              Well,
that was a pleasant interval,
but it's time we went inside.
*Captain* [*aside to his men*]. Men, this is it now; let's go.

[*The* SOLDIERS *burst in, restraining* CRESPO *and*
INÉS, *and seize* ISABEL.]

*Isabel.* Let me go, villain! What does this mean,
sir?

*Captain.* Mean? Love's frenzy and
delirium is what it means!

[*He carries her off.*]

*Isabel* [*offstage*]. Villain, let me go!

*Crespo.*                              Cowards!

*Isabel* [*offstage*]. Father, father!

*Inés* [*aside*].                        I'll slip away now.

[*Exit*

*Crespo.* Damned traitors! You dare do this to me
because you see that I'm unarmed!
You rogues! You cowards!

*Rebolledo.*                  Out of my way,
or take this final blow and die!

[*Exeunt kidnapers*

*Crespo.* Go ahead! What use is there
in living now my honor's dead?
Oh, if I only had a sword!
There's no point in running after them
unarmed, and if I dashed inside
to get my sword, they'd soon be
out of sight. Ill luck has it—
what am I to do? I must lose,
whatever way I choose.

*Enter* INÉS, *with a sword.*

*Inés.* Here is your sword now.

*Crespo.*                        Ah,
you've brought it just in time.
Now I have this sword to follow them,
my honor is restored.

[*Exeunt*


*In an open field*

CRESPO *is fighting with the* SERGEANT, REBOLLEDO, *and*
*the* SOLDIERS; *the voice of* ISABEL.

*Crespo.* Cowards! Dogs! Release the daughter
you have stolen from me!
I'll free her, or else die in the attempt.

*Sergeant.* It's useless: you're outnumbered.
*Crespo.* The injuries you've done me
are legion; they'll fight for me . . .            [*He falls.*]
*Rebolledo.* Finish him off!
*Sergeant.*                          No, let him live.
It's bad enough for him
he's lost his honor. Better
tie him up and leave him in the woods
where he won't attract attention.
*Isabel* [*offstage*]. Oh Father, help me!
*Crespo.*                          Dearest daughter!
*Rebolledo.* Drag him off, as you say!
*Crespo.* Oh, my daughter, only
my sighs can follow you now!

                              [*He is carried away.*]

ISABEL *and* CRESPO *offstage; then, enter* JUAN.

*Isabel* [*offstage*]. Oh, my God!
*Juan* [*entering*].                 What sad cry is that?
*Crespo* [*offstage*]. Oh, my God!
*Juan.*                          The moan is human!
My horse was galloping so fast
when we came into these woods
that he stumbled and both of us
went down. Now I can't see where he went
through the thickets. Someone is weeping
here—and there, someone else is groaning
in great misery. I hear
both voices but can't tell where they are,
they're so muffled. Two human voices
invoke my aid with equal
urgency. One of them's a man's,
the other, a woman's.
I shall help her first, and this way
obey my father twice:
"Respect all women, and fight
only when you have just cause."
So now to help this woman,
then have just cause to fight.

## ACT THREE

*In a forest*

Isabel, *weeping.*

Isabel. Oh, never let the glorious day
touch my eyes again nor waken me
to know my shame beneath its shade!
Oh morning star, harbinger of so
many fleeting planets, stay and give
no quarter to the dawn which now
invades thy bluest canopy.
Let it not erase thy quiet face
with dewy smiles and tears.
But as I fear this must come to pass,
admit no smile at all, dissolve
in tears. Now, sun, thou greatest star
of all, delay, hold back,
and linger yet a while below,
in the ocean of cold foam.
Let night for once protract
its hushed and trembling empery,
and thus, attentive to my prayer,
assert thy majesty by will
and not by sheer necessity.
Why shouldst thou wish to rise and witness
in the tale of my calamity
the vilest, most terrible
enormity, the maddest violence
that Heaven ever hoped to publish
on the shame of all mankind?
But alas, thou art cruelly
despotic, for despite my pleas
to stay thee, I detect thy face
now rising luminous beyond
those hills. Alas, must I contend
with thy wrathful gaze now fixed upon
my extinct honor while so many
wretched ills, such horrible
adversities pursue me?
What am I to do? Where shall I go?
If my errant feet turn homeward,

I intensify the injury
against my poor dear father,
whose only joy and fortune
was to see his purest honor
mirrored in my own, once white and chaste
as is the moon, now so sadly palled
and, to my shame, totally eclipsed.
But if respect for him and my own
tormented fear prevent my going
home, I thereby invite the world
to name me as accomplice
to my own disgrace, and by so blind
an inadvertency let
innocence attest to slander.
How wrong I was, how wrong
of me to flee my brother!
It would have been much better
had I told him of my plight, and so
move his proud wrath to kill me.
I must cry out now; let him return,
furious and vengeful, to kill me.
Let the echo of my voice
clarify these mutterings,
and by repeating them proclaim . . .

### CRESPO *and* ISABEL

*Crespo* [*offstage*]. Come back now and finish me.
Come, be merciful and kill me.
It is no kindness to allow
a man so wretched as I am to live.

*Isabel.* Whose voice is this, so thick
and broken? I cannot make it out.

*Crespo* [*offstage*]. Kill me, I say. Oh, that
I might urge you to be so kind!

*Isabel.* Heavenly God! Here is another
who yearns to die, another so
miserable he lives against his will.

[*She parts the foliage and discovers* CRESPO,
*bound.*]

Ah, what do these eyes of mine behold?

*Crespo.* Whoever you are, so timidly
approaching through the wood,
for pity's sake, come here and kill me.
Heavens! who is this I see?

    *Isabel.* And both hands bound up behind you
to this heavy oak . . .
    *Crespo.*           And her voice
so sweet, so heavenly . . .
    *Isabel.*           Father!
    *Crespo.* Ah, Isabel my dear.
    *Isabel.* My own dear father!
    *Crespo.*            Come closer.
Here. Good, now untie me.
    *Isabel.* I dare not do it. Once my hands
untie the bonds that grip you now,
I shall never have the courage,
Father, to tell the story
of my grief, recounting
all my sorrows to you.
Once your hands are freed, and you find
strength regained but honor lost,
your revenge entails my death.
Sooner than have you learn of it
through someone else, I must tell
my wretched story to you now.
    *Crespo.* No more of this, Isabel my dear.
You need not say another word.
There are often tales that tell themselves;
they need not be spoken.
    *Isabel.* There are many things you must be told
which even as I mention them
can hardly fail to move you
to revenge before you've heard them all.
Only last night I sat
in perfect safety, sheltered
by your reverend love and all
the promise which it held in store
for me; then all at once they fell
upon us, those muffled villains
whose only law is that honor
must succumb to force; and so
they carried me away. I think
of them only as ravenous wolves
who steal inside the fold
and snatch away the suckling lamb.
There the Captain, the wretched
ingrate, who on the very day
he came to lodge with us

brought with him such unheard of,
such unspeakable discord
(full of guile and treachery,
outbursts and violence),
the Captain plunged ahead, seized me
in his arms while his cohorts, those
other rogues of his, protected him.
He brought me to this dense dark forest,
the haunt he'd chosen near the town.
When are such dim retreats not used to
perpetrate the vilest infamies?
There I found myself, incredulous,
half-crazed, when even the sound
of your voice trailing behind me
disappeared. The words you shouted
one by one faded in the distance,
dispersed upon the wind.
Then what were words became
the merest sounds, and finally
not even sounds but simply
the muffled echoes of alarms
scattered through the air, as when
trumpet sounds have died away and
one still hears the ringing afterward,
but not the notes themselves.
Then when that villain sensed there was
no one following behind him
and no one to defend me
(for now the moon itself withdrew,
cold and vengefully behind dark clouds,
the very light it borrows
from the sun), he attempted, to my
eternal sorrow, to justify
his guilty love with grievous lies.
Who'd not be shaken with disgust
by the patent effrontery
that converts the crudest
violence to tender love?
Beware of him, I say beware
the man who seeks forcibly
to win a woman's heart:
he cannot see nor understand
that love's victory is not
in snatching up the spoils

but in securing the affection
of the loveliness that's treasured.
When desire seeks to gain
such loveliness dishonorably,
by force, it then becomes
a lust for beauty that is dead.
How I pled with him and wept—at first
spoke humbly, then cold and cuttingly.
But all in vain. And then
(now let my voice grow dumb),
the arrogance (and grieving cease),
the insolence (let my heart moan),
the impudence (let my eyes shed tears),
brutality (rumor shut its ears),
cruelty (and breath fail to tell it),
and shamelessness (and I wear mourning) . . .
But what words cannot express
my gestures and emotions may.
I hide my face in shame.
I weep tears of bitter outrage.
I wring my hands in anguish.
Rage has cracked my heart. You know
my meaning; there are no words
to utter it. Enough to say
my cries, so wearily
repeated on the wind, no longer
begged for help but justice.
Dawn came, and lit my way; I heard
the branches rustle; I turned to look
and saw my brother standing there.
Heavenly God! When, oh bitter fate,
was such favor ever shown
so quickly to one in misery?
In the uncertain morning light,
while only dimly visible,
he swiftly guessed my plight
without needing to be told.
Sorrow's looks are lynx-eyed:
they penetrate at a glance.
Wordlessly he drew his sword, the one
you'd girded round him that same day.
Then the Captain, recognizing now
that someone had at last come
to my aid, replied with his sharp blade.

They closed and fought, thrust and parried.
But while they fought relentlessly,
in my grief and fear I recognized
that my brother would not know
if I was or was not
guilty of complicity.
And so, not to risk my life before
I could explain the circumstance,
I turned into the forest's
tangled underbrush and fled.
And yet, not completely, Father;
for it was also my desire
to know what would ensue behind me
that prompted me to turn and watch them,
screened behind a latticework of vines.
Soon I saw my brother wound
the Captain, who stumbled backward; and
just as Juan prepared to follow through
the Captain's men, who had been searching
for him, burst in, furious
to avenge him. At first, Juan stood
his ground, then saw himself outnumbered
and swiftly disappeared.
They resolved to aid their officer
rather than pursue his assailant.
Heedless of his crime, they lifted up
the Captain and brought him back
to town, deciding that the safest
course, however hazardous,
would be the most expedient.
When I considered how one's worst fears
increase, and link by link are forged
to one another, I ran off
blindly, confused and stumbling
in distraction, and unguided
wandered dimly through woods and fields
and undergrowth until
I reached your side, where
having told my bitter tale at last,
I lie prostrate at your feet
awaiting the stroke of death.
Now you know my grievous story,
summon up your courage, take your sword
and end my life. Do it boldly

as my own hands untie your bonds.

*[She unties his bonds.]*

Bind this cord around my neck
and choke my wretched life out.
I am your dishonored daughter.
Now you are free, kill me
and thereby let the world
commending you say this: "To resurrect
his honor, he took his daughter's life."

  *Crespo.* Stand up, Isabel, my child. No,
do not kneel before me on the ground.
If it were not for such torments
and afflictions, all our sufferings
would go unrewarded, and all
our joys quickly turn to ashes.
This is the lot of man,
and we must gird ourselves
to bear it deep within our hearts.
Come, Isabel, let us go home
quickly now; the boy's in danger
and we must make every effort
to find out where he is
and bring him back in safety.

  *Isabel [aside].* Oh, stars above, does this show
true concern or simply caution?

  *Crespo.*                    Come.

*[Exeunt*

### A *street leading into town*

#### CRESPO *and* ISABEL

  *Crespo.* As sure as there's a God above,
that Captain's been driven back here
just to get his wound attended to,
and I suspect before he's through
he'll wish he died of it
and spared himself the thousand
and one wounds in store for him.
By God, I shan't rest till I see him
dead! Come, come child, we're almost home.

#### Enter *the* TOWN CLERK.

  *Clerk.* Ah, Master Pedro Crespo,
I've good news for you.

*Crespo.*                    Yes, clerk—
good news of what?

*Clerk.*                   You were selected
Mayor of the town today,
and to mark your debut in office
you've two important functions
to perform now. The first concerns
the King, who is expected to arrive
either today or tomorrow;
the second concerns the Captain
who with his company was
billeted in town here yesterday.
Some of his men have brought him back
in secret; he needs urgent treatment,
for he's been wounded, though he
refuses to declare who did it.
If this can be established,
there will have to be a trial.

*Crespo* [*aside*]. Just when my honor was to be
avenged, the staff of magistrate
is thrust into my hands!
How can I exceed the law myself
when I am committed to the role
of keeping others within its bounds?
But such matters need further
mulling over. —I am extremely
grateful to the Council
for the honor they've bestowed on me.

*Clerk.* Let us proceed to the Town Hall
and your official installation,
after which you may look further
into these affairs.

*Crespo.*          Come along, then.
[*To* ISABEL.] You'll go directly home.

*Isabel.* Heaven preserve me! Should I not go
with you now?

*Crespo.*          Child, now your father's
mayor here, he'll see to it
there'll be justice done you.

[*Exeunt omnes*

### The CAPTAIN's lodging

*The* CAPTAIN, *wounded, wears a bandage; the* SERGEANT.

*Captain.* Why, there's nothing to this wound at all.
Why did you have to bring me back here?
*Sergeant.* Who could tell it was so slight
before we had it looked at?
Now that we know you're perfectly
all right, we must consider there is
further danger to life and limb
since you had the wound patched up.
But think how much worse off you would be
if you'd been left to bleed to death.
*Captain.* Well, it's wrong to stay here any
longer now that I've been treated.
Let's get out before the word
goes round we're here. Are the others
waiting outside?
*Sergeant.*          They are.
*Captain.* Only a swift escape will save us
from running into all those peasants.
Once they discover I am here, we'll
have to fight our way out barehanded.

### Enter REBOLLEDO.

*Rebolledo.* The officers of the law are here.
*Captain.* Civilian law! What's that to me?
*Rebolledo.* I only said they've just arrived.
*Captain.* Good, I could wish for nothing better.
Since they've found me out, there's no need
to worry now about the townsfolk.
The law obliges them
to turn me over to
a military court, and there,
although the case is awkward,
I'll be perfectly safe.
*Rebolledo.* The peasant's probably
registered some complaint.
*Captain.* That very thought's occurred to me.

### Enter the CLERK and FARMERS.

*Crespo* [*offstage*]. Lock the doors! Don't let any soldier
out of here, and if any
tries to leave, kill him.

*Captain.* What right
have you to be here? [*Aside.*] Good Lord!
Now what's this I see?

*Enter* PEDRO CRESPO *with his magistrate's staff
and flanked by* FARMERS.

*Crespo.* And why not?
As magistrate, I think I have
sufficient reason to be here.
*Captain.* If you look into this,
I believe you'll find that
a civilian judge (though you've been one
only for a day or so)
has no jurisdiction over me.
*Crespo.* My word, sir—do calm yourself!
I've come here with but one concern,
and that's a matter, if
you don't mind, for your ears only.
*Captain* [*to the* SERGEANT *and* REBOLLEDO]. You may
leave us now.
*Crespo* [*to the* FARMERS]. Yes, and you too.
[*Aside to the* CLERK.]
Watch those soldiers carefully.
*Clerk.* Yes, indeed.
[*Exeunt* FARMERS, *the* SERGEANT, REBOLLEDO,
*and the* CLERK

CRESPO *and the* CAPTAIN

*Crespo.* Having used the authority
of my office to avail myself
of your attention, I lay
this staff aside, so [*putting his staff aside*], and speak
to you simply as one man to
another, unburdening his heart.
We're quite alone now, Don Álvaro.
Let us both speak more candidly,
but yet not utterly permit
our deepest feelings, locked up
in the dungeons of our hearts,
to break at once the bars of silence.
I am an honest man
and, as Heaven is my witness,
despite the drawbacks of my humble
origin, I have never had

the slightest reason to regret
the station I was born in.
My fellow townsmen have never failed
to treat me respectfully. The town
church and Council have even thought me
worth honoring. I've been blessed
with a considerable estate
and, I thank Providence, there's no man
wealthier in all this district.
I have raised my daughter,
if I may say so, to be modest,
virtuous, and universally
esteemed—as was her mother,
God bless her soul in Paradise.
I think it will suffice, sir,
to prove the truth of what I've said
if I add that though I'm rich,
nobody here resents me,
and though I'm frank and unassuming,
nobody uses or insults me.
Odd, perhaps, especially
considering we live
in a small community,
where our only fault is prying
into one another's business—
and I could wish to God, sir,
it would only stop at that!
There is, of course, my daughter . . .
She is most attractive—
your own infatuation
will attest to that . . . although,
in saying so, perhaps I should
more stringently deplore it,
since that was her undoing.
But I shall not now pour all
the poison into a single cup;
let some of it remain
to test our fortitude.
We cannot leave everything to time,
sir; we must do something to conceal
its cracks, its imperfections.
One such crack, as you can see, gapes
so wide I cannot hope to mend it,
however hard I try.

If I might keep it hidden,
buried in my heart's deep core,
God knows I'd have no need to come
to you. I'd learn to bear it if
only I might hear nothing further
said of it. Well, then: to redress
so manifest a wrong,
to seek some way of righting
the insult done to me,
is not to look for remedies
but for revenge. So, having cast
about, this way and that,
I have hit upon one recourse—
and one only—that satisfies me,
and should not displease you much.
That's to have you take over
all my property at once,
and unconditionally.
Not a penny will I ask
for my own sustenance or my son's
(whom I shall bring here to beseech
forgiveness at your feet).
On the contrary: we'll be content
to beg out on the street
if there is no other way
to sustain ourselves. What's more:
if you decide you wish
to brand us as slaves and sell us
immediately, you may add
those proceeds to the dowry
I have offered you. Repair
the damage you have done
to my good name. I cannot think
that doing so will detract
one whit from your honor, sir.
For what your sons may lose in
quality by being my grandsons,
they'll make up by that prestige to which
being your sons would entitle them.
As they say, and truly, in Castile,
"It's the stallion that redeems the mare."      [*He kneels.*]
Look, on my knees, and by
an old man's tears that even
seem to melt the snowy beard

they fall on, I beg you. What is it
I beg? Only to restore
the honor you deprived me of.
And though that honor is my own,
I beg for its return so humbly
it must appear I beg for yours.
You know that I can seize it from you
forcibly, but I would have you
yield it willingly instead.
    *Captain.* Tiresome old man, you've babbled on
until you've worn my patience out.
You can count your lucky stars
I've spared your lives so far—
you and that son of yours.
And you ought to know you owe your luck
to Isabel and her beauty.
As for your threat of using force
to retrieve your honor,
that moves me very little.
And when it comes to legal matters—
you've no authority over me.
    *Crespo.* You mean my misery does not
affect you?
    *Captain.* An old man's like
a woman or a child: his fears
are easily dissolved in tears.
    *Crespo.* For all my wretchedness, you've not
a single word of sympathy?
    *Captain.* What more sympathy do you need?
I have spared your life.
    *Crespo.*        Look, sir:
I am down upon my knees.
I beg you to restore my honor.
    *Captain.* How tiresome can you be?
    *Crespo.*        Look, sir:
I am Mayor of this town.
    *Captain.* I am not subject to
your jurisdiction—only
to a military court's.
    *Crespo.* Is that all you have to say?
    *Captain.* That's it, you tedious old babbler!
    *Crespo.* Is there no remedy at all?
    *Captain.* Yes, indeed. The best remedy
for you is silence.

*Crespo.*            Nothing else?
*Captain.*                          No.
*Crespo.* Then, by God, I swear you'll pay
for all this dearly. Ho, there, come in!

> [*He rises, picking up his staff.*]

FARMERS, CRESPO, *and the* CAPTAIN

*Farmer* [*offstage*]. Sir!
*Captain* [*aside*].          What are these peasants up to?

*Enter the* FARMERS.

*Farmer.* What are your orders, sir?
*Crespo.*                          I
order you to arrest the Captain.
*Captain.* Indeed! You know you're acting rashly.
You cannot arrest someone like me,
an officer of the King.
*Crespo.*            We'll see.
But you either leave this place as
my prisoner or as a corpse.
*Captain.* I warn you I am a captain,
and quite alive and in commission.
*Crespo.* Well, what do you take me for—
a dead mayor, out of commission?
Surrender, you're in my custody.
*Captain.* Since I cannot defend myself,
I have no other choice.
I shall complain of your insult
to the King.
*Crespo.* And I'll complain to him
of yours. It's good he's in
this vicinity: he can listen
to us both. And incidentally,
better leave your sword.
*Captain.*                You have no right . .
*Crespo.* Why not, since you'll be in jail?
*Captain.* Now treat it with due respect . . .
*Crespo.* Right you are! I heartily agree.
Take him to his cell, with due respect.
Then, with due respect, shackle him.
With due respect, see to it
he does not communicate
with any of the soldiers.
Then put the other two in jail

as well, and, as it befits their case,
keep them duly separated
so that afterward, with due respect,
they may each of them submit
their sworn depositions,
whereupon if any two of them
evidence their culpability,
by God, I'll hang them one and all
at once—with due respect.
    *Captain.* Oh, these peasants drunk with power!
        [*The* CAPTAIN *is led away by the* FARMERS.]

    REBOLLEDO, LA CHISPA, *the* CLERK, *and* CRESPO

    *Clerk.* The page and this soldier here
were finally apprehended.
The other one got away.
    *Crespo.* That's the rascal who sings; a little
stretching of the voice box
and he'll never sing again.
    *Rebolledo.* Since when is it a crime to sing, sir?
    *Crespo.* Singing's fine, I'm sure. In fact,
I've a little instrument here
to improve your singing. Make up
your mind now, and tell . . .
    *Rebolledo.*            Tell what?
    *Crespo.* All about last night . . .
    *Rebolledo.*            Your daughter
knows more about that than I do.
    *Crespo.* Otherwise you die.
    *La Chispa* [*aside to* REBOLLEDO]. Don't
admit a thing! Deny it all,
and if you do you'll be the hero
of a ballad I'll make up and sing.
    *Crespo.* Later you'll be obliged to sing
a little too.
    *La Chispa.* You can't torture me.
    *Crespo.* Why not, may I ask?
    *La Chispa.*            It's a
pretty well accepted thing.
And there's no law against it.
    *Crespo.* What alibi have you?
    *La Chispa.* A great big one.
    *Crespo.*           What is it? Speak up.
    *La Chispa.* I'm pregnant.
    *Crespo.*           And bold as brass, I see!

This is the last straw! Aren't you
the captain's groom?
    *La Chispa.*       Not at all, sir:
I'm nearer to another's bridle.
    *Crespo.* I want your testimony—both of you.
Now make up your minds to tell me
all you know.
    *La Chispa.* Of course we'll tell you
all we know—and even more.
That's much better than being dead.
    *Crespo.* It will save you from the rack, at least.
    *La Chispa.* If it does, by Heaven, I was born
to sing, and so I'll sing
as I have never sung before! [*She sings.*]

"*Now since they want to torture me . . .*"

    *Rebolledo* [*singing*]. "*What do you think they'll do to
      me?*"

    *Crespo.* What's all this?
    *La Chispa.*          Just tuning up now—
then we'll go right on to sing.

                              [*Exeunt omnes*

### A room in CRESPO'S house

    *Juan.* After wounding that villain
in the forest and turning back
when all his henchmen came,
I've scoured the woods, slashing
every thicket, but in vain.
My sister has disappeared.
Since I have returned to town,
I am resolved to tell my father
everything, here and now.
God in Heaven, I shall learn
from him what must be done
to restore my honor and my life.

      *Enter* INÉS *and* ISABEL, *downcast;* JUAN.

    *Inés.* You grieve and sigh so heavily,
my dear, your suffering
is like a living death.
    *Isabel.* Inés, who told you I find my life
anything but odious?
    *Juan.* I'll tell my father . . . [*Aside.*] Alas,

that's Isabel! It's plain as day.
What am I waiting for? [*He draws his dagger.*]
 *Inés.* Cousin!
 *Isabel.*   Brother! What do you mean
to do?
 *Juan.* Avenge the life and honor
which you compromised today.
 *Isabel.*     But wait . . .
 *Juan.* In Heaven's name, I'll see you dead first.

   *Enter* CRESPO *and the* FARMERS.

 *Crespo.* What's this?
 *Juan.*     This is to expiate
a terrible offense, to avenge
a heinous crime, and punish . . .
 *Crespo.* Enough, enough. You were wrong
to come here and so rashly . . .
 *Juan.* But what's this I see?
 *Crespo.*     . . . present yourself
before me now, having just wounded
a captain in the forest.
 *Juan.* I attacked him, sir, but
my cause was just: your own honor
was at stake . . .
 *Crespo.*   That's enough now, Juan.
Here, arrest him—take him off
to prison.
 *Juan.*  Father! Is this the way
to treat your own flesh and blood?
 *Crespo.* I wouldn't hesitate to treat
my father this way, if I had to.
[*Aside.*] I do it to save his life,
but it will probably be taken
as the oddest piece of justice
ever wrought!
 *Juan.*  Let me at least explain
why I first attacked the Captain,
then tried to kill my sister.
 *Crespo.* I know all about that now, but
knowing personally about it
won't do at all. I must be
officially apprised of it
as Mayor, and then investigate
the evidence. Until your guilt,

if any, has been duly proven
at the trial, I must see to it
that you're detained. [*Aside*.] I'll find a way
to clear him.
   *Juan.*      Your object is
utterly incomprehensible.
You arrest a man and strip him
of his honor for attempting
to restore your own, while you
protect the very culprit
who relieved you of it.

                    [*He is taken off in custody.*]

        CRESPO, ISABEL, *and* INÉS

   *Crespo.* Come, Isabel, go in and sign
your name to the complaint you lodged
against the man who injured you.
   *Isabel.* You who wished to keep that grievous
insult secret, how can you now
persuade yourself to publish it?
If you cannot manage
to avenge it, at least try
to say nothing more about it.
   *Crespo.* No, I cannot treat the matter now
in any other way. As Mayor
I can no longer satisfy,
as I might wish to do
in private, an attack
against my honor.

                      [*Exit* ISABEL

            Now, Inés,
bring that staff inside; since he's refused
to make personal amends for this,
he'll learn how hard the law can be.

                      [*Exit* INÉS

    DON LOPE, SOLDIERS, *and* CRESPO

   *Don Lope* [*offstage*]. Stop! Stop!
   *Crespo.*            What's that? Now who,
who in the world is shouting
as he dismounts outside? And who's this
coming in?
       *Enter* DON LOPE *and* SOLDIERS.

   *Don Lope.* Ah, Pedro Crespo!

Here I am again. I wasn't
very far along the way when
a most alarming piece of news
brought me back to town. I wouldn't think
of stopping elsewhere, Pedro,
since you and I are such good friends.

    *Crespo.* God bless you, Don Lope. Your presence
always does me honor here.

    *Don Lope.* I miss your son; I wonder that
he has not joined me as yet.

    *Crespo.* I shall readily tell you why,
but first, sir, I hope you'll let me
know the news that brought you back.
You seem desperately disturbed, sir.

    *Don Lope.* It's the most disgraceful thing
you can possibly imagine,
the most confounded, harebrained
nonsense anyone could think of!
Why, listening to that sergeant
who overtook me on the road . . .
I tell you, I won't, I can't . . .
I could burst with rage . . .

    *Crespo.*                    Indeed, sir!

    *Don Lope.* Well, some little jackass
of a mayor here threw the Captain
into jail. I swear to you,
this blasted leg of mine
never shook me as it did today;
otherwise I'd have been here
on the spot a long time ago
and have done that mayor in. Sweet
Jesus, I'll flog that rogue to death!

    *Crespo.* Then I think you've come in vain
because that mayor won't let himself
be flogged.

    *Don Lope.* Then he'll get it willy-
nilly.

    *Crespo.* That seems very drastic,
and I can tell you there's no one
in the world who wouldn't say so.
Do you know why he seized the Captain?

    *Don Lope.* No, I don't; whatever the reason,
the injured party must look

to me for justice, and if
beheading is what's called for,
I know a bit about that too.

*Crespo.* I'm afraid you do not understand,
sir, the functions of a mayor
in a town.

*Don Lope.* What else can he be
but another country bumpkin?

*Crespo.* A country bumpkin he may be,
but once his mind's made up
the prisoner deserves
garroting, I swear he'll do it.

*Don Lope.* And I swear he won't! Perhaps
you'd like to see whether
he gets away with it or not.
Well, just tell me where to find him.

*Crespo.* He lives quite close by.

*Don Lope.*                          Come now,
tell me who this mayor is.

*Crespo.*                    Myself.

*Don Lope.* By God, I suspected it!

*Crespo.* By God, I've just told you so!

*Don Lope.* Now, Crespo, I meant exactly
what I said.

*Crespo.*    Now, Don Lope,
I meant exactly what I said.

*Don Lope.* I've come to take the prisoner
away and punish his keeper.

*Crespo.* And I'll keep the prisoner right here
for all the wrongs he's done us.

*Don Lope.* Don't you understand he is
an officer of the King
and I'm his judge?

*Crespo.* Don't you understand
he broke into this house
and snatched my daughter from me?

*Don Lope.* Don't you know I'm sole arbiter
in any case?

*Crespo.*    Don't you know
he ravished my daughter in the woods?

*Don Lope.* Do you know how much greater
my authority is than yours?

*Crespo.* Do you know how much I pleaded

with him first and he refused me,
which left no other course than this?
    *Don Lope.* No matter how you argue it,
you've trespassed on my authority.
    *Crespo.* He's trespassed on my good name,
which is beyond your authority.
    *Don Lope.* I assure you I'll settle that account;
he'll be made to pay for it in full.
    *Crespo.* I've never left to someone else
what I can do myself.
    *Don Lope.* I tell you once for all:
the prisoner is mine.
    *Crespo.* I am drawing up the evidence
of this trial right here.
    *Don Lope.*              What evidence?
    *Crespo.* Certain papers I am gathering
from witnesses to support the case.
    *Don Lope.* I am going straight to your jail now
and take him away.
    *Crespo.*            I cannot
prevent your going there,
but remember this: my orders are—
shoot anyone who's caught approaching.
    *Don Lope.* I am fairly well accustomed
to the threat of bullets,
but there's no point to risking
anything in this little fray
of ours. You there, soldier!
Run as fast as your legs
will carry you, and inform
all the companies lately
billeted here and on the march
today to return directly here
in battle formation,
all muskets and cannons loaded
and ready to be fired.
    *Soldier.* Sir, there's no need to summon them.
The troops have heard what happened here,
and they're in town already.
    *Don Lope.* Then, by Heaven, let's see whether
I get the prisoner now or not!
    *Crespo.* Then, by Heaven, before that happens,
I mean to do what must be done!

                                  *[Exeunt omnes*

*Inside the prison*

[DON LOPE, *the* CLERK, SOLDIERS, CRESPO *are all
heard offstage. The sound of drums.*]

*Don Lope.* Men, here's the prison where
the Captain's being held.
If they refuse to let him go,
set fire to the place at once;
burn it to the ground. If they resist,
burn down the town—all of it.
*Clerk.* Let them set fire to the jail;
he's beyond their help now.
*Soldiers.* Death to the peasants!
*Crespo.*                    What's death?
Come now, is that all?
*Don Lope.*          They've got
reinforcements now. Go at it, men!
Break the jail down; smash the door!

*Enter the* SOLDIERS *and* DON LOPE *on one side;
the* KING, *his retinue,* CRESPO, *and the*
FARMERS *on the other.*

*King.* What is going on here? Is this
the way to greet your King?
*Don Lope.*                This, Sire,
is the most insolent piece
of peasant villainy
that has ever been reported.
You may take my word for it,
Your Majesty, had you reached
this town a moment later,
your progress here would have been marked
by row on row of blazing houses.
*King.* What has happened here?
*Don Lope.*                The Mayor
has imprisoned a captain
and refuses to release him
at my command.
*King.*          Who is this mayor?
*Crespo.* I.
*King.*      And what have you to offer
in defense?
*Crespo.* This evidence,
by which the crime is proven

conclusively, and the death sentence
clearly called for. The girl
was abducted, then ravished
in a lonely wood; the culprit
refused to marry her,
despite her father's earnest plea
and offer to forgive him.

    *Don Lope.* This man is the Mayor
and the girl's father as well.

    *Crespo.* It does not matter one way
or the other; if any stranger
brought the same complaint, would he not
deserve to have like justice done him?
Of course he would; then why
should I not treat my daughter's case
as I would any stranger's?
Besides, I've put my own son
in prison, which should show
I'm impartial to the issue
where the family tie's concerned.
Here, let Your Majesty himself
decide if the trial was fair,
or if anyone can say that
malice has misled me,
if I have suborned a witness,
beyond the facts I have given you.
And if so, I shall pay for it
with my life.

    *King.*          The verdict
is justified. However,
you have no authority
to execute it; that's a matter
for another court's decision
and jurisdiction. And so,
you must release the prisoner.

    *Crespo.* I can hardly do that now,
Your Majesty. We have only
one tribunal here, which executes
whatever verdict has been passed.
And so the sentence in this case
has already been carried out.

    *King.* What's that you say?

    *Crespo.*                    If you doubt my word,
Sire, turn this way and look.

That's the Captain there.

> [A *door is opened and the* CAPTAIN *is revealed
> garroted in a chair.*]

*King.*                    You've dared do that?

*Crespo.* You yourself have said the verdict
was justified; I cannot then
have been far wrong to do it.

*King.* Why did you not leave this for
the military court to decide?

*Crespo.* All royal justice, Sire, is contained
in one body with many hands.
What difference can it make then,
if one arm of justice perform
the job intended for some other
arm? What harm's been done
if some detail is slighted
in accomplishing the broader
purpose which justice must serve?

*King.* Well, suppose I grant you that.
But how is it you did not behead
the prisoner as he deserved,
being a captain and a nobleman?

*Crespo.* I am sorry you should doubt me
on that score, Your Majesty.
In these parts the noblemen
are so well behaved, it happens
our executioner never learned
how to go about beheading
anyone. In any case,
that scruple should properly concern
the dead man—it's within
his jurisdiction, one might say;
but since he's not complained yet,
I trust others need not be concerned.

*King.* Don Lope, the deed is done.
The execution was fully
justified; to deviate
in some particular
is unimportant so long as
justice is upheld in principle.
Let no soldier stay behind now;
order all to march at once.
We must reach Portugal without
another moment of delay.

[*To* CRESPO.] And you are hereby appointed
permanent Mayor of this town.

    *Crespo.* Sire, only you would know how
to honor justice so completely.

                 [*Exit the* KING, *with his retinue*

    *Don Lope.* You can thank your stars His Majesty
arrived here when he did.

    *Crespo.* Even if he hadn't come,
by Heaven, there still would not have been
any other way to settle this.

    *Don Lope.* Wouldn't it have been better
if you'd consulted me
and released the prisoner?
Then he would have been compelled to mend
your daughter's reputation
by marrying her.

    *Crespo.*       She has chosen
to enter a convent now
where she will be the bride of One
who cares nothing for the differences
in social origin among us.

    *Don Lope.* Well, let's have the other prisoners.

    *Crespo.* Bring them out at once.

                     [*Exit the* CLERK

DON LOPE, CRESPO, SOLDIERS, FARMERS;
REBOLLEDO, LA CHISPA; *later* JUAN

    *Don Lope.*              I see your son's
still missing. Now that he's a soldier
he cannot be detained in prison.

    *Crespo.* Sir, he must be punished
for disrespect; he attacked
his captain, though it's true
he was obliged to do so
since his honor was at stake.
Still, he might have found some other way.

    *Don Lope.* Pedro Crespo, never mind that.
Call him in.

    *Crespo.*   Here he is.

*Enter* JUAN.

    *Juan.* I humbly thank you, sir. I am
your devoted servant always.

    *Rebolledo.* I don't think I'll ever want

to sing another note again.

*La Chispa.* As for me, I think I will—
every time I see the image
of that rack before my eyes.

*Crespo.* With which our author says
this true history now ends.
For its errors, pardon us, dear friends.

# THE PHANTOM LADY

## (LA DAMA DUENDE)

# DRAMATIS PERSONAE

DON MANUEL
DON JUAN, *his friend*
DON LUIS, *brother of Don Juan*
COSME, *clownish servant to Don Manuel*
RODRIGO, *servant to Don Luis*
DOÑA ANGELA, *sister of Don Juan and Don Luis*
DOÑA BEATRIZ, *her cousin*
ISABEL, *maid to Doña Angela*
CLARA, *maid to Doña Beatriz*
*Servants*

The scene is laid in MADRID.

# ACT ONE

## A *street*

*Enter* DON MANUEL *and* COSME, *dressed as travelers.*

DON MANUEL. We've come an hour late and missed
the grand festivities Madrid
is celebrating in honor
of Prince Balthazar's christening.
    *Cosme.* As far as that's concerned, things often
went awry before because
someone lost an hour more or less.
If Pyramus had reached the fountain
an hour earlier, he wouldn't
have discovered Thisbe dead there.
But the berries didn't leave a stain,
you know, for according to
the poets that tragedy
was written with blackberry juice.
If Tarquin had delayed an hour,
Lucretia would have found seclusion,
and our classic authors would never
know—unless they turned vicariates
before a court of law—whether it
really was a case of rape or not.
If Hero had spent an hour
considering the wisdom
of leaping from her tower,
I'm certain she never would have
done it, in which case the good Doctor
Mira de Amescua
would have been excused from offering
the theatre such a finely
executed play, and likewise,
the Amarylis Company,
from playing it so credibly
that even the acrobat at
Carnival—which corresponds to Lent—
was more than once observed
to lose his head applauding it.
But as we've missed the grand
festivities, let's not also come

219

an hour late to our lodging, or else,
like the Moorish hero of romance,
we'll find ourselves outside the gate.
Besides, I'm curious to see this
friend of yours, whose regal
hospitality awaits us—
God knows how or why—just when
we need it most, like two
knight-errants being feted
for the tournaments.
    *Don Manuel.*       You mean Don Juan
of Toledo; Cosme, he is my
dearest friend, and so zealous
in professing our amity
as to challenge any of
the closest friendships, celebrated
down the ages, in antiquity.
We went to school together,
and later followed the career
of arms; we were comrades in the field
at Piedmont. When the Duke of Feria
honored me as captain
in the infantry, I made Don Juan
my color guard. As field ensign
he was badly wounded
in a skirmish, and it was I
who nursed him in my tent.
Thus he has always felt that,
next to God, he owes his life to me.
I refrain from mentioning
certain other obligations—
all quite trivial, of course.
A gentleman does not discuss
such matters. In that regard,
the Academy portrays
a wealthy matron turning her back
upon her own benefaction,
thus showing the discretion
of one not wishing to be
reminded of her gift.
When, in brief, he heard that
I was coming to Madrid
in order to accept
His Majesty's preferment

for service to the Crown,
Don Juan, wishing to acknowledge his
gratitude on various counts,
insisted I take up lodging at
his house during our sojourn here.
And though his letter I received
in Burgos indicated
how to find his street and house,
I did not think it fitting
to ask about such matters
while we rode along the way.
That is why I left our bags
and horses at the inn, and how,
in coming here, I noticed
the celebration and everyone
in gala costume. Learning
of the holiday, I resolved
to catch a glimpse of it,
which is why we've been delayed . . .

*Enter* DOÑA ANGELA *and* ISABEL, *both veiled
and dressed in long skirts.*

*Doña Angela.* Sir, if you are the gentleman
your manner and attire indicate,
defend a woman urgently
in need of your protection.
My very life and honor are
at stake if I am overtaken
by that hidalgo at my heels.
By all that's sacred, I implore you:
save a noblewoman from
coming to grief; then some day, perhaps,
she will . . . Farewell. Alas,
I must run or I am lost.

　　　[*Exeunt* DOÑA ANGELA *and* ISABEL *in great haste*
*Cosme.* Was that a lady or a whirlwind?
*Don Manuel.* How very strange!
*Cosme.* 　　　　　　　　What will you do?
*Don Manuel.* What a question! As a man
of honor, what else can I do
but defend the lady
from misfortune and disgrace?
No doubt the man in question
is her husband.

*Cosme.*          And how
do you propose to stop him?
*Don Manuel.* By some stratagem or other,
but if that won't do it,
I shall have to use my sword,
and no further questions asked.
*Cosme.* If you're looking for a stratagem,
leave that to me: I've got one ready.
I'll use this letter from a friend
recommending me to one in town.

*Enter* DON LUIS *and* RODRIGO, *his servant.*

*Don Luis.* I must discover who she is,
if only because she's so intent
upon avoiding me.
*Rodrigo.* Overtake her, and you'll find out.
          [COSME *approaches while* DON MANUEL *with-*
                *draws.*]
*Cosme.* Sir, pardon my temerity,
but may I ask Your Grace
if he will kindly help me read
the address written on this letter?
*Don Luis.* I've no patience for such stuff now.
*Cosme* [*detaining him*]. Well, if it's patience you lack,
I've plenty. I'll give you half of mine.
*Don Luis.* Out of my way!
*Don Manuel* [*aside*]. How long and straight this street
     is!
And there she is: still in sight.
*Cosme.* Be so good, sir . . .
*Don Luis.*                    By God,
if you pester me any more
I'll break your head! . . .
*Cosme.*                    Well, then,
I'll pester you a little less.
*Don Luis.* This is insufferable.
Get out of here!

                                        [*Beats him.*]

*Don Manuel* [*aside*]. I must intervene,
throw caution to the winds,
and face up to him. —Sir,
that's my servant you're knocking about.
I should like to know how

he has offended you to warrant
such ill treatment.

    *Don Luis.*          I never deign
to satisfy a man who questions
any act of mine. Good day!

    *Don Manuel.* If I decide such satisfaction
is in order, you may be sure
your arrogance will not persuade me
to depart without it.
The question I put to you—
namely, in what manner
were you injured or offended—
deserves a much more civil answer.
Now, it would seem to me
to be an insult to the Spanish Court
if a stranger in Madrid
were forced to teach the gentlemen
who live here better manners.

    *Don Luis.* How dare you think I need be taught . . .

    *Don Manuel.* Hold your tongue, and let your sword
      reply.

                          *[They draw swords.]*

    *Don Luis.* You put it well.

    *Cosme.*                              Oh, how lustily
they take to fighting.

    *Rodrigo.*                    Come now,
let's see your sword.

    *Cosme.*                    Since mine
is still a blushing virgin
whom no one's spoken for as yet,
I cannot expose her
to public view.

      *Enter* Doña Beatriz, *who tries to hold back*
        Don Juan; *and* Clara, *her servant.*

    *Don Juan.*     Beatriz,
let me go.

    *Doña Beatriz.* You must not do it.

    *Don Juan.*                              Look,
it's my brother he is fighting with!

    *Doña Beatriz.* Gracious me!

    *Don Juan* [*to* Don Luis]. I'm at your side.

    *Don Luis.* Hold on, there, Don Juan. Stop!

Your support has hindered me;
it makes me out a coward.
Noble stranger, you will understand
how one who had just cause to cross swords
with you in single combat
must now, in being seconded,
either withdraw or else be taken
for a craven coward. Go your way,
sir. My sense of honor
disallows my taking
unfair advantage of any man,
especially of one who shows
such spirit and such valor.
God be with you.
    *Don Manuel.*   I appreciate
your gracious courtesy.
But if, by chance, you are troubled
by any scruple later,
you may count on finding me
whenever you desire.
    *Don Luis.* My respects to you, sir.
    *Don Manuel.* And mine to you.
    *Don Juan.*           What's this
I see and hear? Don Manuel!
    *Don Manuel.* Don Juan!
    *Don Juan.*        My heart is full of doubt,
buffeted by fear and joy.
I cannot understand the cause
of such violent disagreement
between my brother and
my bosom friend.
    *Don Luis.*    It was simply
that this gentleman took
his servant's side, whose impertinence
provoked me; and that's all
there was to it.
    *Don Juan.*   In that event,
I trust that I am free at last
to embrace my friend, Don Manuel,
our noble and eagerly awaited
guest. Having fought as equals,
may you henceforth become
the faster friends for it;

you know each other's valor now.
Your hand!

    *Don Manuel.* Before I shake your hand,
may I say how much I admire
Don Luis for his bravery.
I am at your service, sir.

    *Don Luis.* I am proud to be your friend,
and am only sorry that I failed
to recognize you, though
your skillful sword should certainly
have told me who you are at once.

    *Don Manuel.* Yours might have warned me, having
left this wound upon my hand.

    *Don Luis.* Ah, I would rather have been wounded
a thousand times instead!

    *Cosme.* So, now they fight with powder puffs!

    *Don Juan.* A wound? We must have it dressed at once!
Stay here, Don Luis, and see
Doña Beatriz to her carriage.
Give her my apologies for this
unseemly haste. Come, Don Manuel,
I shall take you to my house—
more properly, your own—
and make sure your wound is dressed.

    *Don Manuel.* Oh, it's nothing at all.

    *Don Juan.* Please come at once.

    *Don Manuel* [*aside*].        How annoying
to be welcomed to Madrid in blood!

    *Don Luis* [*aside*]. How tiresome to lose the
opportunity of finding out
who that lady was!

    *Cosme* [*aside*].    How
appropriate! It serves my master
right for playing Don Quixote
to every passing Dulcinea!

                [*Exeunt* DON JUAN, DON MANUEL, *and* COSME,
                  *while* DON LUIS *joins* DOÑA BEATRIZ, *who has*
                  *been waiting nearby*

    *Don Luis.* Now the storm is past and gone,
I entreat you, madam, to allow
the tinctured hue of roses
once again to warm those cheeks made wan
and desolate by the onset
of so much icy apprehension.

*Doña Beatriz.* Where is Don Juan?

*Don Luis.*                          He begs
your indulgence. Certain
obligations and his
solicitude for a wounded
friend compelled him to depart at once.

*Doña Beatriz.* Wounded? Alas, is Don Juan wounded?

*Don Luis.* No, madam, not Don Juan.
If my brother had been wounded,
I would not be standing here
so calmly. Do not be alarmed,
for it seems to me unjust that
when my brother feels no pain at all
we two should be suffering
with sorrow and anxiety.
My sorrow's cause is seeing you
too much overcome, too deeply
sensible to some imagined harm
which penetrates more cruelly
than any actual wound.

*Doña Beatriz.* Don Luis: I am of course obliged
to you for these compliments,
granting that they mean to show
your heart, and are all your own.
But you should know I cannot
otherwise respond to them:
they address the stars, which may comply,
but no mortal woman surely.
If I seem to take your words
so lightly, that's because the Court
commonly regards nothing else
so highly. Therefore, be grateful
for my frankness, which is, at least,
as rare a thing as you will find
these days at Court. Good day, sir.     [*Exit with* CLARA

*Don Luis.* Good day, madam. Everything I do
goes wrong, Rodrigo. If I see
a lively woman passing by
and try to know her better, some fool
or duel comes up to stop me—and
which of them is worse I do not know.
If I am fighting, then my brother
must rush in, and my antagonist
turns out to be his bosom friend.

If he suddenly departs,
and I am left to soothe his mistress
with apologies, she proceeds
to treat me like a dog. And so:
the veiled lady runs away from me;
the meddling fool stops to drive me mad;
the stranger attacks me;
and my brother leads him off
to be our noble guest at home,
while a second lady leaves me
writhing in her scorn. I've had
a heap of sorry luck indeed.

   *Rodrigo.* Do you care to know which
of all those slights I think
has pained you most?

   *Don Luis.*      You wouldn't know.

   *Rodrigo.* Well, isn't it that you are jealous
of your brother's winning Beatriz?

   *Don Luis.* No, you're quite mistaken.

   *Rodrigo.* What is it, then?

   *Don Luis.*        If I must speak
candidly—and this I say
in strictest confidence—
what pains me most of all
is my brother's heedlessness.
Consider it, Rodrigo:
he brings a gay young gentleman
to stay with us at home where,
as you know, my lovely sister lives,
who though she is a recent widow
still is under age. Scarcely a soul
knows of her presence there, she lives
in such seclusion. At that
the only visitor she sees
is Beatriz, whom we allow
because she is our cousin.

   *Rodrigo.* Yes, I know that Doña Angela
came secretly to live here
in Madrid. Her husband's death,
while Collector of the Royal Ports,
left a large deficit of funds
still owing to the Crown; meanwhile,
as she hopes to settle this affair,
she is living in strict seclusion

under your brother's roof
and his close surveillance.
This being the case, sir, remember
that the situation which forbids
her seeing anyone
will not be threatened by the presence
of Don Manuel at home.
Indeed, sir, since he will not know
she's even there, what harm is done
in his staying at the house?
Besides, special pains were taken
to make the door to his apartment
lead into the street. Then,
to conceal the second doorway,
which leads into the other rooms,
while allowing for its later use,
a paneling of glass mirrors
has been installed in that space.
And the panel's been designed
so that no one would suspect
there'd ever been another door there.
    *Don Luis.* And do you suppose all this
will reassure me? Such precautions
only double my uneasiness,
for what you tell me, in effect,
is that the only thing now standing
as bulwark to my sister's honor
is a frame of glass a single blow
will shatter in a thousand pieces.

                           *[Exeunt*

DOÑA ANGELA's *apartment in* DON JUAN's *house*

*Enter* DOÑA ANGELA *and* ISABEL.

    *Doña Angela.* Here, Isabel, give me back
my widow's hood, worse luck!
And wrap me up again
in that black shroud; as cruel fate
will have it, I must be buried
in this way, alive.
    *Isabel.*        Put them on
quickly. If your brother entered now
with any reason to suspect you,
your dress would tell him at a glance

you were the one he met today
at the palace.
 *Doña Angela.* Heaven help me!
The two of them will be
the death of me. They have cooped me up
behind these walls where I can scarcely
see the light of day, and when night falls
my aching heart is fit to burst
this dungeon—here where the fickle moon
herself, imitating me,
can never boast she saw me mourn
my turn of fortune. Imprisoned here,
what freedom have I gained in
widowhood when my husband's death
releases me simply
to be wedlocked to a brace
of brothers? And then, if I happen
to go out, in perfect innocence,
to see the plays which everyone
in town's been flocking to,
authority decrees that though
I go there veiled, it's as if
I'd just committed murder. My luck's
so miserable and so unfair!
 *Isabel.* But madam, it should not seem so strange
to you. After all, your brothers,
considering your youth, your charm,
and your vivacity, must take
precautions to protect you.
For such attractions are just
calculated to arouse some crime
of passion, especially here
at Court. For don't I cross myself
a thousand times a day in passing
those blossoming young widows?
There they go, flouncing down the street,
pretending they're so prim and chaste,
so holier-than-thou, you know,
when all they really care about
is showing off their latest gown.
Yet let them once take off their toques
and those airs of being so devout,
and they'll go bouncing off agog,
from one young fellow to another,

like a football. But madam, let's drop
this subject for a while; instead,
let's discuss the gallant stranger
whom you begged to be your champion
and in whose keeping you recently
deposited your honor.

  *Doña Angela.* Why, Isabel, that's just the thing—
you seem to read my mind.
My one concern is what he must
have thought of me, for when
I heard the sound of clashing swords
behind me, I wondered, Isabel—
though you may think this fanciful—
whether he was not after all
so far taken by my pleas
that he was forced to draw his sword
on my account. I was mad
to urge him on so; but then, how can
a woman, scared to death, ever stop
to weigh the consequences?

  *Isabel.* I do not know if you
incited him, but I do know
that afterward your brother
stopped pursuing us.

  *Doña Angela.*   Wait, someone's there!

*Enter* DON LUIS.

  *Don Luis.* Angela!
  *Doña Angela.*   Why, brother,
you seem so upset. What's happened?
Is anything the matter?
  *Don Luis.* Everything's the matter
when one's honor is at stake.
  *Doña Angela* [*aside*]. Good Lord, now it's out—he saw
   me!
  *Don Luis.* I am concerned because
your honor is so lightly treated
in this house.
  *Doña Angela.* Is there reason
for you to think so? What troubles you?
  *Don Luis.* The worst of it, Angela, is
that when I come to see you, I am
no less vexed than I was
before I came.

*Isabel* [*aside*]. This is it now!

*Doña Angela.* But brother, how can I possibly
have offended you? Consider . . .

*Don Luis.* You are the cause, and when I look
at you . . .

*Doña Angela.* Oh, dear me!

*Don Luis.*                    . . . Angela,
I realize how little
my brother thinks of you.

    *Doña Angela.*          That is true.

    *Don Luis.* For see how he now adds new sorrows
to those which brought you to Madrid.
And so I was not so wrong
in turning my annoyance with
Don Juan against his guest and friend
whom, out of some presentiment,
I wounded in a duel today.

    *Doña Angela.* Indeed? How did that happen?

    *Don Luis.* Well, sister: this afternoon
I walked to the palace grounds,
up to the stage reserved
for the public performances.
A flock of carriages
and gentlemen were crowded
all around, and it was there I found
a number of my friends conversing
with a lady in a veil,
whose wit they all seemed to relish
and admire. But I had no sooner
joined them than the lady grew silent.
And though someone begged her to explain
why my presence should have struck her dumb,
she would not say another word.
This appeared so odd to me
that I moved closer, thinking
I might know the lady—but in vain.
She only wound the veil about her
more securely, turned, and fled.
To determine who she was,
I followed her. And as she ran,
she turned continually to glance
behind at me, as if in utter
terror; yet her dismay
simply spurred my curiosity.

I continued in this way
until some stranger stopped me;
as I discovered later, it was
the servant of our present guest.
The fellow asked me to read
some letter; I said that I was
in a hurry, though I suspected
he meant to stop me purposely,
for I had seen the lady
speak to him in passing.
His persistence angered me, and I
told him—I can't remember what.
But at that point our guest came up,
looking fierce and military,
to defend his servant. Well,
we drew our swords and went at it.
That's all there was, although
it might have been much worse.

    *Doña Angela.* I declare! To think that wicked
woman led you into such a trap!
Why, of all the shameless, conniving
wenches who. . . . I'll wager
she did not even know you,
and only ran away
to make you follow her.
Now this is why I've often warned you,
as you recall, not to lose
your head over hussies whose
only thought is how to wreck men's lives.

    *Don Luis.* How did you spend your afternoon?

    *Doña Angela.* I spent it here at home,
and entertained myself by weeping.

    *Don Luis.* Did our brother come to see you?

    *Doña Angela.* He has not been here since morning.

    *Don Luis.* I cannot tolerate his neglect
of you.

    *Doña Angela.* Well, you had better not
be vexed, and finally accept
the situation. Remember,
he is our elder brother
whom we count on for our keep.

    *Don Luis.* If you can reconcile yourself,
I shall have to do the same,
since it is only on your account

that I've been vexed. And now
that you've advised me of your feelings
in the matter, I shall go
to see him, and even pay
my compliments to his friend.

[*Exit*

    *Isabel.* Well, madam, what have you to say
to everything that's going on here?
After suffering such a fright,
you have the very gentleman
who saved your life, and was even
wounded for it, lodged here now under
this very roof!
    *Doña Angela.* I suspected
as much, Isabel. The moment
my brother mentioned the quarrel,
I gathered that the wounded man
was to be our guest. And yet,
I can scarcely bring myself
to believe the story. It seems
so incredible that a stranger
just arriving in Madrid
should instantly find himself
enjoined to save a lady's life,
then be wounded by her brother,
only to become her other
brother's house guest. Strange, though
not impossible—and yet
I shan't believe it's happened
till I see it with these eyes.
    *Isabel.* If that's the way you feel,
I know how to satisfy your doubts.
You can have a look at him—
a good one, and even something more.
    *Doña Angela.* Isabel, you are mad. How can I
see the gentleman when his room's
so far away from mine?
    *Isabel.* There is a passage between the two.
Don't look so alarmed.
    *Doña Angela.*        It's not because
I wish to see him, but simply
out of curiosity. . . . Tell me,
how can this be? I heard you well,
but don't believe a word you say.

    *Isabel.* Did you know your brother's had
a paneling of mirrors made
to hide the inner guest room door?
    *Doña Angela.* Oh, I think I understand you now.
What you are saying is that
we can bore a hole behind the door
and manage then to see
our guest through it.
    *Isabel.*              I think
we can manage much more than that.
    *Doña Angela.* Tell me.
    *Isabel.*                 Well, as I say, your brother
has built a movable panel
to shut off and conceal the door
leading this way to the garden.
The panel is movable so that
it may be easily removed,
and the door, later be replaced.
And though made of glass mirrors,
it may now be moved at will.
I discovered this myself
in cleaning up the guest room.
I had a ladder propped against it
when the paneling gave way.
Before I knew it, ladder,
paneling, and I, all at once,
went tumbling to the floor.
When I replaced the frame,
I left it hanging somewhat ajar,
so that now anyone who'd like to,
madam, can go in and out.
    *Doña Angela.* Doing that would be quite rash,
though we might discuss it.
Suppose then, Isabel, I'd some idea
I wished to get into that room.
I unhinge the panel from this side.
Now, could one also do the same if
one were standing on the other side?
    *Isabel.* Why, yes—exactly! But just
to make quite sure no one else
can move it, we must fit two nails
in place, which only we
would know about, for prying loose.
    *Doña Angela.* Now tell the servant when he comes
to light the candles and prepares

the bedroom for our guest,
to come back here and let you know
if the gentleman has left the house.
I'm sure his wound was slight
and won't keep him in bed.

    *Isabel.* Gracious, madam, do you really
mean to go inside?

    *Doña Angela.*    I have
the foolish notion that
I must discover if this man
is indeed the one who saved my life.
For if he spilled his blood on my behalf,
as his wound would testify,
I shall do everything I can
to show my gratitude—provided
I may do so without the fear
of being apprehended.
Come, Isabel, I must inspect
the panel; and if I can really
get into his room without
his knowing I am there at all,
I shall repay him for his kindness.

    *Isabel.* Indeed, that would be a tale to tell.
But what if he should tell it?

    *Doña Angela.* That he will not do, Isabel.
He has proved himself a gentleman,
a man whose courage is only equaled
by his sense of honor
and discretion. From the very first,
his noble qualities touched my heart.
Bold and chivalrous, gallant, prudent—
why, I do not for a moment doubt
that a man so liberally endowed,
could possibly expose me.
So many fine qualities
would never have been wasted
on a man who babbles all he knows.

                      *[Exeunt*

Don Manuel's *apartment; a movable glass panel hooked
   in place is visible; also a brazier, and so forth.*

*Enter* Don Juan, Don Manuel, *and a servant with lit
   candles;* Don Luis *and another servant follow.*

    *Don Juan.* You must lie down, I tell you.

    *Don Manuel.* Ah, Don Juan, it's nothing but a scratch,
like the memory of a lady's
ribbon dropped by chance and forgotten
long ago.
    *Don Juan.* Thank goodness it's no worse
than that. I could never
forgive myself had I gained
the pleasure of your company
at the cost of any injury
to you, particularly since
it was my brother who wounded you,
however innocently.
    *Don Manuel.* No, he's a gentleman. I envy him
his pluck and swordsmanship,
and could wish for nothing better
than to be his most devoted friend.

*Enter* DON LUIS *and a servant who is carrying his belt*
*and scabbard with the sword in it.*

    *Don Luis.* I am your humble servant, sir,
one who still grieves the injury
he has caused you; do let me
repair it now. You must take this
from me; I can no longer bear
this instrument which wounded you.
It cannot please me nor be
of further service to me, and so
I must discharge it as a master
would some tiresome unruly servant.
Therefore I place this miscreant sword
here at your feet to beg forgiveness
for itself and for its master.
Take it, and if your cause requires
vengeance, turn it on its master.
    *Don Manuel.* As once your valor, **now**
your courtesy has conquered me.
I accept your sword and will wear it
always at my side where it will
teach me how to be courageous.
My life henceforth will be immune
to danger, for I am confident
your noble gift contains the power
to repel it, as I myself
have recent cause to know.

*Don Juan.* Since Don Luis has shown me
how to prize a guest, I shall feel
remiss until you have received
some further gift from me.
    *Don Manuel.* How will I ever repay
such favors when you rival
one another in showering me
with kindness?

        *Enter* COSME, *burdened with baggage.*

    *Cosme.*       May an army
of devils straight out of hell
sweep me up like a squadron
of fiery dragons on high
and tear me to pieces meanwhile,
as the wrath of God, for good
and sufficient reasons, declares
they must do till all eternity,
if I wouldn't rather live
ungalled in Galicia,
or even in Asturias, than here
at Court in the capital.
    *Don Manuel.* Now, check yourself . . .
    *Cosme.*              Let this baggage
check itself.
    *Don Juan.* What do you mean?
    *Cosme.* I mean what I say. Any man
who makes up to his enemy
is nothing but a villain.
    *Don Luis.* Hold on now. What enemy?
    *Cosme.* The fountain, of course. The water
in that wretched fountain.
    *Don Manuel.* Is that enough to throw you off?
    *Cosme.* There I was, stumbling along the street
under that load of baggage,
when suddenly I tripped against
the foot of a fountain and fell,
pell-mell, hook, line, and sinker,
as they say, straight into
the muddy drain. Now the stuff's not
fit to bring into a decent house.
    *Don Manuel.* All right, then—off with you.
You're drunk!
    *Cosme.*      If I were really drunk,

I wouldn't half mind being dunked
in water. Once I read a book
about a thousand flowing fountains,
and the water had the power to change
itself into every sort of shape
and form. So I wouldn't be surprised
if the water I was soaked in
had suddenly been changed to wine.
    *Don Manuel.* Once he opens up his mouth,
there's no stopping him.
    *Don Juan.*            The fellow's
humor is oddly fluent.
    *Don Luis.* There's only one thing I want to know.
If you can read, as your reference
to that fountain book would indicate,
how is it you pestered me to read
that letter? And why so silent now?
    *Cosme.* Because I can read books, not letters.
    *Don Luis.* A smooth reply, indeed.
    *Don Manuel.* Gentlemen, please, pay no attention
to him. As you'll discover,
he is simply a buffoon.
    *Cosme.* I'm proud to say my jests are legion,
and you're welcome to them, gentlemen.
    *Don Manuel.* I must pay a visit
this afternoon, while there's still time.
    *Don Juan.* I shall be expecting you at supper.
    *Don Manuel.* Cosme, unpack the bags
and lay out my clothing,
but make sure you clean them first.
    *Don Juan.* Here's the key to your rooms,
if you wish to lock the door.
I've a master key myself,
which I sometimes use when I return
home late. There are no other keys,
however, and no other door
to get in by. [*Aside.*] Now that's clear.
—If you leave yours in the lock,
the servants will come in daily
and attend to your apartment.
                       [*Exeunt omnes, except* COSME
    *Cosme.* First things first—so now for a look at
my own private little stock.

It's time we got together, you
and I, to reckon up how much
we pilfered on the road.
At the inns they don't look after
every little item the way
they do at home, where one is always
pinching pennies like a drudge.
There's more elbow room at those inns,
where a chap can really turn his hand
to some advantage—not just standing
there akimbo, but busy working
in his neighbor's pocket.

[*He opens a traveling bag and takes out a purse.*]

There you are, my dear, my precious joy:
you've come into your own!
You started out this morning
thin as any untried maiden;
now you swell and bulge like a wench
that's nine months gone. Should I
count the money? No, that would be
a waste of time; after all, it's not
as though I'd just sold my master's
flock of sheep and had to figure out
the sum, down to the last
wretched little penny.
Whatever it comes to, that's it.
So. Here's my master's traveling bag.
I ought to open it at once
and lay out all his clothes. Why? Because
that's just what he ordered me to do.
But will I do it simply because
he wants it done at once? No.
There's no reason why a master's word
should interfere with what his servant
actually does. Now then,
I've every reason in the world
to go out and find some nice
worshipful little shrine
where I can get a drop or two
to slake this awful thirsty soul
of mine. How'd you like that, Cosme?
Ah, I'd love it! Well then, Cosme,
hurry along; pleasure

before business, you know—
especially where the first's your own
and the other is your master's.

[*Exit*

DOÑA ANGELA *and* ISABEL *enter by unhinging
the glass panel.*

*Isabel.* This is the room; you see, it's empty.
As Rodrigo said, the gentleman's
gone out with your brothers.
    *Doña Angela.* I never would have dared come here
otherwise.
    *Isabel.* Do you agree there's
no difficulty getting in?
    *Doña Angela.* Yes, Isabel. I was so wrong
to doubt it. Why, there's nothing to it.
The panel moves so easily,
we can go in and out this way
without the slightest fear
of being seen by anyone.
    *Isabel.* Now tell me why we've come here.
    *Doña Angela.* Why, only to go back again.
When two women get together
and decide upon some mischief,
the thing's as good as done
once they've talked it over.
Since you proposed this to me
and I've come, there seems no reason
why we should come again—
except that if he really is
the gallant gentleman who boldly
risked his life to save me,
I still think, as I have told you,
I owe him something for his kindness.
    *Isabel.* See how nicely your brother
furnished this apartment. That's
the gallant's sword upon the desk.
    *Doña Angela.* Come here, Isabel. Isn't this
my writing box?
    *Isabel.*          It was your brother's
whim to put it there. He said
the gentleman needed such
materials for writing,
together with Lord knows how many

different books which I brought in.

*Doña Angela.* Two traveling bags are on the floor.

*Isabel.* And opened too, madam. Shall we look
and see what's inside of them?

*Doña Angela.* Yes, let's do that. I'm dying to see
the clothes and finery he's brought.

*Isabel.* A soldier and petitioner
wouldn't have much finery to bring.

> [*After discussing the articles in question, they
> fling them one after the other around the
> room.*]

*Doña Angela.* What's that?

*Isabel.* A bundle of papers.

*Doña Angela.* Are they love letters?

*Isabel.* No, madam.
I think they're legal briefs of some sort.
They're sewn together and quite heavy.

*Doña Angela.* They'd be light enough if some woman
had written them. Put them back.

*Isabel.* Here is some of his linen.

*Doña Angela.* Is it scented?

*Isabel.* It has the scent
of being clean.

*Doña Angela.* That's the sweetest
scent of all.

*Isabel.* It also has
three other qualities: it's white
and soft and very fine. But madam,
what do you make of all
the instruments inside this case?

*Doña Angela.* Let me see. Ah, this one seems to be
a tooth-puller; those are tweezers;
and that's a curling iron
for his forelocks, and another
for his mustache.

*Isabel.* Item:
hairbrush and comb. Gracious,
but this guest of ours has come
so well equipped he hasn't left
a shoelast out.

*Doña Angela.* How's that?

*Isabel.* Look, I'm holding it in my hand.

*Doña Angela.* Is there anything else?

*Isabel.* Oh yes,

madam: another bundle
of papers. These do look more like
love letters.
    *Doña Angela.* Give them to me.
Yes, this is a woman's handwriting.
But there's something more to it than that.
Wait, it's a portrait.
    *Isabel.*          What
fascinates you?
    *Doña Angela.* The sight
of beauty, which even
in a picture is intriguing.
    *Isabel.* I'd say you look disappointed
at having found it.
    *Doña Angela.*    How silly
you are! That's enough looking for now.
    *Isabel.* What will you do next?
    *Doña Angela.*          Write him a note.
Take the portrait with you.

                    *[She sits down to write.]*
    *Isabel.* I'll look into his servant's
traveling bag meanwhile. Ah,
here's money, and quite heavy, too.
Oh, but how mean of him!
It's full of wretched coppers,
plebeian money, and no royal
gold or silver. I know what.
I'll play a trick on him;
I'll take the money out
and fill the lackey's bag with charcoal.
*[To the audience.]* You'll say, "Where the devil
did that woman find the stuff?"
But you didn't notice, did you,
that the month's November and there's
a little brazier in this room?
        *[She empties the money out of the purse and
          fills it with charcoal.]*
    *Doña Angela.* There, the letter's finished.
Where do you think I ought to leave it
so that my brother, if he happens
to come in, won't see it?
    *Isabel.* There, by the pillow, under
the coverlet. He's sure to find it
when he goes to bed, and yet no one

will discover it till then.

*Doña Angela.* An excellent idea! Here,
put it in there now, and pick up
all these things.

*Isabel.*          Oh, but there's someone
at the door!

*Doña Angela.* Then leave them here,
just as they are, and let's go back.
Isabel, quick!

*Isabel.*          Open, sesame!

    [*Exeunt through the panel, which is left intact
      as before*


*Enter* COSME.

*Cosme.* Well, now I've served myself,
I won't niggle any more about
serving my master, gratis. What's this!
Who's been tossing our things around?
You'd think there'd been an auction here.
Hell's bells! They've made a flea market
of our stuff. Is anybody here?
Good Lord, nobody! Or at least
if anyone is here,
he's not in any mood to say so.
In that case, I'll say this much for him:
he must know I'm not the sort of man
who likes an idle babbler.
Well, be that as it may,
the truth is, here I stand
trembling like a leaf. But come
to think of it, why should I be?
As long as that baggage juggler's left
my purse intact, let him return and
juggle all the rest until he bursts.
Oh, but what's this I see? Good God!

    [*Examining the purse.*]

He's turned my money into charcoal!
Goblin, ghost, or sprite, whatever
you are or happen to be,
you can do what you like
with this money you've left,
but what in the world can you want
with that money I filched?

*Enter* DON MANUEL, DON JUAN, DON LUIS.

*Don Juan.* What are you shouting about?

*Don Luis.* What's the matter?

*Don Manuel.*                    What's happened to you?
Speak.

*Cosme.* Oh, this is a fine little game
you play! But sir, if you must
keep a sprite in your house,
why invite us to share its quarters?
I was only gone for a moment,
but when I returned, look what I found:
all our clothing scattered about,
as though it had been up for auction.

*Don Juan.* Is anything missing?

*Cosme.*                    No, only
the money I had in this purse
of mine was turned into charcoal.

*Don Luis.* I see what you're driving at now.

*Don Manuel.* What sort of stupid joke is this?
How gross and how ridiculous!

*Don Juan.* How lame and how impertinent!

*Cosme.* By God, I tell you it's no joke!

*Don Manuel.* Silence, I say! This is
just like you—always the same.

*Cosme.* Very well, sir, but one of the ways
I'm the same is that I don't take leave
of my senses all of a sudden.

*Don Juan.* I bid you good night, Don Manuel,
and trust my ghostly lodger
will not disturb your sleep.
But do inform your servant
that he must improve his wit.

[*Exit*

*Don Luis.* It is fortunate you are
valiant, sir, since everywhere you go
you are forced to draw your sword
to settle every quarrel
this fool must get you into.

[*Exit*

*Don Manuel.* Do you see what they take me for
because of you? Well, I must be
an idiot to tolerate it!
It never fails—wherever we are,

your behavior exposes me
to ridicule like this.

    *Cosme.* But we're alone, sir. How can you
suppose I still want to pull your leg?
Besides, there wouldn't be much fun
in tripping up one's lord and master
when no one's there to laugh at it.
The devil take me if I lied
in saying someone, whoever
it was, came in when I went out,
and played this trick on us.

    *Don Manuel.* Don't think you'll get out of it
by repeating that foolish tale.
Come, pick up all this stuff you dropped,
and then prepare for bed.

    *Cosme.*               Sir,
sell me for a galley slave if . . .

    *Don Manuel.* Silence! You've said enough.
Another word and I'll break your head!

                        *[He goes into the alcove.]*

    *Cosme.* If you did, no one would be
sorrier than I. Well, well,
so it's back you go again,
one by one, into the bags.
God, how I wish these toggeries
had sense enough to answer
to a bugle call; then they'd all
fall in at once.

          *[Don Manuel returns with a sheet of paper.]*

    *Don Manuel.* Bring a light, Cosme.

    *Cosme.* What's up, sir? Have you stumbled
on anyone in there?

    *Don Manuel.*      I found
this sealed letter, Cosme,
when I was opening the bed.
It was lying by my pillow,
underneath the coverlet.
But stranger still is this inscription
on the envelope.

    *Cosme.*        And who's it to?

    *Don Manuel.* To me, but put so oddly.

    *Cosme.* What does it say?

    *Don Manuel.*         I don't know what
to make of it. *[He reads.]* "Do not touch me,

anyone; I am meant
for Don Manuel alone."
     *Cosme.* God help you, sir, now that
you must believe me! Stop,
don't open it until
you have it exorcised!
     *Don Manuel.* It wasn't fear that stopped me
but surprise. Two different things, Cosme.

                              [*He reads.*]
     "Your well-being is a matter of some concern to me,
who count myself responsible for putting it in jeopardy.
With gratitude and regret, I beg you to advise me if
you are well or not, and how I best may serve you. To
inform me further of such matters, leave your reply exactly
in the place where you found this letter. Remember: secrecy is all-important, for on the day you breathe a word
of this to either of your friends, my life and honor immediately are forfeit."

     *Cosme.* Isn't that astonishing?
     *Don Manuel.*                    What's
astonishing?
     *Cosme.*    Aren't you surprised?
     *Don Manuel.* On the contrary: this letter
simply reaffirms something
I'd already suspected.
     *Cosme.* How's that?
     *Don Manuel.*         It's quite clear, Cosme,
that the veiled lady whom we found
so blindly fearful in her flight
from Don Luis must be his mistress,
for since he is a bachelor,
I suppose she cannot be his wife.
If that's the case, all surprises
end at once, for then the lady
would naturally have free access
to her lover's house.
     *Cosme.*          So far, so good;
that's neatly reasoned out,
but my fears go much further.
Suppose she is his mistress
(and incidentally, sir,
congratulations, since now
she smiles at you), how could she
possibly have known beforehand

what was to happen on the street
so that she'd have the letter written
and waiting for you here?

*Don Manuel.* She could have had it written later,
after seeing me, then had
her servant bring it here.

*Cosme.* Yes, the servant might have brought it,
but how would he have got in here
if nobody has stepped inside
this room all the while that I've been here?

*Don Manuel.* There was time enough for doing that
before we came.

*Cosme.*          Very well.
Writing the letter's only one thing,
but how do you account for
the scattering around of all
our traveling bags and clothes?

*Don Manuel.* Go see if the windows are closed.

*Cosme.* Barred and bolted, sir.

*Don Manuel.*                    It's puzzling.
Now I'm flooded with new suspicions.

*Cosme.* About what?

*Don Manuel.*          I can't say exactly.

*Cosme.* Well, what do you intend to do?

*Don Manuel.* Oh, I shall answer her, of course,
but in such a manner that
there'll be no question of
her having pierced my armor
with apprehension or surprise.
For as long as we engage
in correspondence, I am sure
some occasion will arise
when we discover who the person
is who brings and takes the letters.

*Cosme.* And we're not to breathe a word of this
to either of our hosts?

*Don Manuel.*          Of course not.
How could I possibly betray
the woman who confides in me?

*Cosme.* Then you'd rather betray the man
you think's her lover?

*Don Manuel.*          No indeed;
all I know is this: I can
proceed honorably

only if I do not betray her.

*Cosme.* No, sir; there's more to this
than you believe. I'm convinced of that
in spite of everything you say.

*Don Manuel.* Exactly what convinces you?

*Cosme.* You can see for yourself:
letters and things going in and out
of this place, and still, you,
with all your brains, cannot explain
how such things happen. What
would you believe?

*Don Manuel.*          Simply
that someone with wit and skill
has found an entrance and an exit
to this room, and some way
of opening and concealing it,
which we as yet have not discovered.
And I'd rather lose all my brains
at once, Cosme, than believe
some supernatural thing
has had a hand in this.

*Cosme.* Did you ever hear of sprites?

*Don Manuel.* No one's ever seen them.

*Cosme.* Household spirits?

*Don Manuel.*          Pure fantasy.

*Cosme.* Witches?

*Don Manuel.*     Even more so.

*Cosme.* Sorceresses?

*Don Manuel.*          Utter nonsense.

*Cosme.* Succubuses?

*Don Manuel.*     No.

*Cosme.*          Enchantresses?

*Don Manuel.* Hardly.

*Cosme.*          Magicians?

*Don Manuel.*          Tomfoolery.

*Cosme.* Necromancers?

*Don Manuel.*     Preposterous.

*Cosme.* Energumens?

*Don Manuel.*     You're mad!

*Cosme.* Aha! Here's where I get you:
what about devils?

*Don Manuel.*     They can't write
letters without a notary.

*Cosme.* Are there souls in Purgatory?

*Don Manuel.* Who write me love letters, you mean?
How utterly stupid can you be?
Go away, you're tiresome.
*Cosme.* All right, but what will you do?
*Don Manuel.* Stay up day and night and never
blink an eye until I solve
this mystery, in spite of every
ghost and goblin in the universe.
*Cosme.* As for me, I still maintain
some sort of devil's at the bottom
of it all; and he can fetch
and carry letters, among
other things, as quick as
anyone would puff tobacco smoke.

## ACT TWO

Doña Angela's *apartment*

*Enter* Doña Angela, Doña Beatriz, *and* Isabel.

Doña Beatriz. What a remarkable story!
*Doña Angela.* Remarkable? Just wait
until you hear the end of it.
Now, where were we?
*Doña Beatriz.*　　　You were saying
you entered his apartment
through the panel, and that
this was more easily accomplished
than you were ready to believe;
then you left a letter for him,
and the next day found his answer there.
*Doña Angela.* Yes, and I must also tell you
I've never read anything so elegant
or so gallantly expressed.
His style is gay and high-flown, both,
much as the knights of old would write
on similar occasions.
Here's the letter, Beatriz;
tell me if you do not find it
absolutely charming.

[*She reads.*]
"Beauteous Damozel: Whoever thou art, in thy com-

passion for this poor ardent knight, whose afflicted heart
thou wouldst mercifully assuage, I beg of thee, reveal to
me where I may go to seek that arrant knave, that pagan
miscreant, who to his infamy holds thee now in thrall, so
that I, now recovered from my recent wounds, may sally
forth beneath the standard of thine honor once again, and
thus engage him to the death in extraordinary combat;
for, depend upon it, such death were sweeter far than life
to thy devoted champion. May the giver of all light preserve thee, and not forsake me. —The Knight of the
Phantom Lady."

*Doña Beatriz.* Why, bless me, the writing's excellent,
and the words so exactly fitting
to the spirit of the adventure.
*Doña Angela.* I really expected his letter
would be full of the gravest doubts and
consternation, but since I find him
so receptive I shall continue
the exchange in the same fashion.
And so, in my reply to him,
I'll say . . .
*Doña Beatriz.* Wait, say nothing more;
here comes Don Juan, your brother.
*Doña Angela.* Now he'll come in, the model lover,
all truth and constancy,
so joyous to see you, Beatriz,
and speak with you in his own house.
*Doña Beatriz.* Well, to tell you the truth,
I shan't take it amiss.

*Enter* DON JUAN.

*Don Juan.* As the common proverb has it,
there is nothing quite so ill
but that some good must come of it.
I see this now confirmed in that
all my happiness proceeds
from your misfortunes. I refer,
my lovely Beatriz,
to that unhappy difference
between your father and yourself
which brought you, sad and vexed,
to find refuge in our house.
Though I should be sorry

to discover happiness
in the very circumstance
which pains you, the pleasure
of your present company
has silenced all compunctions.
The effects of love, you see,
are so subtly various
that the reason for your sorrow
becomes the substance of my joy,
and in this is like the asp
whose bite discharges both the venom
and the antidote to cure it.
In brief, you are most welcome,
and though our hospitality
leave something wanting, there is
this compensation: that you are
Beatriz, the happy sunlight,
who have come here to dwell
with Angela, our angel.

    *Doña Beatriz.* Your greetings and condolences
are so graciously commingled,
I do not know what I can say.
It's true I've come because my father
is displeased with me. But you
must take the blame for that.
When he learned I'd spoken
at my balcony last night
to some gentleman (not knowing
the gentleman was you) he promptly
sent me here, while he cools his rage,
to stay with my cousin,
in whose virtue my father has
the highest confidence.
This much I'll tell you, but only this:
I can value my misfortunes too.
For like you I've come to see that
love's effects are subtly various,
and in this are like the sun
whose bounteous rays wither up
one flower at the very moment
they create another. So now
as with a single ray
love strikes against my heart,
it both withers up a sorrow

and gives birth to that joy
I find in being welcomed here.
In this your house is like
the jeweled firmament,
affording ample refuge
to a jealous sun as well
as to a certain angel.
 *Doña Angela.* It seems a profitable day
for lovers, and even I receive
a windfall merely by standing
here between the gusts of
overwhelming compliments.
 *Don Juan.* Sister, do you know what I think?
To punish me for the inconvenience
which my guest has caused you,
you have retaliated
by keeping this lady here
as a guest of yours.
 *Doña Angela.*  Quite right;
I've done it simply to put you to
the trouble of entertaining her.
 *Don Juan.* I welcome such happy punishment.
           *[He turns to leave.]*
 *Doña Beatriz.* What's this, Don Juan? Where are you
   going?
 *Don Juan.* Only to arrange for your further
comfort here. Beatriz, you know
that nothing else would make me leave you.
 *Doña Angela.* Let him go.
 *Don Juan.*      Well, till later.
               *[Exit*

 *Doña Angela.* Yes, the good Lord only knows
what troubles Don Juan's guest has caused me.
Troubles enough to last me
all my life, but no less so, I see,
thank God, than those Don Juan
now suffers because of you;
so that guest for guest I'd say
the two of us are even.
 *Doña Beatriz.* The only reason I can stand
for your sending him away
is that I'm curious
to know how your story ends.
 *Doña Angela.* Well then, I won't tax your patience.

Letters have been flying thick and fast
between us ever since, and his,
at least, so admirably
ingenious, half jesting
and half serious, I've never
seen the likes of them before.

*Doña Beatriz.* And what do you suppose
he thinks of you?

*Doña Angela.*    That I am most
certainly Don Luis' mistress,
because I've been in hiding
and because, as he imagines,
I have another key
to his apartment.

*Doña Beatriz.*    There is
only one thing puzzling me.

*Doña Angela.* And what is that?

*Doña Beatriz.*                          Knowing that
someone must be bringing
all those letters back and forth,
how is it he has not found you out—
indeed, not yet caught you in the act?

*Doña Angela.* It's really very simple.
I have a servant posted
near his door whose job it is
to tell us when the coast is clear.
Then Isabel can get into
his rooms, knowing no one's in them.
Even now, my dear, the servant
has been waiting out there all day long
to give us word when everything
is safe, but we've heard nothing yet.
And that reminds me, Isabel,
be sure you get the basket to him
when you have the chance to do it.

*Doña Beatriz.* Another question: how can you think
the man so clever when he hasn't
even shown the simple wit to
find out where your secret panel is?

*Doña Angela.* Have you ever heard the story
of Columbus and the egg?
Well, the wisest men alive
had exhausted all their wits
endeavoring to set the egg

upright on a jasper table when
Columbus came along, gave the egg
a simple tap, and solved the problem
once for all. The greatest
difficulties solve themselves
once you know the simple answer.

    *Doña Beatriz.* Another question, if you please.
    *Doña Angela.* Oh, do ask it.
    *Doña Beatriz.*                What do you suppose
you'll gain by all this foolish nonsense?
    *Doña Angela.* I don't know. I might say, of course,
to show our guest my gratitude
or while away the weary hours
I am doomed to spend in solitude,
but I confess there's more to it
than that. At first, I was prompted
by my silly curiosity,
but now that has turned to jealousy.
There's a portrait of a woman
in his room I yearn to see again.
And I'm determined to go in
and take it, just as soon as
I can do so. Indeed,
I don't know how to put it,
but I am equally determined
I must see and speak to him
in person.
    *Doña Beatriz.* And tell him who you are?
    *Doña Angela.* Oh no, Heaven forbid! But even
if I did, I would not think him
capable of revealing it
or indulging in such treachery
where his host and friend's concerned.
I'm sure the very thought
that I may be the mistress
of Don Luis has already
made him fearful and uneasy,
and explains the reason why
he writes me in so guarded
and overwrought a manner.
But I would never be so crude
as to tell him who I am.
    *Doña Beatriz.*           Well then,
how is he to meet you face to face?

*Doña Angela.* Now listen, this will be the most
remarkable device of all:
I shall walk straight into his room,
with no danger of his seeing me;
then he'll walk into mine,
but not know where he is.

*Isabel.* According to the script, insert
the other brother's name at this point
in the margin, for here comes
Don Luis.

*Doña Angela.* You'll hear all
about this later on.

*Doña Beatriz.* How differently the stars
influence our characters! For in
two men of equal gifts and merits
exist such inequalities of
disposition that what pleases us
in one annoys us in the other.
Come now, Angela, I want
no words with Don Luis.

*[They turn to leave.]*

*Enter* DON LUIS.

*Don Luis.* Why leave so suddenly?

*Doña Beatriz.* Simply because you have appeared.

*Don Luis.* Then when I enter you withdraw
the loveliest, pure light from which
the sun itself has learned to shine.
Am I then the lowering night?
If so, let your loveliness forgive
my boldness and discourtesy
for detaining you a while,
since I cannot ask your person
to indulge a presence
which it would refuse. Knowing
your severity, I must
unhappily forego the impulse
to ascribe any note of favor
to the merest courtesy.
I also know, of course, how little
my wildest love is capable
of rousing from your scorn
a single spark of hope.
Yet on that account precisely,

my love for you increases
as if it would retaliate
against your rigorous disdain.
The more you torment me,
the more I glory in my state;
the more you would abhor me,
the more my passion for you grows.
Say that you complain of this,
say that the same intensity
of passion in us (my love, your hate)
merely drives us to extremes.
Very well, then: teach me how to hate,
or I shall teach you how to love.
Let me learn severity from you,
unless you'd have me teach you kindness.
Let me learn all you know of harshness;
I'll teach you simple tenderness;
your contempt or my affection,
your neglect or my constancy.
And yet, however much you sought
to steep us both in profane
cruelty, the deity of love,
whom I have glorified,
still would elevate us, you and I,
in token of my faithfulness.

    *Doña Beatriz.* You manage to complain
so eloquently, I feel
I should requite you for your pains.
But I cannot bring myself
to do so, simply because
it happens to be you.

    *Don Luis.* I warn you, if you persist
in treating me so coldly,
I too know something of the language
of disdain.

    *Doña Beatriz.* Very well, then: use it.
Perhaps your eloquent disdain
will cure your ill-bred disposition.

          [Don Luis *stops her as she is about to leave.*]

    *Don Luis.* Listen to me: if this is your
revenge, you must suffer it with me.

    *Doña Beatriz.* I've no intention to. Good Heavens,
Cousin, can't you stop him?

             [*Exit*

*Doña Angela.* What little self-respect you have
to ask for such humiliation!

*Don Luis.* Oh, Sister! What am I to do?

*Doña Angela.* Forget your foolish passion.
To love someone who hates you
is an ordeal worse than death.

*[Exit with* ISABEL

*Don Luis [addressing the absent* DOÑA ANGELA]. Forget
her when my heart is choked
with rage? Impossible! Who could?
First let her be kind to me,
then I'll forget her, gladly.
But after she insults me? Never!
The wisest man alive, no less
than I, would tell you this:
kindness is easily forgotten,
since it never sticks or sinks
so deeply as an insult.


*Enter* RODRIGO.


*Rodrigo.* Where have you been?

*Don Luis.*                          I don't know.

*Rodrigo.* You seem so sad; can you tell me why?

*Don Luis.* I was speaking with Doña Beatriz.

*Rodrigo.* Say no more. Her answer's
written on your face. But where was that?
I haven't seen her here at all.

*Don Luis.* The vixen's come here as my sister's
guest for a few days—as if
one guest already were not enough
to drive me mad. My family
is purposely conspiring
against me. They invite
a different person every day,
just to torment me: first
Don Manuel, and now Beatriz.
Heaven must have brought
all my suspicions home to roost;
I cannot understand it
otherwise.

*Rodrigo.* Look, here comes
Don Manuel. He'll hear you.

*Enter* DON MANUEL.

*Don Manuel* [*aside*]. Why should such strange things happen
           happen
only to me? Good Lord,
how can I proceed, undetected,
to discover if this woman
really is the mistress of
Don Luis, or what secret
strategy she uses
to bring off her intrigue?
    *Don Luis.* Well, Don Manuel.
    *Don Manuel.*                 Ah, Don Luis.
    *Don Luis.* And where have you been, sir?
    *Don Manuel.* At the Palace.
    *Don Luis.*                 Pardon me;
it was gross of me to ask
a man of your affairs
where he goes and where he comes from.
It should be obvious
all paths lead to Court as surely
as all rays do to Heaven.
    *Don Manuel.* If my visits were restricted to
the Palace I'd feel much easier.
But the nature of my business
now requires further action.
I find His Majesty removed
his Court this afternoon
to the Escorial, which means
I must make haste to follow him
there tonight with my dispatches.
And this matter cannot be delayed.
    *Don Luis.* If I may be of service, sir,
in whatever way at all, you need
only say the word, you know.
    *Don Manuel.* I am much obliged to you.
    *Don Luis.* It is no mere courtesy,
I assure you.
    *Don Manuel.* I am certain
you have my interests at heart.
    *Don Luis* [*aside*]. Yes, indeed—and the sooner I am
rid of you the better.
    *Don Manuel.* But it would be unfair of me
to infringe upon the time

of so fine a gallant as yourself.
Surely you must now be engaged
in much pleasanter pursuits
than this tedious affair
you offer to support me in.
    *Don Luis.* Had you heard me speaking with
Rodrigo when you came in,
you would never think so.
    *Don Manuel.*           Do you mean
I am mistaken?
    *Don Luis.*    Yes, indeed;
though I am presently involved
with a lovely lady, it is
only in bitterness,
not gratitude, for she is
utterly determined to treat me
with contempt.
    *Don Manuel.* I did not imagine
you could think yourself so helpless.
    *Don Luis.* I am doomed to love a lady
as wholly cruel as she is
beautiful.
    *Don Manuel.* You are joking, surely.
    *Don Luis.* I wish to God I were.
But my unhappy fate is such
that this beauty flies from me
as the glorious daylight flies
the fall of night, and her scorching rays
consume me. Would you care to know
how miserable a man can be?
Lately, when I followed her,
torn by love and jealousy,
she bade another person intervene
to stop me. Consider
how completely she detests me,
for where others use a go-between
to achieve fonder proximity,
she uses one to flee from me.
                [*Exeunt* Don Luis *and* Rodrigo
    *Don Manuel.* What further evidence do I need?
A woman who fled the sight of him
and had to have another person
stop him! This refers to me and her.
Well, at least I've cleared up one doubt.

If it's true she is that lady,
then she cannot be his fiancée:
he would not have her living
in his house if she detested him.
But here's an even crueler doubt:
if she is not his mistress
and does not live here in the house,
how can she correspond with me?
Ah, so one mystery ends
only to give way to another.
What am I to do or think?
I am more confused than ever. God
help me, for there's a woman in it!

*Enter* COSME.

 *Cosme.* What's become of the phantom, sir?
Perhaps you've seen him hereabouts
again? Please say no, sir,
and I'll be overjoyed.
 *Don Manuel.*   Lower
your voice.
 *Cosme.* Because I've lots of work
to do in our rooms, but can't go in.
 *Don Manuel.* Well, what's the matter?
 *Cosme.*       I'm frightened.
 *Don Manuel.* Is it becoming in a man
to be afraid?
 *Cosme.*  No indeed, sir;
it's not at all becoming!
But here's a man afraid because
it's warranted.
 *Don Manuel.* No more nonsense now.
Go and fetch a light. I've several
things to write and papers to arrange
before we leave Madrid tonight.
 *Cosme.* Yes, I'm sure, and the reason why
you change the subject is that
you're every bit as scared of spooks
as I am.
 *Don Manuel.* I've told you once before
I do not share your interest
in that subject, and when you speak
of it my mind wanders
to more important matters.

And now, of course, I'm wasting
precious time. Light the candle while
I go to say good-by to Don Juan.

[*Exit*

   *Cosme.* Yes, I'll do that, by all means;
it's time to light a candle
for that phantom; he'd be annoyed
if we left him in the dark.
There ought to be one here.
I'll light it in that lamp there
where the wick is dying down.
Now, let's be very cautious!
Well, here goes, I'm on my way—
and my heart pounding like a drum.

[*Exit*


### DON MANUEL'*s apartment*

*Enter* ISABEL *through the panel, carrying a basket.*

   *Isabel.* They've gone out, just as the servant
said they have. Now to put
this basket full of linen
in the right place. Oh, gracious me!
It's so ghastly dark here at night,
I'm afraid of my own footsteps.
Good God, I'm all atremble!
I must be the first phantom
to put its trust in God.
Oh, now I can't find the panel.
How can that be? In all this darkness
and confusion, I've lost my sense
of where things are. I don't know where
I'm standing or even where
the table is. Heavens,
what will I do now? If I can't
get out and they find me here,
the jig is up and everything
is ruined. I'm shaking like a leaf!
Worse yet, I think there's someone
at the door. He's opening it.
He's carrying a candle.
It's all over now, I'm done for!
There's nowhere I can hide
and no way to get out.

*Enter* COSME *with a light.*

*Cosme.* Oh, phantom, please sir: I hope you are
a well-bred phantom who perhaps
are used to such devotions;
I humbly beg of you, count me out
of all those tricks you'd like to play.
Here are four good reasons why:
First, because I know why myself;

> [*As he advances,* ISABEL *follows close behind him
> so that he won't see her.*]

second, you know why yourself;
third, as they say, "a word
to the wise . . ."; and fourth, because
I know these old verses:

> *Oh Phantom Lady, Phantom Lady,*
>    *Have pity on me please,*
> *I'm just a poor lad, all alone,*
>    *And quaking in the knees.*

*Isabel* [*aside*]. Now, thanks to the light,
I can make out where I am again,
and he hasn't noticed me as yet.
If I could only manage
to blow out the candle,
I'd surely get out of here
while he is trying to relight it.
He may hear me, but won't see me,
and that's the lesser of two evils.
   *Cosme.* Fear plucks me like an instrument!
   *Isabel* [*aside*]. And here's the tune it plays.
> [*She strikes him and blows out the light.*]
   *Cosme.* Oh, my God, I've been killed!
Call a priest! Confession!
   *Isabel.*              Now
I can escape.

*Enter* DON MANUEL.

   *Don Manuel.* What's going on here?
Cosme! What are you doing
in the dark?
   *Cosme.*    The phantom's
snuffed us out—the candle and me both.
   *Don Manuel.* Fear puts such nonsense in your head.

*Cosme.* In my neck, you mean!
*Isabel.*                           Oh,
if I could only find the panel!
*Don Manuel.* Who's this here?

> [ISABEL *runs into* DON MANUEL, *who catches
> hold of the basket.*]

*Isabel.*                         Worse luck! Now
I must deal with the master.
*Don Manuel.* Bring the light, Cosme. I've got hold
of him, whoever it is.
*Cosme.* Well, don't let go.
*Don Manuel.*                I won't.
Fetch that candle now.
*Cosme.*                    Hold him tight.

> [*Exit*

*Isabel* [*aside*]. He's got hold of the basket.
I'll leave it in his hands.
Now there's the panel. Good-by.

> [*Exit, leaving him with the basket*

*Don Manuel.* Whoever you are, you'd better
be still until the light's brought in.
If not, by God, I'll run you through
with this sword! But I'm only grabbing
the air now, and nothing alive
but this linen and something
very light. What can it be?
Good God, I'm at a total loss.

*Enter* COSME *with a candle.*

*Cosme.* Now we'll see the spook
by candlelight. But what's become
of him? I thought you'd caught him.
What happened, sir?
*Don Manuel.*      What can I tell you?
He left me with this basket and fled.
*Cosme.* Well, what have you to say to all this?
You yourself just told me
that you'd got hold of him,
and here he's vanished into thin air.
*Don Manuel.* All I can say is that the person
who makes it his business to get in
and out of this room was somehow
shut in here tonight, and to find
his way out, doused your light,

left me this basket, and escaped.

 *Cosme.* Which way?

 *Don Manuel.*     Through that door.

 *Cosme.* You'll drive me out of my mind!
Good God, I saw him myself,
in the twinkle of an eye,
when he nearly pounded me to death
and the candle was just going out.

 *Don Manuel.* Well, then, how did he look?

 *Cosme.* He looked like a huge friar,
and he had on an enormous cowl,
which is why I believe
he was a Capuchin ghost.

 *Don Manuel.* Fear can make you see anything!
Well, give me the candle
and we'll see what the good friar's
brought us. Pick up the basket.

 *Cosme.* Me? Touch baskets the devil's been at?

 *Don Manuel.* Come on, pick it up.

 *Cosme.*         Oh, sir,
my hands are all greasy
with tallow, and I'd soil
that nice taffeta covering.
Better leave it on the floor.

 *Don Manuel.* It's full of fresh linen
and a letter. Let's see
how discreet your friar can be.

            [*He reads.*]

 "During the short period you have been living in this
house, there has not been time enough to provide you
with much linen; as it is made up, it will be brought
to you. Concerning what you have said about Don Luis
and myself, your notion that I am his mistress is, I assure
you, not only untrue but can never ever be true. I shall tell
you more about this when I see you, which will be very
soon. Heaven protect you."

This is a good, baptized phantom.
It commends me to God.

 *Cosme.*       See, sir?
I told you it's a Capuchin.

 *Don Manuel.* It's very late. Pack the bags
and secure those papers in a pouch.
They contain all the reason

for our going. Meanwhile,
I'll write an answer to my phantom.
            [*He hands the papers to* COSME, *who puts them
                on a chair, and* DON MANUEL *starts writing.*]
    *Cosme.* I'll put them right here now,
so they'll be close at hand
and then I shan't forget them.
But still, sir, I'd like to pause
just long enough to ask you this:
Do you still believe that phantoms
don't exist?
    *Don Manuel.* What utter nonsense!
    *Cosme.* Nonsense, is it? When you yourself
have seen all the evidence,
how gifts are thrust into your hands
out of thin air, and still you're doubtful?
But perhaps it's just as well you are,
since you benefit by all
that happens while I who have no doubts
am being constantly deprived.
    *Don Manuel.* In what way?
    *Cosme.*                    I'll prove it, in this way:
when our clothes are scattered all about,
the sight can only make you laugh,
but I must pick them up and set them
right again, which takes some doing.
While letters suddenly appear for you
and your witty answer's carried back,
my money's stolen and my purse
is filled instead with clinkers.
You get sweetmeats brought to you
which like a monk you gobble up
while I, who cannot touch them, stand by,
grow thin, and suffer like a pimp.
Where you get fine collars, handkerchiefs,
and shirts, I only get the shivers
for listening and observing
what goes on about me.
If we happen to arrive here
almost at the same time,
you get a basket full
of nice soft linen, while I get
a monstrous whack on the back
of my head, enough to make me

cough my brains out. You, sir,
get all the pleasure and the profit;
I get all the punishment and pain.
It's just as if that spook
were treating you with silken gloves
and me with iron claws.
So the least that you can do
is to permit me to believe
what I believe; I get drained
and purified by suffering,
which is a state denied to those
like you, who refuse to see the things
that pass before their very eyes.
    *Don Manuel.* Pack the bags and come along;
I'll wait for you in Don Juan's
rooms.
    *Cosme.* But what's there left to pack?
The Court's in mourning; and all you need
to take along is your black cape.
    *Don Manuel.* Shut the door and lock it;
take the key. If someone wishes
to get in meanwhile, Don Juan
will have the other key.
—I'm perplexed at leaving now,
not knowing what's behind
these strange occurrences,
or, indeed, which matter
is more pressing. Well,
one involves my family honor
and estate, and the other
some passing divertissement.
They are really two extremes,
and obviously where honor
is concerned, it must precede
every other consideration.

                                  *[Exeunt*

#### DOÑA ANGELA's *apartment*

*Enter* DOÑA ANGELA, DOÑA BEATRIZ, *and* ISABEL.

    *Doña Angela.* And that's what happened to you?
    *Isabel.* Yes, I could have sworn the jig was up,
because if I'd been found there, madam,
that would have been the end

of everything, but as I've said, I
was lucky, escaping when I did.
    *Doña Angela.* How extraordinary!
    *Doña Beatriz.*                              And now
he's sure to be more puzzled
than ever, finding the basket
in his hand and no trace
of anyone anywhere!
    *Doña Angela.* And after all this, if I can
manage that interview with him
in the way I've indicated,
he'll surely go out of his mind.
    *Doña Beatriz.* At this rate, Angela, the sanest
man alive would be completely stumped.
Imagine his wanting to find you
and not knowing where, and then
meeting a beautiful woman
who's rich and elegant besides,
and not knowing who she is or where
she comes from (all of this
according to your little plan),
and finally, being led
blindfolded in and out of the room
so that he isn't sure where he is!
Oh, who could possibly stand it?
    *Doña Angela.* Everything's ready, and if you
had not been here, he'd have come
to see me for the first time
this very night.
    *Doña Beatriz.* Don't you trust me
to keep your pretty secret?
    *Doña Angela.* Oh, Cousin, I do; that's not
what I mean. It's simply that
your presence here keeps my brothers
in the house; they're so in love with you,
they burn with starry-eyed devotion,
and while they do, they're in my way
and I can't risk doing anything.

          *Enter* DON LUIS *behind the arras.*

    *Don Luis* [*aside*]. God, how can I hide my feelings?
How can I rein in my thoughts, drive back
my tongue, and bridle my emotions?
Although I have not done so yet,

I must at least begin to try to
check my passion and collect myself.
    *Doña Beatriz.* I shall tell you how indeed
you may arrange these matters
so that although I'm present I
shan't become unwanted company.
For I wouldn't want to go away
and miss what happens.
    *Doña Angela.*          Well then,
what do you suggest?
    *Don Luis* [*aside*].   What is it
they're whispering? It is as if
they had only one voice between them.
    *Doña Beatriz.* We'll pretend my father's sent for me
and while your brothers think I've left,
we'll manage things so that
I really stay behind here . . .
    *Don Luis* [*aside*]. Heavens, what is she plotting
against me now?
    *Doña Beatriz.* . . . so I can watch
what happens, secretly,
and meanwhile not be in your way.
    *Don Luis* [*aside*]. My unlucky star, what's this I hear?
    *Doña Beatriz.* You've no idea how much I'd like that!
    *Doña Angela.* But then what could we say
if they saw you here again?
    *Doña Beatriz.* Well, why should that surprise you?
Don't we have brains enough to think
of some other little stratagem?
    *Don Luis* [*aside*]. I'm sure you have. The more I hear
of this, the more I feel old griefs
and torments welling up within me.
    *Doña Beatriz.* And that is how, my dear,
unknown to anyone,
I shall secretly await the end
of your remarkable affair.
For when I'm out of sight
and everyone has gone to bed,
I am sure that he can safely slip
into your room from his,
and not give rise to any scandal.
    *Don Luis* [*aside*]. Ah, now I understand it all,
only too well. Coward that I am,
I'll die bravely yet. Though my brother

more happily deserves her,
I am consumed by jealousy.
So she desires some occasion
to delight him, and while she plans
to meet him secretly in here,
I grovel in humiliation.
To achieve their secret end
without arousing my suspicions,
those two enemies of mine
are plotting to deceive me.
Well, if this is what they wish,
by God, I'll see to it
their little tryst is broken up.
Let her hide then, no matter where;
I'll discover some excuse to search
the house, from room to room. Oh,
I'll do it thoroughly and boldly
till I find her. This passion
burning in my heart must break out.
I have no other choice; the last
resort of jealousy is to ruin
the happiness of others.
Saints alive, support me now!
Since I am torn apart by love,
I must die of jealousy.

[*Exit*

Doña Angela. Fine, then it's all arranged: tomorrow
we will say you've gone away.

*Enter* DON JUAN.

Don Juan. Sister! And my lovely Beatriz.
Doña Beatriz. We have missed you all this while.
Don Juan. Madam, while your words do so much
to magnify my fortune's star,
by contrast they appear to dim
the sunlight of your favor
toward my humble person;
and thus grown jealous of myself,
I distrust my happiness.
For it seems impossible my love
should merit so much of your concern,
and while I am engulfed in such
a tender trap (the object
both of envy and of love), I must

both pity and distrust myself.

*Doña Beatriz.* I would never think of questioning
so flattering a compliment,
Don Juan, except of someone
who has delayed his visit
and forgotten me. For of someone
of that sort I must believe that
he was elsewhere better entertained.
So it would seem more fitting
to distrust his dalliance there,
and pitiful to see him lose
the beauteous object which
delighted him. There is, you see,
a certain syllogism proving
how one might pity and distrust
himself at once.

*Don Juan.*        If it would not
offend us both, I could attempt
to satisfy you, Beatriz,
by saying that the person
who detained me was my guest,
Don Manuel, with whom
I had until this moment
been engaged before he left
Madrid tonight.

*Doña Angela.* Oh, good gracious.

*Don Juan.* Sister, why is that so startling?

*Doña Angela.* Good news may be as startling as bad.

*Don Juan.* Then I'm sorry if you take it so,
for there's more to it you will not like:
Don Manuel returns tomorrow.

*Doña Angela* [*aside*]. And so my dying hope revives.
—I was surprised only because
the source of so much turbulence
at home should disappear so quickly.

*Don Juan.* I cannot understand why
you found it troublesome at all.
Yet you and Don Luis appear
to be annoyed only, as it seems,
because the presence of our guest
gives me so much pleasure.

*Doña Angela.* I might easily say more to that
but shan't, and that's because
I wouldn't dream of interfering

in the game of love; as anyone
should know, I'd only be
a nuisance where three's a crowd,
for lovers' blandishments, like tricks
at cards, are more slyly interchanged
between a twosome pure and simple.
[*Aside to* ISABEL.] Come with me, Isabel.
I must carry off that portrait
tonight. While the coast is clear,
I can do that more easily.
Make sure you have the candle ready,
and we can go in unobserved.
I take it as an insult
that a gentleman who corresponds
with me should keep the portrait
of another woman.

[*Exeunt* DOÑA ANGELA *and* ISABEL

  *Doña Beatriz.* I doubt your protestations are as
pure and weighty as you make them seem.
  *Don Juan.* Then to prove to you I am sincere,
I'll weigh each one until they're clear.
May I proceed?
  *Doña Beatriz.* Why, yes indeed!
  *Don Juan.* Then listen to me carefully.

Fair Beatriz, I swear my faith's so true,
My love's so firm, my deep regard's so rare,
That if I tried to bury love's desire
I'd find, despite myself, I must love you.
  This then is my condition: if decree
Bade me forget you, I'd forget you clear—
That I might choose to love you, made more dear
In consequence of this than formerly.
  Who's bound to love his mistress only when
He can't forget her is not bound by love.
Deprived of will, he cannot love her then.
  But I who can't forget you, dear, see proof
Of love's proud victory betokened in
Consenting eyes, like twinkling stars above.

  *Doña Beatriz.*

If will is all you need to make your choice,
And eyes like fitful stars to give consent,
It seems to me your precepts both are spent

Upon uncertainties, nay, mere caprice.
Therefore, I must distrust your courtesies;
The impossible is what my faith must bend,
And if my will fell short of such intent,
Good grief! I'd view it with distinct surprise.

And as for that brief moment's lapse, aimed at
Forgetfulness so I might love you dearer,
I fear all fondness would evaporate.

And thus I find I cannot but deplore
Forgetfulness, for while I'd be engaged
In that, I wouldn't love you any more.

[*Exeunt*

A *street*

*Enter* COSME, *running, and* DON MANUEL, *chasing him.*

*Don Manuel.* Good God! If I didn't think . . .
*Cosme.* That's it, sir, do stop and think.
*Don Manuel.* . . . how degrading it would be
to strike you . . .
*Cosme.*            Consider
how faithfully I've served you
and that a good Christian's not to blame
if he's got a bad memory.
*Don Manuel.* Who'd have any patience with you,
tell me who, when you forget
the very thing that's most important,
which I clearly ordered you to bring.
*Cosme.* Yes, that's just why I forgot it—
because it *was* so important.
If it hadn't been, how could I
forget it? Hell's bells, it was
my taking such special pains
that made me put those papers
carefully aside. So it was
being thoughtful caused all the mischief.
Otherwise I would not have packed them
separately, and they'd have been here
now with all our other things.
*Don Manuel.* At least it's fortunate you thought
of them while we are still en route.
*Cosme.* I was worried there was something wrong,
but didn't know just what.
I thought it must be something foolish

till it dawned on me—like that!
And then I knew it had to do
with all that fuss about
remembering to bring those papers.
   *Don Manuel.* Tell the boy to tie the mules
and wait for us; there's no point
in our making any noise
and rousing the family.
They must be fast asleep by now.
Since I have the key, I can get in
and find the papers without
disturbing anyone.

[Exit Cosme, who returns at once

   *Cosme.* I've told the boy to wait.
Now consider, sir, it would be
a very bad mistake to think
of doing this without a light.
You cannot possibly avoid
making some noise without one;
and if we do not get a light
from Don Juan's apartment,
how are we to find a thing?
   *Don Manuel.* How tiresome you are!
Are you suggesting that I shout
and wake Don Juan? Can't you conceive,
you simpleton, you clumsy fool,
we've got to make our way
by groping in the dark and find
the papers where you left them?
   *Cosme.* That's not what I'm afraid of. Of course,
I know I left them on the table
and can find them in the dark.
   *Don Manuel.* Now open the door, at once.
   *Cosme.* What bothers me is that I won't know
where the spook has hidden them.
Indeed, when have I ever put
anything down there and not found it
lying somewhere else again?
   *Don Manuel.* There'll be time enough to ask for
candles if the papers aren't there.
Until then, I shall not rouse
our gracious host to whom
we owe so much already.

[Exeunt Don Manuel and Cosme

## DON MANUEL's *apartment*

*Enter* DOÑA ANGELA *and* ISABEL *through the panel.*

*Doña Angela.* Isabel, everyone's retired
and sunk in sleep that steals
half their lives away. Now our guest
has left, I must carry off
the portrait I saw here last time.

　　*Isabel.* Gently now, let's not make a sound.

　　*Doña Angela.* Go back and bolt my chamber door.
I'll stay here till you return.
I shan't take any further risks.

　　*Isabel.* Be sure and wait for me here.

　　　　　　　　[*Exit* ISABEL, *closing the panel behind her*

*Enter* DON MANUEL *and* COSME *in the dark.*

　　*Cosme* [*whispering to his master in the doorway*]. It's
　　　　open, sir.

　　*Don Manuel.* Step lightly.
Any noise heard coming from this room
would throw the house into a turmoil.

　　*Cosme.* Would you believe it? I'm not afraid.
At least that spook might have
the decency to light a candle
for us now.

　　*Doña Angela.* I may as well take out
the candle I brought along.
No one will see it now.

　　　　　　　　[*At the opposite end of the room from* DON
　　　　　　　　MANUEL *and* COSME, *she lights the candle in
　　　　　　　　a lantern she has brought.*]

　　*Cosme* [*aside to his master*]. No sooner said than done!
That spook was never so obliging.
See, sir, how fond he is of you?
When you appear now, a light is lit;
when I appeared before,
he snuffed out mine.

　　*Don Manuel.*　　　God help me, but this
is really supernatural!
Suddenly a light appears—
it's just not human!

　　*Cosme.*　　　　　Aha,
and so you finally admit
that I was right.

*Don Manuel.* I'm petrified!
I'm for getting out of here.
  *Cosme.* So, you're only human after all.
You're scared.
  *Doña Angela.* I see the table there,
and there are papers lying on it.
  *Cosme.* It's moving toward the table.
  *Don Manuel.* Good God! Can I believe my eyes?
How can I take all this in?
  *Cosme.* Do you notice how it leads us on
to the very thing we came for,
and yet we can't make out who
it is carrying that light?
  *Doña Angela.* [*She takes the candle out of the lantern,
    puts it into a candlestick on the table, pulls up a
    chair and sits down, with her back towards them.*]
                      I'll put the light here now
and go through these papers.
  *Don Manuel.* Hold on! Everything comes clear now
in the candlelight. I have
never seen such perfect beauty
in all my life. God in Heaven,
what am I to make of this?
Wonders seem to spring up
Hydra-headed all about me.
What in the world shall I do?
  *Cosme.* She surely takes her own sweet time.
Now she's moved the chair.
  *Don Manuel.*                    The hand of God
has never drawn a creature
half so beautiful before.
  *Cosme.* True enough: there's nothing earthly
to her.
  *Don Manuel.* Her lustrous eyes
outshine the candlelight.
  *Cosme.* I'd say her eyes are lamps
like Lucifer's that fell from Heaven.
  *Don Manuel.* Her radiant hair glints like sunlight.
  *Cosme.* Also stolen from above, no doubt.
  *Don Manuel.* Her curls, a diadem of stars.
  *Cosme.* She very likely swooped them up
and brought them here as well,
from Paradise, Limbo, or Hell.
  *Don Manuel.* I never saw such utter loveliness!

*Cosme.* I'll wager you wouldn't say so
if you could see her feet;
the likes of her are always sure
to have a pair of cloven hooves.

*Don Manuel.* Wondrous beauty, angel fair!

*Cosme.* Yes, it's as I say: an infernal
angel, cursed in the hoof.

*Don Manuel.* I wonder what she means to do
with all my papers.

*Cosme.*          I would guess
she simply wants to go through them
and find the things you're looking for,
just to be saving you the trouble.
Oh, she's a helpful little devil.

*Don Manuel.* God only knows what I should do.
I've never thought myself a coward
till this moment.

*Cosme.*          Unlike me,
who always have.

*Don Manuel.*   I feel as though
my feet were bound in icy chains,
my hair, standing on its ends,
and every breath I draw,
like a dagger thrust straight
to the heart, or like a rope
tightened round my throat.
Must I go on like this, a prey
to my own fears? No, by Heaven,
I'll break this spell, I will!

          [*He moves forward and seizes her arm.*]
Angel, woman, or devil,
I swear you won't slip by me this time!

*Doña Angela* [*aside*]. Good God, I'm lost! He didn't
go away—he just pretended to.
And now he's outwitted me.

*Cosme.* In God's Name (that should bring
a devil to its knees), tell us . . .

*Doña Angela* [*aside*]. But I'll brazen it through.

*Cosme.* . . . who thou art and what it is
thou seekest here.

*Doña Angela.* Most noble
Don Manuel Enríquez:
an enormous treasure lies in store

for thee. Therefore, unhand me,
come no closer, under pain
of forfeiting the very fortune
Heaven has reserved for thee,
in token of so favorable
a destiny and its
immutable decrees.
It was I who wrote to thee
this evening, and in that letter,
foreseeing this occasion,
promised we two soon would meet.
Since I have kept my word and come,
as now thou seest me, in the most
tangible of human forms
I could have chosen, depart in peace
and leave me. For the time
is not yet come when thou may'st fairly
seek to learn more concerning me.
Tomorrow thou shalt know all. Meanwhile,
forbear to breathe a word of this
to anyone, or thou shalt lose
thy greatest treasure. Go in peace.

    *Cosme.* Well, sir, what is it you're waiting for?
She's told us twice we're free to go
in peace.

    *Don Manuel* [*aside*]. By God, I am ashamed
such idle fears deluded me.
Now that I've regained my sanity,
I must get to the bottom
of this mystery once for all.
—Lady, whomsoever thou art
(and I cannot bring myself
to think thou art anything
less tangible), I am resolved,
by all that's sacred, to discover
thy name, by what means thou camest here,
and with what intent. And I shall not
wait another day for such
enlightenment. Speak as a devil,
if thou art one, or as a woman,
if such thou art. If thou art
the very devil, my valor
will not flinch or quail at any threat

or menace thou canst utter.
I know well enough that whilst thy shape
remains corporeal,
thou art no devil, but a woman.

   *Cosme*. It's one and the same.

   *Doña Angela*.                Forbear
to touch me, or lose thy joy at once.

   *Cosme*. This devil gives you good advice.
Don't touch her; she's not a harp
or lute or rebeck.

   *Don Manuel*.   Indeed,
we'll let my sword decide this.
Art thou a spirit? Then [*drawing his sword*]
though this blade penetrate,
it cannot do thee harm.

   *Doña Angela*. Mercy me! Drop your sword,
your cruel, bloodthirsty arm.
How can you kill a poor unhappy
woman? I confess that's all I am.
If it is a crime to love someone,
it is surely not so heinous
as to deserve such punishment.
Please, do not stain or tarnish
with my blood the roset
of your sword.

   *Don Manuel*. Tell me who you are.

   *Doña Angela*. It seems at last I'm forced to do so,
and thereby call a halt to all
my fancies' fond designs,
the purity of my desire,
the sweet and earnest pledge of love.
But, sir, we are now in mortal
danger if we're seen or overheard.
I am much more than you take me for.
So let me entreat you, sir,
lest we be discovered here,
secure that door and the entrance
to the alcove also.
Then, if anyone should happen by,
our light will not be visible.

   *Don Manuel*. Go, Cosme, bring the candle
so we can bolt the doors.
It's a woman now, you see,
and not a phantom.

*Cosme.*          But didn't I
admit they're one and the same?
                    [*Exeunt* Don Manuel *and* Cosme
*Doña Angela.* Gracious, Isabel has shut
the panel on the other side,
and now there's no way out.
I'm obliged to tell our guest the truth.
I've been caught redhanded in his room.

          *Enter* Isabel, *through the panel.*

*Isabel.* Hist, hist, madam! Your brother
is asking for you.
*Doña Angela.* In the nick
of time! Come now, and be sure
you shut the panel behind us.
Ah, my love, you must entertain
your doubts a little longer.
                    [*Exeunt* Doña Angela *and* Isabel *through the
                    panel just as* Don Manuel *and* Cosme *enter
                    the room*
*Don Manuel.* Now the doors have all been bolted,
madam, you may proceed to tell . . .
But what's this? Where is she?
*Cosme.* How should I know?
*Don Manuel.*                    Perhaps
she's gone into the alcove. Go ahead
and look.
*Cosme.* It would be discourteous
of me to walk ahead of you.
*Don Manuel.* I'll search this place from top
to bottom. Hand me that light, I say.
*Cosme.* Oh, but you're welcome to it.
                    [Don Manuel *seizes the candle, goes into the
                    alcove and returns again.*]
*Don Manuel.* No luck—how cruel!
*Cosme.*                    This time, at least,
you cannot say she went out the door.
*Don Manuel.* Well, how did she get out?
*Cosme.* That's beyond me, sir. But do you see?
It's just as I've always said:
she's a phantom, not a woman.
*Don Manuel.* By God, I'll search through every nook
and cranny in this apartment.
Surely there's an opening behind

some picture frame on those walls
or a trapdoor of some sort
underneath those carpets—
perhaps an archway through the ceiling!

    *Cosme.* The only thing that I can think of
is that large mirror.

    *Don Manuel.*      No, it's clear
there's nothing there but one large surface
made of smaller panes of glass.
We must look elsewhere.

    *Cosme.*           Sir,
I've always been averse to prying.

    *Don Manuel.* I am still convinced she is no phantom.
She had sense enough to fear death.

    *Cosme.* She also had another sense by which
she could foretell we'd be obliged
to come back here tonight and see her.

    *Don Manuel.* There was something ghostly in the way
she suddenly appeared
in that fantastic light,
but there was also something human
in the way that she avoided
being seen and touched—
something mortal in her fear,
something feminine in her distrust.
Yet she simply came apart
like an illusion, and
like a spirit vanished in the air.
By God, if I gave this matter
any further thought, who knows,
who knows if I could any longer
separate credulity from doubt.

    *Cosme.* It's all quite clear to me.

    *Don Manuel.*               What?

    *Cosme.* That the lady is the devil.
But there's nothing unusual
about it: when women are such devils
all year round, I wouldn't blame
the devil if he turned woman
to get even with them once for all.

## ACT THREE

Doña Angela's *apartment*

*Enter* Don Manuel *in the dark, being led by* Isabel.

Isabel. Wait here in this room, sir;
my mistress will see you shortly.
                    [*Exit, closing the door behind her*
Don Manuel. Well, this time I've not been tricked.
Did you lock the door? She did.
The suspense is more than I can bear!
I found this note awaiting me when
I returned from the Escorial;
it was written by the same
bewitching pilgrim, that wondrous
beauty who last night lit the light
but still keeps me in the dark.
Yet her words are very tender:
"If you would dare," she writes,
"to come and see me, you must go
out this evening with your servant
until you reach the graveyard"
(that's the odd part!) "behind
the Church of Saint Sebastian,
where two men will be waiting for you
with a sedan chair." And she
was serious. I was brought there,
stumbled about, and lost my bearings
totally. Then I found myself
before a grisly-looking doorway, and
went through it full of grim forebodings.
In pitch darkness I found a woman
(or so she seemed) waiting there alone.
And without a word she led me
from one room to another.
I said nothing, heard nothing,
saw nothing. I only groped my way
behind her till I came here.
Ah, now I see a light glimmering
through the keyhole.
                    [*Looking through the keyhole.*]
          Ah, love, at last

you've conquered me; there's the lady now.
The risks were all worth taking.
What a magnificent house!
What an exquisite table!
And what lovely women! Look
how elegant they are!
How they glitter as they walk!
Such complete magnificence!

> [*The door is opened, and several ladies enter
> carrying napkins, sweetmeats, and water, curt-
> seying as they pass* DoÑa Angela, *who is
> seated, elegantly dressed, before them.*]

*Doña Angela* [*aside to* DoÑa Beatriz].
Since my brothers assume you've gone home,
you'll be safe and sound here.
There'll be no excuse for their intruding,
and nothing at all for you to fear
while you stay here with me.

*Doña Beatriz* [*aside to* DoÑa Angela]. And what's my
role to be?

*Doña Angela* [*aside to* DoÑa Beatriz]. First, you'll be
my servant;
then you may withdraw and watch
everything that happens later.
[*To* DoN Manuel]
Are you weary of waiting for me?

*Don Manuel.* Not in the least, madam.
Whoever would await the dawn
knows full well that he must fret away
the cold and dismal night, by which he
is the more rewarded for his pains;
indeed, the longer he must wait,
the more surely will he
appreciate the day.
Yet I hardly think I need have
suffered through such darkness
had I known how much dazzling light
your beauty held in store.
For now I realize the splendor
of your all-pervading radiance
would not be dimmed by any
of the deepest shades of night.
Madam, you are the day itself
and have no need for sun to rise.

The night flies, madam, before the dawn's
sweet smiling promise; it will shine,
and yet will not illuminate.
Then when dawn gives way to morning,
its niggard rays illuminate,
and yet they will not burn.
Then morning light gives way
to the very sun itself,
and only such a sun
can shine, illuminate, and burn.
Dawn, if it would shine, must send night
packing, and morning, in its turn,
merely follow in the tracks of dawn,
if it would illuminate.
But where the all-pervading sun
defies them both, you in turn
defy the very sun,
which is why I say I need not
have suffered through the cold night darkness
had I known your sun of suns
would now arise to crown the day.

    *Doña Angela.* Although I'm grateful to you, sir,
for such a pretty speech, I am
afraid your flattery's excessive
and rather questionable.
We do not dwell in Heaven's mansion
where the noblest passion
is so stormily expressed it would
reduce a tempest to exhaustion.
We live in this poor humble house
where such exaggerations
as you offer sound suspicious.
Do not compare me to the dawn
whose fixed smile I do not share,
for I am not frequently so blissful.
Nor am I like the early morning
light in shedding pearly tears;
I hope you have not found me weeping.
Nor can I like the sun divide
the light of truth I love
into so many parts.
And so, although I cannot say
exactly what I'm like,
I only know I'm not the dawn,

the morning, or the sun of day.
At least I cannot think I am
the sunlight all aglow,
or weeping like a stream.
In sum, my dear Don Manuel,
the only thing I'd have you say
of me is that I've always been
and am a woman, and you are
the only man I have ever asked
to visit me in private.

   *Don Manuel.* But that comes to very little,
madam, for though I've come to see you
finally, I might say your
indulgence gives me more grounds
for regret than pleasure.
Indeed, you have offended me.

   *Doña Angela. I,* offended *you,* sir?

   *Don Manuel.* Yes, because you do not trust me
well enough to tell me who you are.

   *Doña Angela.* That is the one thing I beg you
not to ask of me, for I cannot
possibly enlighten you.
If you wish to visit me,
you may do so only
on condition you do not seek
to know or ask my name.
I can only tell you this now:
Accept me as something enigmatic,
for I am not what I appear
to be nor does my appearance now
belie the person that I am.
So long as I remain in hiding,
you may see me, and I see you;
but once you satisfy
your curiosity and learn my name,
you shan't be fond of me again,
though I continue fond of you.
When death has limned the features,
what one sees is not a portrait.
The life descried in one light
is transfigured when it appears
in any other. The same is true
of Love, the painter, for whom I sit
portrayed in double light,

which is why I fear that what you
delight to see in me at present
is but one aspect of me, and that
perhaps you will detest me when
you come to see me in the other.
All that I can tell you now
which matters to me is that
your notion about my being
the mistress of Don Luis
was utterly mistaken.
You have my word, there is no ground
for any such suspicion.
    *Don Manuel.* Then, madam, what drove you
to escape from him?
    *Doña Angela.*       It may be
my reputation was at stake,
something I risked losing if I were
recognized by Don Luis.
    *Don Manuel.* Well, then, tell me at least
how you managed to enter this house?
    *Doña Angela.* I cannot tell you that just yet—
another troublesome detail.
    *Doña Beatriz* [*aside*]. That's my cue to enter graciously.
—The sweetmeats and iced water are served.
Will Your Excellency observe
if there is anything . . .
        [*The ladies come forward with napkins, water,
           trays of sweets.*]
    *Doña Angela.* How gauche, how impertinent of you!
Idiot! Whom are you addressing
as Your Excellency? Is this
the way you would deceive
Don Manuel to make him think
I am a lady of some rank?
    *Doña Beatriz.* Indeed, I did not mean . . .
    *Don Manuel* [*aside*]. There, that was a slip, enough to
        lift
the irksome veil on all my doubts.
Now I know she is a noblewoman,
which is why she's so intent
on cloaking her identity;
and so, it was her money
that devised and kept her secret
plan in motion all this while.

[*The voice of* DON JUAN *is heard; general consternation ensues.*]

*Don Juan* [*offstage*]. Isabel, open this door.
*Doña Angela* [*aside*]. Good Heavens! Who's knocking?
*Isabel.* I shall die!
*Doña Beatriz* [*aside*]. I am frozen stiff!
*Don Manuel* [*aside*]. God preserve me, my troubles
aren't over yet.
*Doña Angela.* That's
my father at the door, sir.
*Don Manuel.* What am I to do?
*Doña Angela.*                    You must go
and hide somewhere out of sight.
Isabel, take the gentleman
to that other apartment—you know
which—and see to it he's well hidden.
Do you understand?
*Isabel.*            Perfectly.
Come along, sir—at once.
*Don Juan* [*offstage*]. Won't you ever open this door?
*Don Manuel.* So help me, there goes my life,
and my honor too, in one fell swoop.

[*Exeunt* DON MANUEL *and* ISABEL

*Don Juan* [*offstage*]. Very well, I'll smash the door in.
*Doña Angela.* You might step into the entry,
Beatriz; they mustn't find you here.

[*Exit* DOÑA BEATRIZ

*Enter* DON JUAN.

*Doña Angela.* Now what brings you to my room
at this hour of the night,
and making such an uproar too?
*Don Juan.* Angela, first you answer me:
what do you mean by wearing
such a dress?
*Doña Angela.* As my grief and sorrow
require me to wear deep mourning
constantly, I imagined I might
lift my heavy spirits by donning
these fineries for a change.
*Don Juan.* I don't doubt it. Though a woman's grief
invariably is cured
once she's decked herself in fineries
and then convalesces with her jewels,

in your case I find such
consolations quite indecorous.

*Doña Angela.* Why should it matter if I change
my gown, when no one comes to see me?

*Don Juan.* Tell me, has Beatriz gone home?

*Doña Angela.* Yes, her father's thought it wiser
to cool his anger and has now
made up with her.

*Don Juan.*      That is all
I wished to know. Now perhaps
I can see and talk to her tonight.
Good night, but remember,
that frippery is not for you.

[*Exit*

*Doña Angela.* Good night to you—and good riddance.

*Enter* Doña Beatriz.

*Doña Angela.* Beatriz, bolt that door.

*Doña Beatriz.* We've got out of that impasse
very nicely. Now your brother's off
to look for me.

*Doña Angela.* Before we rouse
anyone else and Don Manuel
comes out to look for me,
let's retire to that little room
where no one will disturb us.

*Doña Beatriz.* If everything turns out the way
you planned it, you'll really earn
the title *Phantom Lady.*

[*Exeunt*

Don Manuel's *apartment*

*Enter* Don Manuel *and* Isabel *in the dark,
through the panel.*

*Isabel.* You must stay here now, sir;
and be careful not to make a sound—
someone's sure to hear you.

*Don Manuel.* I'll be still as marble.

*Isabel.* Dear God, let me stop trembling
so I can shut this panel tight.

[*Exit*

*Don Manuel.* Lord, what risks a man takes
who dares intrude inside a house

where he can never know or sense
the pitfalls that await him,
the dangers lurking all around him.
So here I am, in some stranger's house,
and the owner a member
of the nobility—at least
she's called Your Excellency—
and this place, so far away
from Don Juan's house, is full of
ominous and flitting shadows.
What's that now? Someone on the other
side is opening the door. Yes,
and now he's coming in here.

*Enter* COSME.

*Cosme.* Thank God I can get into
my room tonight so handily [*groping*]
and not be frightened, though I come
and go without a light; but since
my lord the phantom seized my master,
what in the world would he want with me?
                    [*Running into* DON MANUEL]
Oh-oh, there *is* something he wants.
Who's that? Who is it?
    *Don Manuel.*              Be still,
I tell you, whoever you are,
or I'll run you through with this sword.
    *Cosme.* I'll be mum as a poor relative
sitting at a rich man's table.
    *Don Manuel* [*aside*]. This must be a servant
who happened to come by.
I'll try to get him to tell me
where I am. —Come now, whose house
is this, and who is the owner?
    *Cosme.* Sir, the house and owner both
belong to Satan, because there is
a lady living here who's called
the Phantom Lady, and she's
the very devil.
    *Don Manuel.* And who are you?
    *Cosme.* An attendant, or you might say
a serving man; I'm a subject
and a slave, and I don't know

how or why I stand it,
but I have been bewitched.

   *Don Manuel.* And who's your master?

   *Cosme.*               A madman,
a fool, a meddlesome idiot,
a perfect ass, and hopelessly
in love with that lady.

   *Don Manuel.* And what's his name?

   *Cosme.*               Don Manuel
Enríquez.

   *Don Manuel.* In God's Name!

   *Cosme.* As for me, my name's Cosme
Catiboratos.

   *Don Manuel.* Cosme,
is that you? How did you get in?
It's your master. Tell me,
did you follow behind my sedan?
And did you come in, like me,
to hide in this apartment?

   *Cosme.* A nice little game you're playing!
Tell me, how did you get here?
Weren't you the brave chap who sallied
forth alone to that distant churchyard?
Then how did you get back so soon?
And how in the world did you
get in here when I had the key
to the apartment all this time?

   *Don Manuel.* Now you tell me: what apartment
are we in?

   *Cosme.* If it isn't yours,
it must surely be the devil's.

   *Don Manuel.* You lie in your throat! Only
a moment ago I was far away
from here, in quite a different house.

   *Cosme.* Well, then the devil's had a hand
in it, because what I've told you
is nothing but the honest truth.

   *Don Manuel.* You'll drive me out of my mind.

   *Cosme.* Do you need further proof? Just step
through that doorway to the alcove,
and see if you don't recognize the place.

   *Don Manuel.* A good idea. I'll go and see.

                           *[Exit*

*Cosme [to the audience].* Ah, ladies and gentlemen:
when shall we be done
with all this sham and muddle?

*Enter* ISABEL, *through the panel.*

*Isabel [aside].* Now that Don Juan's returned,
I must get Don Manuel away
so that he won't be found here.
—Hist, sir, hist.
*Cosme.*          Oh, worse and worse: those *hists*
go straight to my sciatica!
*Isabel.* My master's gone to bed, sir.
*Cosme [aside].* What master's that?

*Enter* DON MANUEL.

*Don Manuel.*                    Yes, this is my
apartment, no doubt of it.
*Isabel.* Is that you?
*Cosme.*          Yes, it's me.
*Isabel.* Then come along with me.
*Don Manuel.* You were perfectly right.
*Isabel.* Don't be afraid. I won't mislead you.
*Cosme.* Oh, please, sir: the phantom
is towing me away.
          [ISABEL *takes* COSME *by the hand and leads him
               through the panel.*]
*Don Manuel.* Won't we ever get to the bottom
of this mystery? You don't answer.
What a blockhead you are!
Cosme, Cosme! Good Lord,
there's nothing but the four walls now.
Wasn't I just speaking with him?
Where did he disappear to
suddenly? Wasn't he just here?
I really must be going mad.
Still, it's clear somebody else came in
from somewhere; I must find out
how and where. I'll hide in this alcove
and wait there patiently
till I can determine
who this wondrous Phantom Lady is.

          [*Exit*

DOÑA ANGELA's *apartment*

*Enter all the ladies, one with lit candles, another with*
*assorted trays, and still another with a pitcher of water.*

*Doña Angela.* Now my brother's left to search for you
and Isabel's gone off to bring
Don Manuel from his room,
everything's in readiness.
He'll find this collation waiting
when he comes. Let us all
prepare to take our places.
    *Doña Beatriz.* I've never seen the likes of this
in all my life.
    *Doña Angela.* Is he coming?
    *Servant.*                 Yes,
I hear his footsteps now.

    *Enter* ISABEL, *leading* COSME *by the hand.*

    *Cosme.* Poor me, where am I going?
This joke's gone far enough.
But no . . . now I'm gazing at
a swarm of perfect beauties!
Am I really Cosme, or am I
Amadis of Gaul? Just little
Cosme, or Belianis of Greece?
    *Isabel.* He's coming in. But what's this I see?
Sir!
    *Cosme* [*aside*]. Now I'm sure I am bewitched.
My soul's about to leave my body.
    *Doña Angela.* What's the meaning of this, Isabel?
    *Isabel* [*aside to her mistress*]. Madam, I went back to
        where I'd left
Don Manuel and brought his servant
here by some mistake.
    *Doña Angela.*       Don't gild
the truth; you've made a mess of it.
    *Isabel.* It was dark.
    *Doña Angela.*       Goodness me,
now it will all come out.
    *Doña Beatriz* [*aside*]. Never mind, Angela.
This is even better. —Cosme.
    *Cosme.* Damiana.
    *Doña Beatriz.*     Come closer.
    *Cosme.* I'm happy here.

*Doña Angela.*          Come, come.
You needn't be frightened.
    *Cosme.* Frightened? A brave man like me?
    *Doña Angela.* Then why stand so far away?
                    [*He advances toward them.*]
    *Cosme* [*aside*]. There's no hanging back where
a point of honor has been made.
—Whenever there's respect you'll find
some awe and fear mixed in with it,
though Lucifer himself
would hardly frighten me
if he were dressed up as a lady.
And he surely tried it once:
brewing up a little stratagem,
he slipped into some petticoats
and a whalebone corset.
For who but the devil himself
could have invented such stuff?
Well, that's just how he appeared,
disguised as some wealthy, fair
young damsel, before a shepherd.
No sooner did the shepherd clap eyes
on her than his heart was swept
by flames of love. After the shepherd
enjoyed the devil-lady,
the devil changed shape, becoming
something horrible and ugly,
and then he raised his voice:
"Miserable creature," he said,
"do you see the sort of beauty,
all dressed up from wig to toes,
that you have fallen for?
Despair now: you have knowingly
committed mortal sin."
Well, the shepherd, less contrite
than he was before he had enjoyed
the lady, told the devil off:
"Oh, vain and insubstantial shade!
if you really wish to drive a wretch
like me to despair, come again
tomorrow morning, dressed up
as you were before. You'll find me
no less loving or obliging
than I was just now. And be

the devil, if you wish,
because however horrible
you are, a woman's just a woman
in a dress."
    *Doña Angela.* Collect yourself.
Here, take a sweetmeat and some water.
Fright sometimes brings on thirst.
    *Cosme.* I'm not thirsty, though.
    *Doña Beatriz.*                 Come here.
You've two hundred leagues to go, you know,
before you can get home again.
    *Cosme.* Heavens, what's that noise?

                            [*Someone calling*]
    *Doña Angela.*              Is there
someone calling?
    *Doña Beatriz.* Yes, indeed.
    *Isabel* [*aside*]. How awful!
    *Doña Angela* [*aside*].      Gracious me!
    *Don Luis* [*offstage*]. Isabel.
    *Doña Beatriz* [*aside*].      Good Heavens!
    *Don Luis* [*offstage*]. Open this door!
    *Doña Angela* [*aside*].          I've a brother
for every shock.
    *Isabel.*        And this the worst
of all.
    *Doña Beatriz.* I'm going to hide.

                                 [*Exit*
    *Cosme* [*aside*]. That must be the honest-to-goodness
Phantom.
    *Isabel* [*to* COSME]. Come with me.
    *Cosme.*                    By all means.
                    [*Exeunt* ISABEL *and* COSME

       *The door opens; enter* DON LUIS.

    *Doña Angela.* What are you doing here
in my apartment?
    *Don Luis.*        My own distress
compels me to disturb
the happiness of others.
I know that Beatriz is back;
I saw her sedan chair here lately
in the house, and I also know
my brother's somewhere hereabout.
    *Doña Angela.* Well, what is it you wish?

*Don Luis.* I heard footsteps overhead, and thought
there must be visitors upstairs;
I came up only to make sure
I was mistaken.

> [*He raises a portiere and finds* BEATRIZ.]
>                    Is that you,

Beatriz? [BEATRIZ *returns.*]
   *Doña Beatriz.* Yes, it's me.
I had to come back. My father grew
annoyed again, and he's still angry.
   *Don Luis.* You both seem quite confused here.
What extraordinary mischief's
going on with all these glasses,
plates, and sweetmeats?
   *Doña Angela.*          Are you simply
asking us to tell you how women
entertain themselves when they're alone?

> [ISABEL *and* COSME *make a sound at the panel.*]

   *Don Luis.* Now that noise, how do you explain it?
   *Doña Angela* [*aside*]. I think I'll die!
   *Don Luis.*                              By God,
there *is* someone lurking there!
I only hope it's not my brother
hiding from me in this fashion.

> [*Takes a lit candle.*]

Merciful Heavens! The foolish
jealousy love planted in my heart
which drove me here to interfere
now gives way to insult.
Yet I must take this candle,
however rashly, and if light
uncovers everything,
light my way to honor lost.

> [*Exit*

   *Doña Angela.* Oh, Beatriz, we're lost
if they should meet!
   *Doña Beatriz.*          You needn't worry;
once Isabel gets him to his
master's room, you can be sure
that Don Luis won't find out
about the secret panel.
   *Doña Angela.* But, as luck would have it, what if
Isabel is so confused
she forgets to bolt the panel,

and then he follows her straight through?

*Doña Beatriz.* Well, then you'd better think
of finding refuge somewhere.

*Doña Angela.* I'll take advantage of your father,
just as he has of me.
Fate has turned the tables now:
if one sorrow brought you to my house,
another leads me home to yours.

[*Exeunt* Doña Angela *and* Doña Beatriz

Don Manuel's *apartment*

*Enter* Isabel, Cosme, Don Manuel; *later* Don Luis.

*Isabel.* Get in, quickly.

[*Exit*

*Don Manuel.*               I hear someone
in the entryway again.

*Enter* Don Luis, *with a lit candle.*

*Don Luis* [*aside*]. I can make out the figure
of a man there. By God!

*Cosme.* This looks bad.

*Don Luis.*               How does this panel come
to be ajar?

*Cosme.* Oh—oh, there's a light.
Here's where that table I found
will come in handy.

[*He crawls under the table.*]

*Don Manuel.*      It's time
to settle this at once.

[*He puts his hand on his sword.*]

*Don Luis.* Don Manuel!

*Don Manuel.*               Don Luis!
What's this all about? I've never
been so mystified before!

*Cosme* [*aside*]. Well, just listen to him admit it!
I could have said so a thousand times.

*Don Luis.* Villain! You do not deserve the name
of gentleman! Traitor, ungrateful
wretch, you who would violate
the friendship and hospitality
of this house! You who would trifle
so shamelessly with the honor

of a man who has trusted
and befriended you!

[*Draws his sword.*]

                    Since you dare
be so offensive, draw
your miserable sword and fight.

   *Don Manuel.* Yes, I shall draw, but only
to defend myself. Can you really
be addressing me? I am
bewildered, and can hardly believe
my senses. Yet you cannot kill me,
though you try; a lifetime spent
in overcoming cruel misfortunes
has made me invulnerable;
nor can your sword, if this be
your intent, unhinge a life
already injured to the quick
by your accusations,
for however capable
your strong right arm may be,
the sorrow which your words inflict
is stronger—indeed, is mortal.

   *Don Luis.* Soft replies will not stop me now;
only your sword will do that.

   *Don Manuel.*                    At least
stop long enough to tell me, Don
Luis: Is there no other way
I can satisfy you in this?

   *Don Luis.* After what you've done, how can you
speak of any other recourse?
Did you not use the secret panel
to enter that wanton's rooms?
Is there any satisfying
such an insult?

   *Don Manuel.* Don Luis,
I would gladly suffer you to run
my body through a thousand times
if I so much as knew that there was
such a panel or that it opened
on anyone's apartment.

   *Don Luis.* Then what were you doing here alone
without a light?

   *Don Manuel* [*aside*]. What shall I tell him?
—I was waiting for my servant.

*Don Luis.* When I myself saw you hiding here?
Shall I doubt my own two eyes?
*Don Manuel.* Yes, for sight is more deceptive
than any other sense.
*Don Luis.* And if my eyes deceived me,
did my ears deceive me too?
*Don Manuel.* Yes, they did.
*Don Luis.*                    They all lie, then,
while only you can tell the truth,
and still it was you alone who . . .
*Don Manuel.* Stop there, or I'll cut you down
before you say another word, or
even think it, or imagine it.
If you want daring, I'm your man.
I've borne enough, for friendship's sake.
If we must come to blows,
let's do it properly. First, we'll
share this light between us, equally;
then, you bolt that door through which
you rashly entered, while I fasten
this other one. Now I'll throw this key
upon the floor. Whoever survives
can pick it up and flee.
*Don Luis.* I'll shut off the entrance
through this panel by placing
the table against it. Then no one
can possibly get in.
                    [*Lifting the table, he finds* Cosme.]
*Cosme* [*aside*]. Well, the jig is up.
*Don Luis.*                    Who's this here?
*Don Manuel.* Oh, my unhappy stars!
*Cosme.*                    No one's here.
*Don Luis.* Look here, Don Manuel. Isn't this
the servant you were waiting for?
*Don Manuel.* There's no point in discussing that now.
My cause is just ; you may think
whatever you wish. Once our swords
are drawn, only one of us will live
to boast about it.
*Don Luis.*      I'm for you, then.
Why are you delaying?
*Don Manuel.* You presume too much. I am
considering what to do about
my servant; if I throw him out,

he'll go for help; if I let him stay,
that puts you to a disadvantage
since he's sure to come to my aid.
  *Cosme.* I won't, if it's inconvenient.
  *Don Luis.* There's a door to that alcove.
If you shut him up inside,
we'll be on equal terms again.
  *Don Manuel.* A good idea. Get in and stay there.
  *Cosme.* What's all this to-do about
keeping me out of the fight,
when my not fighting is
a foregone conclusion?

                                        [*Exit*

  *Don Manuel.* Now we're alone at last.
  *Don Luis.* Well then, let's go to it.

                                [*They fight.*]
  *Don Manuel.* I have never seen a swordsman
with a steadier wrist!
  *Don Luis.* I have never seen a swordsman
with a stronger thrust!
            [*The sword is knocked out of his hand.*]
                You've disarmed me.
I'm defenseless now.
  *Don Manuel.*        That's the merest
accident, and no aspersion on
your valor. Go find another sword.
  *Don Luis.* You are courteous as well as brave.
[*Aside.*] My luck! What shall I do
in this emergency?
He has robbed me of my honor
but lets me live when he has
vanquished me. One way or the other,
I must find some excuse
to resolve this question and
determine what it is I owe him.
  *Don Manuel.* Are you going for your sword?
  *Don Luis.* Yes, and if you will wait for me,
I shall return with it at once.
  *Don Manuel.* Sooner or later, when you come,
I shall be waiting.
  *Don Luis.*        God keep you,
Don Manuel.
  *Don Manuel.* And you, Don Luis.

                                [*Exit* DON LUIS

*Don Manuel.* Meanwhile I'll lock the door
and keep the key so that no one
can get in and find me here.
What illusions and confusions
go tumbling through my head!
How right I was to think
there was a secret door
where she got in, and that the lady
was his mistress after all!
Indeed, everything's turned out as I
imagined it. But then, our worst
imaginings often come true.

> [COSME *peeps out over the doorway.*]

*Cosme.* Oh, sir! For pity's sake,
now that you're alone, let me
out of here. I'm afraid that phantom
will creep into this narrow place—
which is no bigger than its own
four walls—and, haggling and squabbling,
one way or the other,
will carry me off at last.

*Don Manuel.* Yes, I'll open it for you.
I am so weary of my own
absurd reflections, I can even
be impervious to you.

> [DON MANUEL *opens the door and enters the
> room behind which* COSME *is shut up.*]

*Enter* DOÑA ANGELA, *veiled and in stocking feet,
while* DON JUAN *stands in the doorway.*

*Don Juan.* You'll stay right here until I find out
why you left the house, dressed as you are,
and at this hour of the night.
Ungrateful wretch, I shall not let you
enter your apartment till
I have satisfied myself
on this account by asking your maid
without giving you the chance to meddle.
[*Aside.*] Since she'll be left in Don Manuel's
apartment, I must post a servant
at the house door to warn him not
to come inside here when he returns.

> [*Exit*

DOÑA ANGELA. How miserable I am!

One by one the doors are closed
against me. Now there's no way out.

*Enter* DON MANUEL *and* COSME.

*Cosme.* Let's go quickly.
*Don Manuel.*                What are you
afraid of now?
*Cosme.*        That that woman
is the devil and she's not finished
with me yet.
*Don Manuel.* But we know now
who she is; and we know the panel
is shut off by a table
while the door itself is locked.
So where do you suppose
she can get in?
*Cosme.*        Wherever
she's a mind to.
*Don Manuel.* You're mad.

[COSME *spies* DOÑA ANGELA.]
*Cosme.* Lord God, save me, save me!
*Don Manuel.* What is it?
*Cosme.*                The unmentionable one's
got in here, pretty as you please.
*Don Manuel.* What are you, woman, a shade
or some illusion sent here
to destroy me? Tell me,
how did you get in?
*Doña Angela.*        Don Manuel . . .
*Don Manuel.* Tell me.
*Doña Angela.*        Then listen patiently.
Don Luis knocked at my door
in great excitement, rushed in
wildly, checked himself,
seemed to overcome his
agitation, paused, spoke calmly;
then turned and rushed out blindly,
searched the house, ran through every room
until he found you, after which
the only sound I heard
was the clash and clatter of your swords.
Aware that two men were locked behind
closed doors, both grimly silent while their
swords proclaimed their quarrel,

one to prove his valor, the other,
his reputation, and knowing
such an issue must terminate
in the death of one or the other,
half dead myself, I fled the house.
There outside, the cold and silent night
became the pallid image of
my former happiness.
I found myself wandering
aimlessly, falling and stumbling,
and all my sluggish senses
muffled in the silken prison
of my clothes. Confused, alone,
and terrified, my errant steps
led me roundabout to some dim
familiar threshold, to the haven,
as it turned out later,
of my former cell, and not
the refuge or the sanctuary
which I sought. But where, indeed,
does any poor unhappy wretch
find refuge? Still, Heaven forges
our misfortunes, link by link,
so carefully, that on that very
threshold stood Don Juan—Don Juan,
my brother . . . At first, I forbore,
then vainly I delayed, to tell him
who I was, though knowing that
my hesitation put us both
in certain jeopardy. Still,
who would think silence in a woman
could be dangerous? Yet it was
precisely this, my being silent
and a woman, which nearly
finished me. For, as I say,
there he stood—good God! waiting in
the doorway just as I arrived—
like a frozen volcano
or an alp on fire. There,
in the dim moonlight he caught
the sudden gleam and flash of jewels
around my neck—not, by any means,
the first time that such baubles
have betrayed a woman. And there

he heard the rustle of my skirts—
nor, there again, was it the first time
a woman's dress gave her away.
He mistook me for his mistress,
to whom he flew directly,
as a moth would toward the flame
it would be consumed by,
the mere ghost of his lustrous star.
Who would suppose a gallant, wracked
by jealousy, should so utterly
mistake his own adverse destiny
as not to know that jealousy
would be his fixed and awful fate?
He tried in vain to speak,
but deepest feeling's always mute.
At last his quaking voice,
which quickly blurred the words
his tongue would utter just
as they reached his lips, inquired
why he had been made to suffer
such an insult. I tried to answer,
but, as I've said, deep emotion
silenced me. I could not say a word.
Perhaps it was because I sought
to color the guilt I felt
that fears came surging up
to cloak my reason. It always
follows that when one must seek
excuses for one's innocence,
they never come, or if they do,
arrive too late, so that
the very crime one would deny
asserts itself more flagrantly.
"Get inside," he said. "My sister
is a wanton, and the first to stain
the honor of our ancient name.
I shall leave you under lock and key,
and while you're safely hidden,
I'll deliberate upon
the wisest course to follow
in redressing this insult."
Whereupon he locked me in here
to nurse my griefs, until,
as luck would have it, you appeared,

to lighten them. To love you
I became a phantom in my own house.
To honor you, I became
the living tomb of my own secret.
Indeed, I could not tell you that
I loved you nor how much
I respected you for fear
that any open declaration
would jeopardize your presence
as our guest, compelling you
to quit the house at once.
I only sought your favor
because I loved you and because
I feared to lose you. My only thought
was keeping you, to cherish
and obey you all my life, to wed
my soul with yours, and so all
my desire was to serve you,
as now my plea is but
to urge you to support me
in my pressing need: in effect,
to save me, comfort and protect me.

 *Don Manuel* [*aside*]. All my troubles seem to rise up
Hydra-headed from dead ashes.
What am I to do, sunk in this deep
abyss, this human labyrinth
of myself? She is the sister
of Don Luis, and not his mistress,
as I thought. Heavens, if I was
so squeamish about crossing him
in love, what can I do now
that his honor is involved?
What an awful impasse!
She's his sister: if I try
to free her and defend her
with my blood, or let my sword
underscore her innocence,
I thereby compound my guilt,
for that's to say that I've betrayed
him as a guest in his own house.
If I plead my innocence
by implicating her, then that's
to say she was the guilty one,
which my sense of honor won't allow.

Then what am I supposed to do?
If I reject her, I'm a villain.
If I defend her, a thankless guest;
and fiendishly inhuman
if I yield her to her brother.
Say I decide to protect her:
that makes me a false friend;
and if I free her, I violate
a noble trust; if I don't free her,
I violate the noblest love.
Whichever way I turn, I'm in
the wrong. So I'll die fighting.
[*To* DOÑA ANGELA.] Madam, have no fear. I am a
gentleman; you shall be protected.

> [*There is a knocking at the door.*]

    *Cosme.* Sir, there's someone knocking.
    *Don Manuel.* It's Don Luis, who went to fetch
a sword. Let him in.
    *Doña Angela.*     Dear me,
my brother!
    *Don Manuel.* There is nothing
to fear. I shall defend you
gallantly. Now stand behind me.

> [DOÑA ANGELA *moves behind* DON MANUEL
> *while* COSME *opens the door.*]

### *Enter* DON LUIS.

    *Don Luis.* I've come back. But what's this?
Oh, you traitress!

> [*Seeing* DOÑA ANGELA, *he draws his sword.*]

    *Don Manuel.*   Sheathe your sword,
Don Luis. In this room, where I've been
awaiting your return, this lady
entered—by what means I did not know.
She informs me she is your sister.
But you have my word, as a
gentleman, that I did not know
of it before. It should suffice
to say that not knowing who she was,
though I could have been mistaken,
I spoke to her. At the risk of
my own life and soul, I must
conduct her now to safety
before we can resume our duel

behind locked doors and avoid
a further scandal. Having freed her,
I shall return here to take up
our quarrel. To one who would sustain
his reputation, the cause of honor
and his sword are his most vital
possessions. Just as I
permitted you to leave this room
to fetch another sword, permit me
now to leave in order to fulfill
the debt I owe my honor.

   *Don Luis.* I went to get my sword, but only
to bring it here that I might lay it
at your feet, and so acknowledge
your generous behavior.
But since you've given me new grounds
for argument, I must pick it up
again. This lady is my sister.
No man in my presence shall lead her
from this house who is not her husband.
Therefore, if you insist on
taking her away, you must first
agree to marry her. Once
I have your word to this effect,
you may take her, then return
for the further disposition
of this matter, if you wish.

   *Don Manuel.* I shall return, but instructed
by your prudence and honesty,
only to throw myself
upon your mercy—thus.

   *Don Luis.* You must not kneel. Rise.

   *Don Manuel.*                                        Further,
in fulfillment of my sworn vow,
I now take your sister's hand.

      *Enter* DOÑA BEATRIZ *and* DON JUAN.

   *Don Juan.* If all that's lacking is her
guardian to give the bride away,
I'm here to do so. I was about
to enter when I heard voices
in the room where I had left
my sister in some displeasure.
So let me enter it again

to give you both my blessings.

*Doña Beatriz.* If congratulations to you both
are now in order, perhaps
we others ought not be omitted.

*Don Juan.* Why, Beatriz, have you come back
to grace this house?

*Doña Beatriz.*          I never left it.
I'll explain this to you later.

*Don Juan.* Well, let us take advantage of
this occasion, which so clearly
bids us insure our happiness.

*Cosme.* Thank goodness, the Phantom Lady's
cleared things up.
[*To* Don Manuel.] Tell me, sir, was I mad
or what?

*Don Manuel.* So long as you're not mad now,
you may marry Isabel today.

*Cosme.* That would only prove I'm really mad.
Besides, I can't.

*Don Manuel.* And why not?

*Cosme.* Because the good time usually
wasted on such nonsense
would be much better spent now
beseeching this audience
to pardon our mistakes,
and to say: our author humbly
thanks you for your kind indulgence.

# APPENDIX

NORMAN MACCOLL's notes to his *Select Plays of Calderón* are still the best general introduction in English to Calderón's drama and period. Excerpts from that material here include the editor's accounts of the character of Spanish drama, the social and dramatic types represented in the cape-and-sword plays, and the theatre of Calderón's time. Maccoll's fondness for generalization is typical of the nineteenth-century Hispanist whose enthusiasm for things Spanish often gave him the feeling he understood the culture better than Spaniards themselves. This attitude shows up in his occasional disparagements of ecclesiastical influence on Spanish life and literature; compared with Ticknor, Prescott, and Borrow, however, Maccoll was only a mild purveyor of the "black legend." But his close descriptions of seventeenth-century Spanish dramatic types and customs have an interest that is not surpassed in more recent writings on the subject.

### I. CALDERÓN AND SPANISH DRAMA

The Spanish drama, like the English, sprang out of the Mystery plays of the Middle Ages, and it began to assume definite shape as early as the commencement of the sixteenth century. For a time its development was checked by the jealousy of the Inquisition, which, while favoring the performance of the mysteries, laid an interdict on secular plays that was not formally removed till 1573. The theatrical tastes of the Spaniards proved, however, too strong to be controlled by their ecclesiastical rulers, and a goldbeater at Seville named Lope de Rueda, who appears to have possessed no common share of genius for acting, obtained great popularity at the head of a strolling company which he formed soon after 1540, and for which he wrote comedies, thus laying the foundation of a national theatre shortly before the time when *Ralph Roister Doister* and *Gammer Gurton's Needle* appeared in England.

The impulse given by Lope de Rueda proved permanent, and the Spanish drama gradually formed itself, not upon literary traditions, but in obedience to the taste of crowds who flocked to the theatre. An endeavor was indeed made by Jerónimo Bermudez, a celebrated professor of theology at Salamanca, and the famous lyric poet Argensola to introduce tragedy provided with choruses and modeled upon the plays which bear the name of Seneca; but although Argensola's tragedies attained a momentary popularity on the stage, and attracted the admiration of Cervantes, the national type prevailed, and in the hands of Lope de Vega it obtained undisputed supremacy. Lope, it is true, professed to believe in the so-called unities, and to write in the popular style only because of the necessity of pleasing the multitude; but it is not likely that, had he ventured to follow in the footsteps of Argensola, he would have succeeded in establishing a classical school of drama; not only because his own temperament unfitted him for such a task, and his greatest qualities would never have been called into activity by "climing to the height of Seneca his stile," but because the Renaissance had gained no real hold in the Peninsula, and the romantic temper was too deeply rooted in the nation not to find expression on the stage. Adopting the popular side, he settled the question once for all, and his successors adhered to the forms he provided for them as long as the theatre preserved its vitality.

The drama, as thus established, was intensely national, and is marked by the qualities which distinguished the Spanish people —a profound sense of personal dignity, strong religious feeling, reckless bravery, ardent love of adventure, fantastic loyalty, and intense patriotism. In its nature it bears an unmistakable resemblance to the ballads and chronicles in which the genius of the nation had originally found expression. This is obvious in matters of form, for not only had the drama no meter peculiar to itself, but the assonant trochaics in which most of the dialogue is written are the measure of the ballads; and the kinship extends beyond matters of form—in its essence the structure of a Spanish play is usually narrative rather than dramatic. The novelty of his plots and ingenuity of his conceptions form, with harmony of style, the great merits attributed to Calderón by the Maestro Joseph de Valdivieso in his note prefixed to the first volume of the published plays, and certainly were what both critics and the public prized. The first demand of the playgoer was for an interesting story of love and adventure, and consequently the first care of the playwright was the formation of his plot. In his endeavor to make that attractive he allowed himself a range of subject such as no other dramatists thought of. He could not only produce a picture of the life of his own day, but the romantic annals of the Peninsula lay open to him from the time of Viriathus; he might range over the whole course of history, sacred or profane; he might lay his scene in ancient Babylon, or cross over to the New World, and bring on to the stage the Incas of Peru; he might seek his theme among the myths of Greece, as he found them in Ovid, or the stories of the Round Table. Characters of all kinds figured on the scene—Oriental Monarchs, Greek Gods, Roman Generals, German Emperors, Moorish Sultans, Popes, Cardinals, or Saints. It must not be supposed that he made any attempt at archeological accuracy. Such efforts would have been unintelligible to the public for whom he wrote, even if he had been capable of them, and consequently not only were the wildest anachronisms allowed, but the characters, whatever they purported to be, were in reality Spaniards of the reigns of the Philips. It was on the construction of the story that the writer concentrated his efforts. That at the outset it should arrest the attention of the audience, that incident should succeed incident so rapidly that the interest once excited

should never flag, and that, although, to arouse the spectator's
curiosity, and to prepare his mind for the *dénouement*, the even-
tual solution was often indicated at an early stage, the exact manner of the catastrophe should remain a mystery till the last
scene; such were the requisites of success, and to them the
*dramatis personae* were often sacrificed, more often indeed by
Lope than by Calderón; yet even with Calderón the development
of character was a secondary matter. Not that he was at all
incapable of character drawing. *The Alcalde of Zalamea* is ample
proof to the contrary; and even in his comedies of intrigue,
although the characters are usually types, not individuals—though
they are, as Goethe remarked, like bullets all cast in one mold,
and the Don Juan of one play is the Don Carlos of another—
they are, taken separately, animated sketches, if not elaborate
studies, thoroughly alive and dashed off with the broad vigor
which we are in the habit of calling Shakespearean. They are
quite free from the exaggeration of Ben Jonson's types; they
are not abnormal beings but representative of the men and
women of Calderón's day, if seldom individualized to the point
of being individuals instead of specimens of their class. But
though Calderón is not neglectful of his *dramatis personae*, it
must be confessed that to him, as to other Spanish playwrights,
the plot is the paramount consideration; that it is as a dramaturge,
as a constructor, that he is greatest. In this respect he stands at
the head of all modern dramatists. In fact, in his best works the
scenes are so admirably pieced together, the whole story is devel-
oped with such perfect regularity, that the ingenuity displayed
seems to be excessive, and the reader is surprised to find so much
real poetry in plays so dexterously framed. . . . A lyrical writer
possessing an inexhaustible fund of metaphor and an almost
infantine love of ornament, indulging in hyperboles that just stop
short of sheer nonsense, he is at the same time one of the most
elaborate and artful of dramaturges.

Calderón owes his great place in literature to his being the last
heir in the direct line of the inheritance of the Middle Ages.
Though he was trained by the Jesuits, and though his plays
are full of classical allusions, and the subjects are often borrowed
from heathen mythology or Roman history, he was in no sense
a child of the Renaissance. His Latin quotations and his allusions to pagan mythology are like Ionic cornices or Corinthian
pilasters placed upon the front of a building of the thirteenth
century. Of all the literature of the ancient world it is obvious
that the only book really familiar to him was the *Metamorphoses*,
which is the part that makes the nearest approach to the Romantic spirit, and the fount of his inspiration was essentially the
same that gives life to the ballads and chronicles and the ro-
mances of medieval Spain. . . . Only in Spain was such a treat-

ment possible in the middle of the seventeenth century. In France a magnificent literature was springing up that was in every respect opposed to the Romantic temper. In Italy the Renaissance had crushed it long before. In England we have in Milton a clear example of the struggle between two opposing influences, the profound appreciation of the value of serenity, of symmetry, and of subdued ornament, and yet the longing glances backwards

> "To Knights of Logres, or of Lyones,
> Lancelot, or Pelleas, or Pellenore."

In Spain, however, till the accession of the Bourbon dynasty, there was no such conflict of tendency, and Calderón gives expression to the Romantic temper of his nation without any conscious effort, and with the additional warmth derived from the Oriental strain that runs through Spanish nature. Yet all this Romantic fervor, this love of the wonderful, this thirst for adventure, is controlled by a consummate artistic faculty that prevents his plays from becoming the formless creations, the series of wild improbabilities, the mere accumulations of horrors or marvels which are common among the inferior Spanish dramatists, for extravagance is the danger to which Romantic literature is especially liable, just as tameness and insipidity are the bane of the classical school. There is, too, in Calderón, nothing of the factitious element which vitiates much of the work of the Romantic revival of the nineteenth century. He does not write as he does because he deems such a mode of writing picturesque or interesting. He writes as his environment bade him write; there is the unconsciousness of real genius in his methods, free from the posing and affectation which wrecked the German Romantics who were ever proclaiming their admiration of him. (pp. xxxi-xxv; xlii-xliv)

## II. SOCIAL AND DRAMATIC TYPES IN THE
### CAPE-AND-SWORD PLAYS

Not only does Calderón confine his *Comedias de Capa y Espada* to one section of society, but he also adheres to one type of plot; and his characters are strictly limited in number, and bear a strong resemblance to one another. The intrigue in the comedies always turns upon the love affairs of two or three young gentlemen and two or three young ladies, a father or guardian or two being added, whose watchfulness the lovers endeavor to circumvent. They are aided by their serving-man—the *gracioso*, common to Spanish tragedy and comedy—and by the maids of the ladies. These *dramatis personae*, who number from ten to twelve, reappear in every comedy, and the national custom of going about masked furnishes the machinery of the plot. Calderon himself frequently laughs at the sameness of his materials. *"Es comedia,"* he says in one place,

> *De don Pedro*
> *Calderón, donde ha de haber,*
> *Por fuerza, amante escondido,*
> *O rebozada mujer.*[1]

The absence of anything resembling family life is another notable feature of these *Comedias de Capa y Espada.* The young ladies who figure in them are invariably motherless. They either live with a father who is a widower, or, if they are orphans, they are under the charge of a brother who is always a bachelor. They have no domestic interests nor household cares, and they are supposed to see, beyond the circle of their relations, little society except that of their own sex. Even the appearance in her father's house of a male visitor who is not a relative is usually the signal for a young lady's withdrawal to her own apartment. When she goes to a party the guests are, as a rule, all women, and the intrusion of a man on such an assemblage is regarded as a breach of decorum.

The seclusion of women was an essential part of Spanish manners, but the absence of a mother is obviously a device of Calderón's to give additional interest to his plays. Unlike other Spanish dramatists, he seldom introduces a duenna. To elude the vigilance of a mother would be a tame proceeding, while the attempt to hoodwink a father or a brother had the piquancy that danger gives, as on discovering the deceit practiced upon him he would be bound, according to the Spanish code of honor, to avenge himself by stabbing the damsel and running his sword through her lover's body.

A sketch of the life of one of Calderón's heroines may serve to make matters more intelligible. Doña Ana rose late and drank a cup of chocolate, which was followed by a glass of iced water. She then went to mass, attended by her maid. Sometimes she was carried to church in a sedan chair, sometimes she walked, and she was often accompanied, for her better protection, by an elderly serving-man equipped with sword and dagger. Her toilet, when she quitted the house, was elaborate. Over her *saben-agua* or petticoat were worn several other petticoats, one of which was of heavy satin or velvet, and the whole mass was supported by five or six hoops. Her train swept the ground both behind and before, so as to conceal her feet, when she did not wear clogs, which she usually did if she walked, as the streets of Madrid were

[1]                 by Don Pedro
                 Calderón, where there must
                 absolutely be a hidden lover
             or muffled lady somewhere.—E. H.

notoriously filthy. The body of her dress was high in front and cut low behind. Her sleeves were so long that her hands were not visible, and so full as to serve in some measure for pockets. Round her throat was wrapped a silk handkerchief. She wore no necklace, but, on the other hand, earrings hideously long and massive. From her shoulders was suspended a gold chain or a string of pearls; her hair hung down her back in plaits (*trenzas*) tied at the ends with ribbons. She was adorned with bracelets and rings, and agnuses were fastened about the front of her dress, while jewels made in the shape of serpents or pelicans or cupids were fixed in her hair, or used as brooches. A long rosary and a fan hung at her waist. When she went out she wrapped a *manto* round her so that she could conceal her face; or if she wore a hat it was adorned with feathers and a diamond clasp. There was much sincere piety in the Spain of Philip IV, yet in the great cities, at least, and the fashionable churches, religion had hardened into a form; and Doña Ana went to mass daily, not because she was particularly devout, but because it was the custom. She squatted on the floor of the church, fanning herself, and looking through the folds of her *manto* at the rest of the congregation, especially at the male part; striking herself mechanically on the breast when the Host was raised. The priest gabbled through the service as fast as his tongue could go (Tirso, *Villana de Vallecas*, I., i.); and, when she had listened for a short time, Doña Ana rose, and on her approaching the basin of holy water, the brush was presented to her by one of the *caballeros*— very likely her lover—who were always loitering there. She returned home and dined lightly, as Spaniards still do, and took the usual siesta. In the afternoon she drove out with one of her friends to pay visits or to attend a party or to shop, and she usually finished the day by proceeding slowly along the *Prado*, generally with the carriage blinds down. This was the ordinary routine, but if there was a religious procession, or an ambassador was to make his state entry into Madrid, she took care to go to the house of some one of her acquaintances from whose balcony she could see the show; or if she knew no one who lived in the streets it passed through, she coaxed her father to hire a window for her; while, if there was a bullfight in the *Plaza Mayor*, she made a point of sharing a window with some of her acquaintances. The time spent in waiting for the spectacle was occupied in consuming sweetmeats, or beguiled by music and singing. When night had fallen her lover—and in the drama every lady has her lover—came to her street, and paced to and fro before her house attended by his serving-man. At the commencement of his suit he was usually allowed to keep his vigil unnoticed, and if he brought a guitar—but Calderón's heroes do not seem to have indulged in serenades—he was more likely to meet with a hostile than a friendly reception. He was compelled to persevere for months in his nocturnal courtship, and Calderón has an abundance of phrases to describe the species of wooing (*festejar su calle, solicitar su calle,* etc.). Years apparently might pass before his constancy was rewarded. In *Con quien vengo, vengo,* for instance, the heroine says:

> *Dos años há que festaja,*
> *Mi calle, dos años há*
> *Que asido hasta el alba está*
> *A los hierros de mi reja.*[2]

He also ran the risk of encountering other suitors for his lady's favor, and these naturally resented his attentions. Calderón compares the uproar caused in the streets by rival lovers to the confusion created by the archangel in the camp of Agramant (*El Galán Fantasma,* I, 294 c):

> *Astolfo una dama ama,*
> *Y tiene un competidor*
> *Poderoso, y en rigor*
> *Hoy la calle de la dama*
> *Con uno y con otro amante,*
> *Ya Moro, ya Paladin,*
> *La esfera de su jardín*
> *Hizo campo de Agramante.*[3]

When at last the lady relented, she condescended to come to the window and talk to her admirer through the bars. This sort of intercourse would go on for some time, and at length an attempt would be made to introduce the favored suitor into the garden, or into the house itself. The maidservant, who was supposed to act as a check on her mistress' movements, had long before been won over, and was ready to aid with all the devices her ingenuity could suggest. An evening was chosen when the men of the household were absent, the *caballero* signified his presence by throwing a pebble against the window, the maid ran down and opened the door, which was closed immediately on his

[2] Two years he's spent wooing me outdoors,
two years now that he's been fastened
every night until the dawn
to my iron window bars.—E. H.

[3] Astolfo loves a lady
but has to face a mighty
opposition, and today, in fact,
what with one lover
grappling with another,
now a Moor and now some paladin,
it's turned his lady's street
from heaven's fairest garden plot
to the battlefield of Agramant.—E. H.

entrance—the lackey remaining in the street to cover his master's retreat should he be discovered, and the successful suitor was ushered into the presence of his mistress. Of course in all the comedies one of these stolen interviews is the moment chosen for the reappearance of the master of the house. The alarm is given, the intruder is hidden behind a curtain, or in another room, and various shifts and devices are resorted to in order to smuggle him out of the house unnoticed. There was no corridor in a Spanish dwelling of that time. The various rooms on each floor opened one out of the other, thus making escape more difficult, and if the master of the house remained in the *estrado* or principal sitting-room, which seems to have been near the entrance, there was no mode of escape except by a back staircase, which was rare, or by jumping out of a window, which frequently was not easy both on account of the height from the ground and because the window was usually barred, or by creeping through the skylight, and clambering along the roof to the next house. Occasionally the father or brother of the heroine returns so suddenly that there is no time for concealment; and then the ready wit of the lady or her maid concocts some falsehood to account for the presence of a stranger, as in the *Maestro de Danzar*, so named because Doña Leonor calmly assures her father that her visitor is a dancing master whom she has engaged to give her lessons.

An additional complication is given to the plot when the interview takes place at the abode of a friend of the heroine who has been persuaded to lend her house for the purpose. In that case the lovers are invariably surprised by the lover of the accommodating friend; he at once suspects a rival, and quarrels with his mistress on the ground of her infidelity.

In all cases, it is to be observed, whatever the apparent complications, the heroine's attachment to her lover is beyond reproach. Jealousy and misunderstanding of various kinds may lead to a quarrel, but the ultimate end is beyond doubt. Doña Ana is never fickle, she loves warmly and steadily, and on the other hand the attachment of her lover is undeniably sincere. He is usually jealous, apt to take offense at the slightest suspicion of lack of loyalty on the part of his mistress, but he is ever willing to sacrifice his life for her sake, and to revenge the slightest approach to an insult, sword in hand. Like his mistress, he is quick to resort to any trick to deceive her guardian; any lie is considered excusable in this regard. But he is equally ready to resent an aspersion on his honor. With a man he will not stoop to argue; the sword is, in his eyes, the best of arguments.

He is oftentimes a young man who has seen a campaign or two in Flanders or Italy, and who has returned to Madrid to seek the customary reward of service in the field—the habit of one of the military orders—a distinction greatly coveted for the privileges it conferred. Frequently he is a resident in Seville or Granada, or some other provincial city, who has come to the capital to look after a lawsuit or an inheritance. Occasionally he has had a quarrel with another *caballero*, and having killed his adversary, has fled his native city in order to escape the police and the relatives of the slain. In that case a tragic interest is imparted to the comedy by the fact that the dead man was the brother of the lady of his love. In *El Escondido y la Tapada* and in some other plays, the fatal fray has taken place at Madrid, the murderer has sought refuge in Portugal, and unable to bear banishment from the presence of his mistress, makes his way back secretly, so that the efforts of the dead man's relatives to avenge his death add to the intricacy of the plot. It is to be noticed that a homicide of this kind is lightly thought of. Calderón's hero is careful to tell us that he killed his man in fair fight (*cara a cara*), and that he did not assassinate him (*a estocadas*): and so long as this was the case he seems to feel little remorse for the deed. It was merely a *trance funesto*, regrettable, no doubt, and involving disagreeable consequences, but still quite a gentlemanly act. The very carelessness with which he hazards his life is in favor of this reasoning. He risked as much as his adversary. He slew his opponent, and may himself be slain tomorrow. The homicide loses nothing in the esteem of his friends, and though the dead man's relatives think it a duty to avenge him if they can, there is no obstinate blood-feud. The murderer has done them a wrong, but on very slight grounds they agree to forgive him and let bygones be bygones.

Two other characters, the serving-man and the maid, call for but brief remark. The *gracioso* is a constant figure in Spanish drama, both tragic and comic. . . . In the comedies he plays a more conspicuous part than in the tragedies. His speeches are longer, and his jokes naturally turn on topics of the day. He does not so much occupy the position of a spectator, and he is more directly set up as a contrast to his master. The characteristics are, however, the same. His poltroonery, real or assumed, serves as a foil to his master's headlong valor. He is greedy, inquisitive, talkative, conceited, as proud of his common sense as the *caballero* of his romantic devotion. He has usually the virtue of fidelity, although in *El Secreto a Voces* he plays the traitor, and reveals his master's secrets without scruple. Often he carries on a flirtation with the lady's maid, which, though not pushed into great prominence, serves as a species of parody on the main plot. In one play his vanity leads him to believe himself a possible rival to his master, but this is a deviation from the general rule, and it is curious that Calderón should have made use of a *motif* that must have seemed wildly improbable in days when distinctions of rank were clearly marked, and no one dreamed of the possibility of their being ignored. It was this strong demarcation of classes which made possible the extremely familiar tone adopted by the *criado*. He advises his master, ridicules him, and complains of his conduct and of that of his friends without any scruple or reserve. Of course a good deal of this is conventional, a part of the regular stage business, and merely intended to make the audience laugh, yet it must have been, to some extent, a correct picture of contemporary manners. As for the humor of the *gracioso*, I cannot think Calderón is, in this respect, successful. The fun is usually forced, and gives the impression of being the result of an effort to entertain the spectators, not of the author's enjoyment of his character: Calderón had wit, but he had little humor, and the jokes of the *gracioso* are apt to be labored.

The *criada* is devoted to her mistress, and enjoys inventing expedients by which to screen her intrigues. She has the keenest sympathy with the lovers, and seldom disapproves of her mistress' choice. She is, for the rest, a colorless character—she has no individuality; and there is no difference between the maid in one play and the maid in another. In her dialogues with the *gracioso* she affects a jocularity similar to his, and her audacity is greater than her mistress', because she has no need to dread the vengeance of an offended father or brother. The fear of this vengeance is one of the main elements in the plot, but, according to Ticknor, it is purely conventional. "The father," he says, "by the old Spanish laws had power to put to death his daughter who was dishonored under his roof, and if the father died the same terrible power was transferred to the brother in relation to his sister; or even to the lover, when the offending party had been betrothed to him. No doubt these wild laws, though formally renewed and re-enacted as late as the reign of St. Ferdinand, had ceased in the time of Calderón to have any force. But, on the other hand, no doubt these laws were in operation during more centuries than had elapsed since their abrogation and the age of Calderón and Philip IV. The tradition of their power, therefore, was not yet lost on the popular character, and poetry was permitted to preserve their fearful principles." (pp. 368–74; 379–81)

### III. THE THEATRE OF CALDERON'S TIME

In Madrid, as in other Spanish cities, the first theatres were simply courtyards in the rear of private houses. The stage was a rough scaffolding, and the mass of the audience crowded into the yard, while some looked on from the windows of the adjoining houses. Stage and yard were alike roofless, and the only spectators who enjoyed shelter from the weather were those who sat at the windows. These primitive arrangements were in their essentials retained in the two theatres which Madrid possessed during the palmy days of the Spanish drama, the Theatre de la Cruz, and the Theatre del Príncipe. The rooms in the upper and lower stories of the houses that overlooked the stage were converted into boxes, and were the only parts frequented by ladies belonging to the higher ranks of society. Of these boxes the upper ones were named *desvanes*, the lower *aposentos*. The first floor of the house immediately facing the stage formed a kind of large box which was occupied by women of indifferent character and their admirers. From the *aposentos* a range of benches styled *gradas* sloped down to the yard or *patio*. These seemed to have been protected from the weather by a projecting roof. Below them was the *patio* or pit, quite open to the sky and filled with the humbler class of playgoers—the dreaded *mosqueteros*. Between the *mosqueteros* and the stage, in the place occupied in modern theatres by the orchestra, were some benches called *bancos*. These were screened from the sun by an awning, but had no roof over them. Further, upon the stage itself, which was wide but not proportionately deep, some of the spectators sat on stools, and the privilege of so doing was so highly valued that it passed like an heirloom from father to son.

There was no artificial light, the performance taking place in the daytime, and commencing about two o'clock in winter and about three o'clock in summer. Originally much longer, the entertainment had been curtailed in Lope's time so as to occupy little over two hours and a half. The proceedings began with a song accompanied by music, and as there was no part of the house reserved for the orchestra, the musicians appeared on the stage on this and other occasions, when their services were needed. Upon the song followed the *loa* or prologue, sometimes a monologue, oftener a dialogue in verse which frequently had little or no connection with the drama which was to be played, and by Calderón's time had nearly fallen out of use. Next came the first act of the *comedia*, after which an *entremes* or *sainete*, a species of farce dealing with low life, was performed for the delectation of the *mosqueteros*. The second act of the drama was then given, and was succeeded by a ballet; the third and final act of the *comedia*, which was always in three acts, was played, and the whole entertainment concluded with a second ballet.

The stage arrangements were of the simplest, and it is almost unnecessary to point out how closely in them, as well as the disposition of the *auditorium*, the Spanish theatre resembled the Elizabethan. There was neither curtain nor drop-scene. In the background was an erection of a nondescript character which served to represent a house, or a castle, or a wall of a town, or even a mountain side, such as that which Rosaura is supposed to descend at the opening of *Life's a Dream*. At the wings and at the back of the stage were hung curtains and tapestries which served to cover the entrances, and formed almost the only scenery. On very special occasions a piece of canvas rudely painted to represent a tree or a house was shoved forward to indicate the locality, and the withdrawal of a curtain concealing one of these pieces of canvas was supposed to mark a change of scene. Generally, however, such luxury of decoration was beyond the means of the manager, and a change was simply intimated by leaving the stage unoccupied for a minute or two. Almost everything, in fact, was left to the imagination of the spectators, and, in order to render the action of the piece intelligible, the dramatist was often forced to put into the mouths of his characters a few lines descriptive of the spot in which the scene was supposed to be laid. The machinery was of the most meager kind. Trapdoors were used, and there were hoists for lowering the mythological characters onto the stage or bearing them aloft. Madame d'Aulnoy ridicules the properties she saw, and the absurdities entailed by the lack of scenic appliances, the gods appearing on horseback on the gallery at the back of the stage, the sun represented by a dozen lamps shining through oil paper, and the demons climbing up ladders from the infernal regions onto the stage: and her account of the poverty of the Spanish theatre is borne out by other contemporary notices.

While the playhouses in Madrid were of this humble character, Philip IV showed his enthusiasm for the drama by erecting at the Palace of the Buen Retiro a much more splendid theatre. It was fairly large, and was gorgeous with carving and gilding, while the stage was supplied with all the machinery that the skill of the time had devised. At the back the stage could be opened, and the garden which lay beyond could be used for the enhancement of scenic effects. The mounting of theatrical spectacles had been for years practiced at the Spanish Court, Italian engineers who excelled in technical ability the Spaniards—never greatly distinguished in mechanics—were largely employed, and we have notices of magnificent entertainments which took place in the preceding reign. The Cardinal Duke especially had distinguished himself by lavishing some of the immense fortune he had accumulated on dramatic performances.

Naturally when a young monarch, fond of pleasure and especially fond of the theatre, mounted the throne, such shows underwent still further development. In 1623, for instance, the birthday of Philip IV was celebrated at Aranjuez by a performance of a play in which the Queen and the principal courtiers took part, and on this occasion an elaborate theatre was erected in the open air by the celebrated architect Fontana. The subjects of the dramas produced on these occasions were, in accordance with the spirit of the late Renaissance, generally mythological, and their resemblance to the masques which were at the same time fashionable at the English Court is obvious. The Spanish king had the advantage of a fuller purse than his brother of England, and, thanks to the southern skies, a large part of the performance could take place out of doors—a distinct advantage in days when the stage even of the king's theatre was comparatively small. As I have said, the back could be thrown open, and the large ponds in the garden were turned to account. Circe's island was frequently constructed in the center of them; Ulysses appeared reclining in a gilded barge that floated on real water; and Sirens, Dolphins, and Tritons disported themselves upon it. But the Spanish climate did not always permit these shows to proceed without interruption. For instance, in 1640 a huge stage had been erected upon boats in the middle of the large lake at the Buen Retiro, provided with curtains, scenery, and machinery: but in the course of the performance a heavy thunderstorm broke over Madrid, the stage and its appurtenances were wrecked, and the spectators had a narrow escape of being drowned. (pp. xlviii-lii)—from Norman Maccoll's *Select Plays of Calderón*. London: Macmillan and Co., 1888.

# DRAMABOOKS

WHEN ORDERING, please use the Standard Book Number consisting of the publisher's prefix, 8090-, plus the five digits following each title. (Note that the numbers given in this list are for paperback editions only. Many of the books are also available in cloth.)

MERMAID DRAMA BOOKS

*Christopher Marlowe* (Tamburlaine the Great, Parts I & II, Doctor Faustus, The Jew of Malta, Edward the Second) (0701–0)

*William Congreve* (Complete Plays) (0702–9)

*Webster and Tourneur* (The White Devil, The Duchess of Malfi, The Atheist's Tragedy, The Revenger's Tragedy) (0703–7)

*John Ford* (The Lover's Melancholy, 'Tis Pity She's a Whore, The Broken Heart, Love's Sacrifice, Perkin Warbeck) (0704–5)

*Richard Brinsley Sheridan* (The Rivals, St. Patrick's Day, The Duenna, A Trip to Scarborough, The School for Scandal, The Critic) (0705–3)

*Camille and Other Plays* (Scribe: A Peculiar Position, The Glass of Water; Sardou: A Scrap of Paper; Dumas: Camille; Augier: Olympe's Marriage) (0706–1)

*John Dryden* (The Conquest of Granada, Parts I & II, Marriage à la Mode, Aureng-Zebe) (0707–X)

*Ben Jonson* Vol. 1 (Volpone, Epicoene, The Alchemist) (0708–8)

*Oliver Goldsmith* (The Good Natur'd Man, She Stoops to Conquer, An Essay on the Theatre, A Register of Scotch Marriages) (0709–6)

*Jean Anouilh* Vol. 1 (Antigone, Eurydice, The Rehearsal, Romeo and Jeannette, The Ermine) (0710–X)

*Let's Get a Divorce! and Other Plays* (Labiche: A Trip Abroad, and Célimare; Sardou: Let's Get a Divorce!; Courteline: These Cornfields; Feydeau: Keep an Eye on Amélie; Prévert: A United Family; Achard: Essays on Feydeau) (0711–8)

*Jean Giraudoux* Vol. 1 (Ondine, The Enchanted, The Madwoman of Chaillot, The Apollo of Bellac) (0712–6)

*Jean Anouilh* Vol. 2 (Restless Heart, Time Remembered, Ardèle, Mademoiselle Colombe, The Lark) (0713–4)

*Henrik Ibsen: The Last Plays* (Little Eyolf, John Gabriel Borkman, When We Dead Awaken) (0714–2)

*Ivan Turgenev* (A Month in the Country, A Provincial Lady, A Poor Gentleman) (0715–0)

*George Farquhar* (The Constant Couple, The Twin-Rivals, The Recruiting Officer, The Beaux Stratagem) (0716–9)

*Jean Racine* (Andromache, Britannicus, Berenice, Phaedra, Athaliah) (0717–7)

*The Storm and Other Russian Plays* (The Storm, The Government Inspector, The Power of Darkness, Uncle Vanya, The Lower Depths) (0718–5)

*Michel de Ghelderode: Seven Plays* Vol. 1 (The Ostend Interviews, Chronicles of Hell, Barabbas, The Women at the Tomb, Pantagleize, The Blind Men, Three Players and a Play, Lord Halewyn) (0719–3)

*Lope de Vega: Five Plays* (Peribáñez, Fuenteovejuna, The Dog in the Manger, The Knight from Olmedo, Justice Without Revenge) (0720–7)

*Calderón: Four Plays* (Secret Vengeance for Secret Insult, Devotion to the Cross, The Mayor of Zalamea, The Phantom Lady) (0721–5)

*Jean Cocteau: Five Plays* (Orphée, Antigone, Intimate Relations, The Holy Terrors, The Eagle with Two Heads) (0722–3)

*Ben Jonson* Vol. 2 (Every Man in His Humour, Sejanus, Bartholomew Fair) (0723–1)

*Port-Royal and Other Plays* (Claudel: Tobias and Sara; Mauriac: Asmodée; Copeau: The Poor Little Man; Montherlant: Port-Royal) (0724–X)

*Edwardian Plays* (Maugham: Loaves and Fishes; Hankin: The Return of the Prodigal; Shaw: Getting Married; Pinero: Mid-Channel; Granville-Barker: The Madras House) (0725–8)

*Alfred de Musset: Seven Plays* (0726–6)

*Georg Büchner: Complete Plays and Prose* (0727–4)

*Paul Green: Five Plays* (Johnny Johnson, In Abraham's Bosom, Hymn to the Rising Sun, The House of Connelly, White Dresses) (0728–2)

*François Billetdoux: Two Plays* (Tchin-Tchin, Chez Torpe) (0729–0)

*Michel de Ghelderode: Seven Plays* Vol. 2 (Red Magic, Hop, Signor!, The Death of Doctor Faust, Christopher Columbus, A Night of Pity, Piet Bouteille, Miss Jairus) (0730–4)

*Jean Giraudoux* Vol. 2 (Siegfried, Amphitryon 38, Electra) (0731–2)

*Kelly's Eye and Other Plays* by Henry Livings (Kelly's Eye, Big Soft Nellie, There's No Room for You Here for a Start) (0732–0)

*Gabriel Marcel: Three Plays* (Man of God, Ariadne, Votive Candle) (0733–9)

*New American Plays* Vol. 1, ed. by Robert W. Corrigan (0734–7)

*Elmer Rice: Three Plays* (Adding Machine, Street Scene, Dream Girl) (0735–5)

*The Day the Whores Came Out to Play Tennis . . .* by Arthur Kopit (0736–3)

*Platonov* by Anton Chekhov (0737–1)

*Ugo Betti: Three Plays* (The Inquiry, Goat Island, The Gambler) (0738–X)

*Jean Anouilh* Vol. 3 (Thieves' Carnival, Medea, Cécile, Traveler Without Luggage, Orchestra, Episode in the Life of an Author, Catch As Catch Can) (0739-8)
*Max Frisch: Three Plays* (Don Juan, The Great Rage of Philip Hotz, When the War Was Over) (0740-1)
*New American Plays* Vol. 2 ed. by William M. Hoffman (0741-X)
*Plays from Black Africa* ed. by Fredric M. Litto (0742-8)
*Anton Chekhov: Four Plays* (The Seagull, Uncle Vanya, The Cherry Orchard, The Three Sisters) (0743-6)
*The Silver Foxes Are Dead and Other Plays* by Jakov Lind (The Silver Foxes Are Dead, Anna Laub, Hunger, Fear) (0744-4)

### THE NEW MERMAIDS
*Bussy D'Ambois* by George Chapman (1101-8)
*The Broken Heart* by John Ford (1102-6)
*The Duchess of Malfi* by John Webster (1103-4)
*Doctor Faustus* by Christopher Marlowe (1104-2)
*The Alchemist* by Ben Jonson (1105-0)
*The Jew of Malta* by Christopher Marlowe (1106-9)
*The Revenger's Tragedy* by Cyril Tourneur (1107-7)
*A Game at Chess* by Thomas Middleton (1108-5)
*Every Man in His Humour* by Ben Jonson (1109-3)
*The White Devil* by John Webster (1110-7)
*Edward the Second* by Christopher Marlowe (1111-5)
*The Malcontent* by John Marston (1112-3)
*'Tis Pity She's a Whore* by John Ford (1113-1)
*Sejanus His Fall* by Ben Jonson (1114-X)

### SPOTLIGHT DRAMABOOKS
*The Last Days of Lincoln* by Mark Van Doren (1201-4)
*Oh Dad, Poor Dad . . .* by Arthur Kopit (1202-2)
*The Chinese Wall* by Max Frisch (1203-0)
*Billy Budd* by Louis O. Coxe and Robert Chapman (1204-9)
*The Devils* by John Whiting (1205-7)
*The Firebugs* by Max Frisch (1206-5)
*Andorra* by Max Frisch (1207-3)
*Balm in Gilead and Other Plays* by Lanford Wilson (1208-1)
*Matty and the Moron and Madonna* by Herbert Lieberman (1209-X)
*The Brig* by Kenneth H. Brown (1210-3)
*The Cavern* by Jean Anouilh (1211-1)
*Saved* by Edward Bond (1212-X)
*Eh?* by Henry Livings (1213-8)
*The Rimers of Eldritch and Other Plays* by Lanford Wilson (1214-6)
*In the Matter of J. Robert Oppenheimer* by Heinar Kipphardt (1215-4)
*Ergo* by Jakov Lind (1216-2)
*Biography: A Game* by Max Frisch (1217-0)

For a complete list of books of criticism and history of the drama, please write to Hill and Wang, 72 Fifth Avenue, New York, New York 10011.